With best
wishes, John

AF342159

Learning in Higher Education: Contemporary Standpoints

Learning in Higher Education: Contemporary Standpoints

Claus Nygaard
John Branch
Clive Holtham

Foreword by Professor Ron Barnett

THE LEARNING IN HIGHER EDUCATION SERIES

LIBRI
PUBLISHING

First published in 2013 by Libri Publishing

Copyright © Libri Publishing

Authors retain copyright of individual chapters.

The right of Claus Nygaard, John Branch and Clive Holtham to be identified as the editors of this work has been asserted in accordance with the Copyright, Designs and Patents Act, 1988.

ISBN 978 1 907471 70 4

All rights reserved. No part of this publication may be reproduced, stored in any retrieval system or transmitted in any form or by any means, electronic, mechanical, photocopying, recording or otherwise, without the prior written permission of the copyright holder for which application should be addressed in the first instance to the publishers. No liability shall be attached to the author, the copyright holder or the publishers for loss or damage of any nature suffered as a result of reliance on the reproduction of any of the contents of this publication or any errors or omissions in its contents.

A CIP catalogue record for this book is available from The British Library

Cover design by Helen Taylor

Design by Carnegie Publishing

Printed in the UK by Short Run Press, Ltd

Libri Publishing
Brunel House
Volunteer Way
Faringdon
Oxfordshire
SN7 7YR

Tel: +44 (0)845 873 3837

www.libripublishing.co.uk

Contents

Foreword   vii
Ronald Barnett

Chapter 1   A Call for Contemporary Practices of Learning in Higher Education   1
John Branch, Clive Holtham and Claus Nygaard

Chapter 2   Student-generated Questions: Enhancing Learning through Vicarious Experience   11
Patrícia Albergaria Almeida and José Teixeira-Dias

Chapter 3   Social-media Learning Environments   29
Christine Lenstrup

Chapter 4   Developing Student Contemporary Leadership Capacity through Teamwork   45
Ieva Stupans

Chapter 5   Learning Design and Transdisciplinary Pedagogical Templates (TPTs)   59
Eva Dobozy, James Dalziel and Bronwen Dalziel

Chapter 6   Designing a Learning-centred Degree: Challenging to Learn and Learning to Challenge   77
David R. Newman

Chapter 7   Strategies for Augmenting Students' Attention in Higher Education   93
Barbara Hong and Catheryn J. Weitman

Chapter 8   Universal Design for Learning in Higher Education   111
John Branch and Alyssa Martina

Chapter 9   Interrelationships between Student Culture, Teaching and Learning in Higher Education   127
Steffen Löfvall and Claus Nygaard

Chapter 10   ePortfolios and the Twenty-first Century: Learning in Higher Education   151
Lori L. Hager

Chapter 11   The Development of "Learning to Be" in Higher Education   167
Yahui Su

Chapter 12 Building Student Capacity for Reflective Learning   183
Kayoko Enomoto and Richard Warner

Chapter 13 Preparing for Learning: Incorporating Academic
Literacies in a Pathway Programme   203
Helen Benzie

Foreword

In placing learning in higher education in a contemporary context, just what might count as 'contemporary'? There is, after all, a paradox here – which this volume adroitly displays: 'contemporary' now includes the future. The future, as has been said before, has come into the present. It is not just that the pace of life is swift, with near instantaneity in communication across the world; it is also that there is now an anticipation of the future built into the organisation of institutions and the framing of policy. Consequently, humanity now lives with the future in its collective bones.

Higher education is not and cannot be immune from these phenomena as, again, this volume makes clear; and on two levels. On the first level, students are themselves in part living in the future; or at least, living against a horizon of the future. Increasingly, they look to higher education to furnish them with resources – understandings, capabilities and even qualities – that will carry them forward in the wider world; and not just in their transitions into the labour market but through life itself. And so, on the second level, curricula need to be designed partly with this orientation towards the future. Just how can curricula be designed to have this future-oriented and life-enhancing potential – and what forms of learning might they sponsor?

So there is this strange combination of the here-and-now (students, lecturers and, indeed, curricula living in the present) and of the future (with the future inscribed in the ethos of the institution). I am not sure that this aspect of institutional life, this conjunction of living *simultaneously* both in the moment and in the future, has been particularly studied; and yet it is a phenomenon that is perhaps particularly characteristic of universities. This volume – *Learning in Higher Education: Contemporary Standpoints* – surely offers us a valuable resource here. Its framing of the matter, in the themes of 'collaboration', 'design', 'identity' and 'transformation', gives us a firm basis on which to tackle this Janus-faced conundrum.

What *is* it both to live in the present and in the future? There lies the matter of *identity*. What transitions are ahead of one, in this strange mix of present and future? How can one perpetually live both in the future and in the moment? There lies the matter of *transformation*. How can one negotiate the awkwardnesses of these transitions? There lies the matter of *collaboration*. And how can one shape curricula not only with an eye on the past and the present but also on the future? There lies the matter of *design*.

In the process of engaging with these large themes, yet others assuredly must emerge, as is evident here. In the context of the liquid environment surrounding us, the matter of *knowledge* turns into knowledges, both practical and cognitive, both emotional and abstract, and both scientistic and humanistic; and so the theme of trans-disciplinarity can never be far away. The matter of *time* – the future, the present and the past – also invokes the matter of space, for time and space interact in complex and intricate ways. After all, living in the future can open spaces for inquiry and for learning, in imparting new horizons of possibility. The matter of learning as a means of furthering the *identity of individual students* poses the matter of universality: just what, if anything, serves to bind learning across the world? Does the idea of the student as a 'global citizen' really carry water? The matter of learning *as an individual and as a collaborative enterprise* prompts, too, the matter of authenticity: how is authentic learning possible? Is it possible? Is the whole idea of any value today? If learning is to be pursued within 'communities of learning', can and should learning be 'for oneself'? And the matter of *the relationship of learning and life* raises the matter as to the spaces of learning and life: might and should learning have a space outside of life? Wasn't this one of the cardinal features and virtues of a university, that it offered, in Oakeshott's memorable phrase, "the gift of the interval", a haven from life, in which one could reflect upon life and even critique it a little?

All of these matters – and several others – are raised either explicitly or implicitly by the contributions to this volume and we are much in debt to Claus Nygaard, John Branch and Clive Holtham for assembling the papers here and to the writers of the chapters for the accessible way in which they have pursued their task. None of the authors and editors here, I'm sure, would want to claim the last word on the important topics that this book opens up. That their offerings may be a spur to further thought, research and educational development in the practices of institutions serves as an indication of their significance.

Ronald Barnett
Emeritus Professor of Higher Education
Institute of Education, London
(r.barnett@ioe.ac.uk)

Introduction
A Call for Contemporary Practices of Learning in Higher Education

John Branch, Clive Holtham and Claus Nygaard

Changes in higher education

Authors of chapters in this anthology – from their own points of view – base their presentation of contemporary practices of learning in higher education on the recent changes in the nature of the student body. These changes are apparent in students' expectations of the nature of university education itself and in their views on their future use of what they learn during their years in university.

Forty-five years ago in the USA, the industrial production of material goods accounted for over 50 per cent of the country's economic output. Today, almost 70 per cent of that economic output comes from production of information products, such as computers, books and software, and services like telecommunications, broadcasting and financial services (Karmarkar & Apte, 2007; Apte *et al.*, 2008). The cases of contemporary practices of learning in higher education included in this anthology come from North America, Europe, Asia and Australia and they all suggest that this development, from industrial production to information economy, challenges higher education and calls for new ways to engage university students in education. Even if it has been argued so many times that it may sound like a cliché, the knowledge society calls for graduate attributes like *"production, distribution and use of knowledge and information"* (OECD, 1996:7) which are seen as the drivers of both productivity and economy. To a contemporary reader this may seem obvious but, indeed, the rise of the knowledge economy has had huge implications for higher education.

When prior generations went to university in order to prepare for industrial production, the world looked quite different. Markets were much more closed than today and the economy was strongly linked to individual national states. In general, consumers had little knowledge of products and developments of trends outside their regional or domestic context and they had to rely on their local and national media (traditional newspapers and a few television channels) for general information about change. The world may well have seemed much larger because news did not travel fast. In other respects, the world was indeed smaller because you could concentrate on your own backyard. Everything seemed smaller, more stable and easier to forecast. In this type of context, the university could thrive as a legitimate provider of methods and models to plan, act, check and do. The university could market itself as the institution in which highly esteemed professors could act as experts transferring their valuable academic knowledge to students. With academic knowledge in academic textbooks, academic textbooks in academic libraries and academic libraries in universities, it was natural to attend university to gain access to that knowledge. It was seen as an honour to be lectured to by professors. University students would be told what they needed to know and why they needed to know it. That was the general way of educating the future white-collar workforce.

Today we face a very different situation. Not only has society changed from industrial production to production of information, the means and methods for doing so have also changed radically. With the Internet enabling a worldwide network of personal communication, information and knowledge today are radically different than forty-five years ago. Markets are open, even in societies where governments still try to close them. The economy is strongly linked to global trends. In general, consumers have instant access to detailed knowledge of products and trend developments from every corner of the globe, and local and national media are no longer information gatekeepers. Traditional newspapers are struggling to survive, and thousands of global television channels are accessible by a few clicks on your computer or smartphone. The world may well be large if you have to travel it, but information-wise you can get global reactions to one particular event in a matter of minutes. There is no such thing as your own backyard anymore. Everything is moving and impossible to forecast.

In today's reality, the university cannot be a legitimate provider of methods and models to plan, act, check and do. The global economic crisis of the last years has shown us that even highly esteemed professors cannot direct a way out. The markets (political, economic, social, cultural, technological, etc.) act as almost autonomous agents changing the foundations for themselves. Instead of acting as experts transferring their valuable academic knowledge to students who have no prior information, university professors need to facilitate students' development of knowledge that enables them to analyse the global context they are in, synthesise what are currently deemed as important knowledge and methods, make qualified decisions for constructive action, and reflect on their normative consequences. This is what Tinkler *et al.* (1996) summarised with the term *"learning for the future"*.

Chapters of contemporary standpoints

Linked to the above presentation of changes in higher education, this anthology is in many ways about developing students' abilities to "learn for the future". This underlying theme runs through all chapters. *The context for teaching and learning in universities has changed over the past decades; we are facing new challenges as universities: what do we do?* The chapters fall into four categories, all central to learning in higher education: 1) Collaboration; 2) Design; 3) Identity; 4) Transformation. Figure 1 shows the four categories, and the keywords addressed within the individual chapters in each category.

	#	Author(s)	Keywords
Collaboration	2	Albergaria Almeida & Teixeira-Dias	vicarious learning; questions; science education
	3	Lenstrup	perceptions of learning; social media; teacher beliefs/roles
	4	Stupans	leadership; scaffolding; teamwork
Design	5	Dobozy, Dalziel & Dalziel	transdisciplinary pedagogical templates; learning design; twenty-first-century skills development
	6	Newman	challenge-based learning; problem-based learning; curriculum design; public policy
	7	Hong & Weitman	attentional strategies; deep thinking; active learning
	8	Branch & Martina	universal learning design; disabled students
Identity	9	Löfvall & Nygaard	student culture; student identity; student learning; curriculum design
	10	Hager	ePortfolios; pedagogy; higher education
	11	Su	higher learning; learning to be; university education
Transformation	12	Enomoto & Warner	reflective learning; lifelong learning; learning processes
	13	Benzie	preparation for higher education; academic literacies; contexts of learning; Pathway programs

Figure 1: Overview of the anthology: sections, chapters, authors and keywords

In the following sections, we take a closer look at each of the categories and the individual chapters contained within them.

Collaboration

The chapters on collaboration argue that an important component in the development of students' ability to learn for the future is their ability to engage, question and work together in teams.

In Chapter 2, Albergaria Almeida and Teixeira-Dias open this section with their study of how vicarious learning supports the development of students' ability to question. They report from an empirical study of first-year chemistry students at the University of Aveiro, Portugal. Their data show that the oral questions formulated by some students during the development of group mini-research projects stimulated other students to raise questions during these sessions and also stimulated students to formulate questions during other class activities. They argue that these questions contributed to i) students' engagement in the discipline and ii) increasing the interaction between students, and between students and the teacher. They see how students who engage in questioning gradually develop their ability to ask better questions, leading to better performance in mini-research projects and, subsequently, improvement in their final marks.

Lenstrup, in Chapter 3, discusses the importance of new ways of teaching and learning in higher education by using social-media learning environments for the new generation of "digitally native" students to become more engaged and motivated through the creation of a meaningful learning experience. She argues that, with the adoption of social-media learning environments, new openings and challenges arise both for the students and for the teacher, changing the role of the teacher from the traditional "expert" deciding the curriculum to one of a facilitator, supervisor or sparring partner for the students. She looks at how meaningful learning in second-language acquisition courses can be achieved through social-media learning environments by discussing some of the results from a teaching project at Copenhagen Business School in which the application of various ICT tools in language learning classes are analysed.

In Chapter 4, Stupans provides considerations for developing learning outcomes, learning opportunities and assessment which provide an opportunity for students to develop leadership. She argues that our universities have yet to consider how leadership should be taught and assessed, since modern leadership theory has shifted from a focus on the individual leader toward the collective act of leadership. She proposes that pedagogically sound teamwork has the potential to contribute to the development of leadership alongside disciplinary knowledge. Her conclusions are threefold. First, teamwork in the higher-education environment, critical to the contemporary leadership development trajectory, needs to be structured so that it facilitates all students to identify with leadership. Second, alignment of learning outcomes, learning opportunities and assessment around teamwork provides a framework for conceptualisation of development of students' leadership capacity. Third, scaffolding student learning – through clarity and explicit communication regarding definitions, benefits, expectations and processes – is critical.

Design

The section of the anthology on design focuses explicitly on curriculum design and learning design which are argued to improve students' ability to learn for the future.

In Chapter 5, Dobozy, Dalziel and Dalziel argue that, in order to professionalise the future workforce, paradigmatic changes are required in the way that university education is conducted. A possible way forward, they argue, is an adoption of Learning Design principles and the successful dissemination of knowledge-centric transdisciplinary pedagogical templates (TPTs) for use in various educational contexts. In their chapter, they explore the implementation of Learning Design principles through the development of such knowledge-centric TPTs and gauges of initial practitioner reactions. They discuss benefits of knowledge-centric TPTs for the renewal of university education and point to some obstacles identified in pilot implementations of scenario-based designs in medical and teacher education.

Chapter 6 sees Newman present the pedagogical considerations behind the development of the curriculum for a new one-year Master of Public Policy degree at postgraduate level. Writing from six months of action research, Newman shows how the degree design, based on transmission of content, could be transformed into challenge-based learning over time. He looks at the degree objectives and the requirements and constraints set by different stakeholders, discusses alternative theory-based pedagogies, and sets out some appropriate combinations of pedagogy and technology that will best support student learning for this new degree.

Hong and Weitman, in Chapter 7, focus on attention as the core of all learning. Without attention, they argue, learning is difficult to achieve, if not impossible, because attention leads to interest, motivation, active and deep thinking. Dealing with design principles, they bring to the forefront key features of cognitive science for faculty members to consider as they design their teaching and ultimately impact students' learning. This is relevant, they argue, as faculty members in higher education yearn for students to pay attention, become interested in the discipline at hand and, in most cases, interact or become engaged with the material. An underlying argument is that, while most faculty members recognise the signs of students who are attentive, responsive and involved, they rarely consider the dynamics of attention and their own impact on the interaction between teaching and learning. Reading this chapter will hopefully inspire faculty members to do so when they engage in curriculum design.

Chapter 8 sees Branch and Martina focus on universal design for learning, a proactive approach to teaching and learning design that benefits students with disabilities. They review the history and principles of universal design and argue that much is yet to be done in order to accommodate the needs of disabled students in higher education. Their chapter presents an important functional, ethical and symbolic challenge to HEIs which, unfortunately, has often been overlooked due to the relatively low proportion of disabled students. However, with the numbers growing, and the rise of inclusive learning design strategies, their chapter becomes increasingly relevant.

Identity

The part of the anthology focusing on the role students' identity plays in their ability to learn for the future argues that students are a heterogeneous group driven in their learning activities by their personal identity projects.

In Chapter 9, Löfvall and Nygaard discuss the possible relations between student culture and teaching and learning at universities. They present four ideal types of student culture and argue how student identity and student learning are affected by the identified student cultures. It is their main argument that universities can play an active role in forming student culture through their curriculum strategies and they present two alternatives (the content stream and the process stream) which inform and guide curriculum development and thus the student culture. They end their chapter on a normative note, introducing six different areas which can be clearly addressed and developed within the university and which have an impact on student culture and, consequently, on teaching and learning: 1) classroom activities; 2) online activities; 3) campus design; 4) teacher training; 5) policy forums; and 6) university branding. These areas are presented as inspirational points for future development of a culture of overall student engagement.

Hager, in Chapter 10, argues that universities and colleges are forced to respond to changes in the workplace demanding that students exit higher education with twenty-first-century skills such as creativity, collaboration and pattern making. This gives rise to a new student body with a new mindset and identity not achieved through traditional lecturing. She introduces the concept of ePortfolio learning as a driver for such transformations in teaching and learning in higher education, resulting in changes in the classroom environment which radically challenge traditional teaching and learning. She examines the ways that faculty and students are responding to these challenges through embedding ePortfolios in teaching and learning. Linking to this, she also discusses the larger implications for transformations in higher education as a result of participation in building interdisciplinary communities of learners through blended learning environments. As such, new roles and identity of students are discussed.

In Chapter 11, Su centralises student identity when arguing that the learning practices associated with a modern university education cannot be sustained only by the acquisition of skills and knowledge. Students should also "learn to be" if they are to find their values and develop identities in the long term in a world of change. Students are expected to learn to deal with authenticity-oriented tasks or projects and to construct and develop their personal meanings and existences in a more engaging and reflective mode in order to meet the possible challenges of future life and career situations. She concludes that learning for oneself by moving beyond disciplinary boundaries should be the focus of university education because, she argues, this will enable students to live authentically and continuously in a reflexive world in an ontologically self-directing manner.

Transformation

The final part of the anthology focuses on transformation into and out of university, explicitly dealing with ways in which students can be prepared to enter university and ways they can be prepared for their future roles in business.

Enomoto and Warner in Chapter 12 explore a reflective learning model to prepare students for lifelong learning. Their model was piloted with a diverse cohort from various cultural, linguistic and disciplinary backgrounds, in a first-year language course in an Australian university. Scaffolds to practise reflection and opportunities to experience interim successes as rewards were systematically embedded in the curriculum. To support their argument about student transformation, they present qualitative analyses of students' reflective writing and show that the reflective learning model effectively developed students' transferable reflective learning skills to learn how to learn – building learning capacity through reflection by transforming individual experiences into learning. The reflective learning model, they argue, encouraged students to understand and value their learning processes, not just marks, as valid manifestations of "learning" directly relevant to their futures.

Chapter 13 sees Benzie focus on the role of preparatory programs for helping students transform from one educational context to another. She argues that just as students enter university from a variety of educational and cultural contexts, the level of preparation they have received before entry to higher education has become a topic of interest. Preparatory programs exist to enable students from disparate educational and cultural contexts to access the academic and linguistic practices that will bring them success in higher education, but preparatory program curricula could flow into disciplinary curricula more explicitly to provide smoother transitions for international students. In her chapter, she focuses on an English-for-academic-purposes preparatory program for international students at an Australian university and its intersection with the Master's in Commerce to which they proceed. Course texts and student interviews are accessed to explore the relevance of the preparation for the Master's program. A series of mismatches in approaches to learning has implications for curricula in both programs. These can, she argues, be minimised through learning processes which make more explicit the practices of the academy.

Possible ways forward

We know from practice that students today are in many ways different from students in the past. Some may say they have a shorter attention span. Others may say they are more focused. Some may argue that they waste their time on the Internet during lectures. Others may argue that, as digital natives, they are using the technology in ways we have not experienced before. Such arguments will continue to thrive in the university sector as it tries to develop and reinvent itself to cope with the change from the industrial era to the digital era. For us, as editors of this book, we find this development of the university sector to be a fascinating challenge. Our argument is that this process will succeed only if student learning is seen as the nexus of both curriculum design and teaching practices. Each of these thirteen chapters shows a possible way forward in that respect. As editors, we have no doubt that the cases on collaboration, design, identity and transformation will serve as inspiration for individual teachers, as well as faculty groups, striving to take their own university teaching to the next level.

About the authors

John Branch is Lecturer of Marketing at the Stephen M. Ross School of Business and Faculty Associate at the Center for Russian, East European & Eurasian Studies, both of the University of Michigan, USA. He can be contacted at this email: jdbranch@umich.edu

Clive Holtham is Professor of Information Management and Director of the Learning Laboratory at Cass Business School, City University, London, UK. He can be contacted at this email: c.w.holtham@city.ac.uk

Claus Nygaard is Professor in Management Education at Copenhagen Business School and executive director of LiHE. He can be contacted at this email: lihesupport@gmail.com

Student-generated Questions: Enhancing Learning through Vicarious Experience

Patrícia Albergaria Almeida and José Teixeira-Dias

Introduction

This study is part of a broader research project, aiming to improve strategies for the teaching, learning and assessing of first-year students in chemistry. It builds upon previous work (Albergaria Almeida *et al.*, 2010; Albergaria Almeida *et al.*, 2011; Albergaria Almeida & Teixeira-Dias, 2011a). This study:

i.   Investigates ways to stimulate students to formulate questions

ii. Identifies factors that may inhibit students' questions

iii. Discusses the role of small-group work for the promotion of vicarious learning.

This project was developed with one undergraduate class (N=100) within a chemistry programme for science and engineering at the University of Aveiro, in Portugal. The study rests upon the conviction that it is possible to improve active learning (Hong & Weitman, this volume; Newman, this volume) by promoting question-asking between teacher and students and between students. With this in mind, several teaching approaches were developed to encourage students to ask questions to their teachers, and between themselves, through all the academic year 2010–11. The majority of these approaches were already tried during previous study phases (Albergaria Almeida & Teixeira-Dias, 2011a) with very positive results. The main approaches were:

i. Lectures (not compulsory attendance, N=100), mainly expositive, with small pauses for student questioning

ii. Laboratory sessions, reformulated in order to enable questioning and to promote student autonomy (compulsory, n=15)

iii. Tutorials (not compulsory attendance), intended to provide an opportunity for students to ask questions, expose their doubts and receive adequate answers

iv. Mini-research projects, developed during second semester (from February to June), small-group work to stimulate investigations on relevant and actual themes (voluntary).

A more detailed description of these strategies can be found elsewhere (Albergaria Almeida *et al.*, 2010).

A discussion forum in the Moodle platform supported these approaches to teaching and learning. In this forum, students were encouraged to write their questions and receive answers provided by peers or by the teacher. This use of the Moodle platform was actively aimed at motivating students to learn (Hong & Weitman, this volume; Lenstrup, this volume).

This work is based upon learners asking questions during the processes of learning. It is work concerned exclusively with those questions asked by learners and not with the routine asking of questions by teachers. A growing body of research suggests that asking questions is an important component of a rich learning experience of the sort one hopes is provided at every level of education (e.g. Albergaria Almeida *et al.*, 2010; Chin & Osborne, 2008; Di Teodoro *et al.*, 2011). Questioning is also considered to be an essential skill for lifelong learning (Enomoto & Warner, this volume).

We are concerned with the questions asked by learners as they embark upon a search for understanding in their studies. In everyday life, questions take on a multitude of forms and purposes. Ordinarily, to question is to ponder, seek answers to a puzzle or a problem, to encounter a perplexity that requires resolution. In this sense, we follow a route which suggests that the questions asked by learners are indicative of their need for some degree of interaction with both teachers and other students within sessions, for understanding within the domains in which they are working and studying and for some resolutions in their thinking.

We have argued elsewhere that the asking of questions is central to a learner's 'enculturation' into the patterns of language and thought (Albergaria Almeida et al., 2008; Teixeira-Dias *et al.*, 2005), discussion and criticism (Albergaria Almeida *et al.*, 2011) that are characteristic of an academic discipline (Albergaria Almeida, 2012; Albergaria Almeida & Mendes, 2010). It is also well known that, on a more detailed and local level, question-asking is often the most effective way for a learner to overcome a gap in understanding (Graesser & Olde, 2003), a particular impasse during problem solving (Ge & Land, 2004) or to resolve a difficult conceptual issue.

In several lecture-hall, tutorial and laboratory studies, we have developed and refined our understanding of how to describe, capture, classify and use learners' questions within higher-education courses (Albergaria Almeida & Teixeira-Dias, 2011a; Albergaria Almeida *et al.*, 2010; Teixeira-Dias *et al.*, 2005).

Questioning is a relatively new research area, although its value is already well recognised. As stated by Cuccio-Schirripa and Steiner (2000:21):

> *"questioning is one of the thinking processing skills which is structurally embedded in the thinking operations of critical thinking, creative thinking and problem solving. It consists of the smaller micro-thinking skills of recall, comprehension, application analysis, synthesis and evaluation… Questions guide knowledge construction in the formation and changing of the cognitive networks or schemata."*

We suggest that question-asking involves some personal risk and can be managed not just by individuals weighing benefits against costs (Pedrosa de Jesus *et al.*, 2006) but also through their observation of others balancing these same issues. This involves two forms of learning:

i.   The (often tacit) negotiation and co-construction of a climate of inquiry (Barbosa *et al.*, 2004)

ii. Vicarious learning (Roberts, 2010).

Vicarious learning occurs when students are influenced by other students' behaviours (Bandura, 1994; Cox *et al.*, 1999). For example, when shy or quiet students in a tutorial group learn from discussions between the teacher and others, or when 'lurkers' on an email discussion list the benefits derived from reading the contributions of others. Through vicarious experience, students may also change their behaviour by replicating an action that was performed by another student. For example, when students ask questions in class because another student posed a question and the teacher revealed appreciation.

In this chapter, we aim to shed light on this process, examining the ways in which we can encourage question-asking through vicarious learning and derive 'teacher-friendly' ways of managing this.

Vicarious learning

Huann-Shyang *et al.* (2009) argue that being able to ask appropriate questions is one of the keys to successful learning. It might be that this involves confidence as much as inquisitorial hunger, and observing other learners engaged in such dialogues provides a model of good learning experiences. Actually, there is an emerging body of research which emphasises that students are able to learn from others' experiences (Cox *et al.*, 1999; Robert, 2010). We have borrowed Bandura's (1986, 1994) term 'vicarious' learning to describe this. Vicarious learning is also known as observational learning or modelling (Bandura, 1994; Cox *et al.*, 1999). According to Bandura (1994:66):

> *"Humans have evolved an advanced capacity for observational learning that enables them to expand their knowledge and competencies rapidly through the information conveyed by the rich variety of models. Virtually all behavioral, cognitive, and affective learning from direct experience can be achieved vicariously [second-hand] by observing people's actions and the consequences for them."*

Vicarious learning, a key component of Bandura's social learning theory, occurs when a person changes after watching the behaviour of another person. Cox *et al.* (1999) highlight the potential benefit to learners of being able to observe or 'listen in' on their peers as they discuss a new topic.

A person's behaviour can be affected by the positive or negative consequences – called vicarious reinforcement or vicarious punishment – of a model's behaviour. Vicarious learning is important because it is typically much more efficient than learning which involves actually experiencing a given situation, particularly where that experience is difficult or high risk.

There are several guiding principles behind vicarious learning:

i.   A person will imitate someone else's behaviour if this role model possesses characteristics (talent, intelligence, power, good looks or popularity, for example) that the person finds attractive or desirable.

ii. The person will react to the way the model is treated and mimic the model behaviour. When the model behaviour is rewarded, the observer is more likely to reproduce the rewarded behaviour. When the model is punished, an example of vicarious punishment, the observer is less likely to reproduce the same behaviour.

iii. Human actions are a complex interaction of the person, the person's behaviour and the environment. A person's cognitive abilities, physical characteristics, personality, beliefs, attitudes and so on influence the observer's ways of behaving. These influences are reciprocal. People can influence feelings about themselves and their attitudes and beliefs about others. Like-wise, much of what a person knows comes from environmental resources such as television, parents, and books.

Our initial question has been: *how does vicarious learning promote learners' question-asking?* There are three kinds of vicarious learning that are of interest to us:

i.   The Modelling Effect occurs when a person almost directly duplicates an action the observer has seen someone else perform. For instance, a young woman student watches a friend asking questions in class and then asks her own questions in a situation where previously she would have simply stayed quiet.

ii. The Eliciting Effect occurs when a person performs an action similar but different to the role model. For example, the same student hears her friend asking oral questions in class and this prompts her to make a written note of her questions and later email these to her teacher for a response.

iii. The Inhibitory Effect occurs when a person refrains from an action after seeing someone disadvantaged for engaging in that action. For example, the young woman might stop asking questions if she saw several other students receive minimal feedback to their queries, given additional assignments to write reports on topics about which they asked questions or, worse, suffered some undue embarrassment in the class (from teacher or peers) in the process of asking their questions.

There is, of course, more to effective teaching than making the implicit meaning of the subject matter more explicit. Indeed, students' enculturation into the archetypes of language and thought, discussion and criticism that are traits of a disciplinary field can be thought of as a higher-level alignment. The learner acquires a new set of norms and procedures, and also a new framework of knowledge. So there are two rather different ways in which we can think about teaching: as a source of knowledge about a specific area and as a way of embedding the student into the culture of a disciplinary field.

Classroom questioning

Much of the literature on questioning approaches the topic from the perspective of teachers rather than students. Student behaviour is most often mentioned in terms of the answers or responses that teachers receive to their questions. Thus questioning seems to be viewed as something teachers do to students, a one-way flow of interrogation that is occasionally interrupted by answers to teachers' questions. It has been documented that teachers typically ask 96 per cent of the questions in a classroom environment (Graesser & Person, 1994). Increasingly, however, teaching and learning are seen as interdependent activities requiring interaction between teacher and students such that teacher–student communication is not a simple one-way process.

There is a series of studies placing the responsibility of questioning onto students rather than their teachers and indicating that this benefits student learning (Chin & Osborne, 2008). Student questioning plays a significant role in motivating meaningful learning and can serve different functions within this. These functions can include confirmation of expectations, answers to unexpected puzzles and filling a recognised knowledge gap (Biddulph & Osborne, 1982). The questions that learners ask are also indicative of their need for resolution in their thinking, for understanding within the domains in which they are working and studying, and for some degree of interaction with both teachers (Pedrosa de Jesus *et al.*, 2003) and other students within sessions (Albergaria Almeida & Teixeira-Dias, 2011b). Student questioning, particularly at the higher cognitive levels, is also an essential aspect of problem solving (Chin & Chia, 2004) and is considered as the most important indicator of critical thinking (Pedrosa de Jesus *et al.*, 2003).

Besides helping students to learn, student questioning can also guide teachers in their work. Some researchers (Crawford *et al.*, 2000) have explored the potential for using students' questions to influence the curriculum. Some questions indicate that students have been thinking about the ideas presented and have been trying to extend and link these with other things they already know. Questions can also reveal much about the quality of students' thinking and conceptual understanding (Albergaria Almeida *et al.*, 2010; Watts *et al.*, 1997), their alternative frameworks and confusion about various concepts (Maskill & Pedrosa de Jesus, 1997), their reasoning (Donaldson, 1978) and what it is they want to know (Elstgeest, 1985). However, according to Graesser and Person (1994:105), it is *"well documented that student questions in the classroom are very infrequent and unsophisticated."* In fact, studies at different educational levels and contexts generally indicate that learners do have questions but avoid asking them (Dillon, 1998; Teixeira-Dias *et al.*, 2005) and report, for instance, that students tend to ask fewer on-task attention questions in higher-education-level classes (Good *et al.*, 1987).

According to Graesser and McMahen (1993) there are three stages to generating a question:

i.   Cognitive disequilibrium occurs when the student detects and is aware of a conflict in knowledge and understanding

ii. Verbal coding occurs when the student articulates this in words, and then

iii. Social editing occurs when the student expresses these words in a social setting.

Needless to say, each of these stages takes time: questions do not always arrive in their best format at the point of utterance. That is, questions can be quickly or slowly formed, with a spectrum in between. Our own taxonomy of question types relates to levels of learning:

    i.   Acquisition questions are factually orientated, being easily and quickly formed

    ii.   Specialisation questions require subject-specific detail

    iii.   Integration questions are critically analytic questions, taking progressively longer (Albergaria Almeida *et al.*, 2008; Albergaria Almeida *et al.*, 2010).

However, this needs not to be the case. Using Graesser and McMahen's three stages, we can see that the:

    i.   Detection of 'cognitive' conflict can be sudden, but can take place over an extended period of time as variations between expectations and counter evidence accumulate. As Miyake and Norman (1979) caution, it can take a large amount of knowledge to know what one does not know.

    ii.   Articulation of questions can also take time. This will depend to some extent upon the complexity of the issues and the presence or absence of a felt need to formulate a fully developed question. While some learners are prepared to herald and then ask a 'naïve' question, others are only willing to prepare fully written and carefully worded questions.

    iii.   The context within which questions are asked can prove an obstacle and therefore slow down the process. In Graesser and McMahen's study, the authors suggest, for example, that questions do not surface when this involves too much mental effort or when it is socially awkward to ask them.

According to these three stages, it is possible to advance several reasons for the absence of students' questions in class. For instance, students won't ask questions if they:

    i.   Cannot detect cognitive disequilibrium

    ii.   Can detect cognitive disequilibrium but this does not raise a question (being perhaps not prepared to admit their own level of uncertainty or lack of knowledge)

iii. Can detect cognitive disequilibrium but want to infer the answer themselves (be cognitively active)

iv. Can detect cognitive disequilibrium but want someone else to answer – preferably the teacher (cognitively passive)

v. Cannot formulate the question

vi. Can formulate a simple question but want to ask an elaborated question

vii. Cannot ask out loud

viii. Can ask questions but prefer asking classmates outside the classroom rather than asking the teacher during classes

ix. Can ask but cannot ask actionable questions.

Although literature about students' questions is not abundant, some authors discuss strategies for involving students in questioning. Early work by Dillon (1988) proposed that teachers encourage student questions by systematically making room for questions in the class agenda, welcoming and inviting questions, and waiting patiently for them. Others have suggested that teachers could improve classroom learning by helping students to learn good questioning skills (Graesser & Person, 1994).

The project: encouraging student questioning

This project rests on the belief that it is possible to nurture a questioning culture in higher-education classes. With this in mind, several teaching and learning strategies were designed to promote student-generated questions.

In addition to the lectures, tutorials and laboratory sessions, students have been asked to undertake mini-research projects on topics in chemistry (Albergaria Almeida & Teixeira-Dias, 2011b) during the second semester of academic year 2010–11. Students were invited to choose from a list of 20 suggested themes such as: 'Nanotechnology and the Double Helix', 'Making New Elements' and 'The Complexity of Coffee'.

The participation in these mini-research projects was proposed on a voluntary basis, coexisting with other students' studies and interests. It enabled students to enhance their assessments by a small margin.

Forty students voluntarily organised themselves in 20 groups with two students each. During one semester, the students developed the tasks proposed by the teacher and had regular meetings with him. At the end of the semester, each group prepared an oral 'poster presentation' for an audience in which all peers and teachers involved were invited. Questions from the audience were encouraged and welcomed.

Participants and data gathering

From October 2010 to January 2011 (first semester) and from February to June 2011 (second semester), all chemistry lessons (approximately 90) from one class were audio-recorded. The researcher (the first author of this chapter, in attendance at all lessons) also used observation grids for every lesson. This way, all oral questions were also collected.

As mentioned, the data were collected from one teacher's class (the second author of this chapter) with 100 undergraduate students (47 female, 53 male; mean age 18 years). All were taking a common programme in chemistry, although following different degree programmes: chemistry, chemical engineering, physics, physical engineering, environmental engineering and materials engineering. From the total sample of 100 students, 20 students were selected for an interview. Ten of them were interviewed at the end of the first semester; the other 10 students were interviewed at the end of the second semester. The main aims of these interviews were to:

   i.   Gather students' opinions about the project

   ii.   Understand the reasons that lead them to ask, or not ask, questions.

Results and discussion

Along the academic year, a total of 354 questions (both oral and written) were registered. During the first semester, all the questions collected were in a written format and were mainly related to topics discussed during lectures and laboratory classes, totalling 80, as shown in Figure 1.

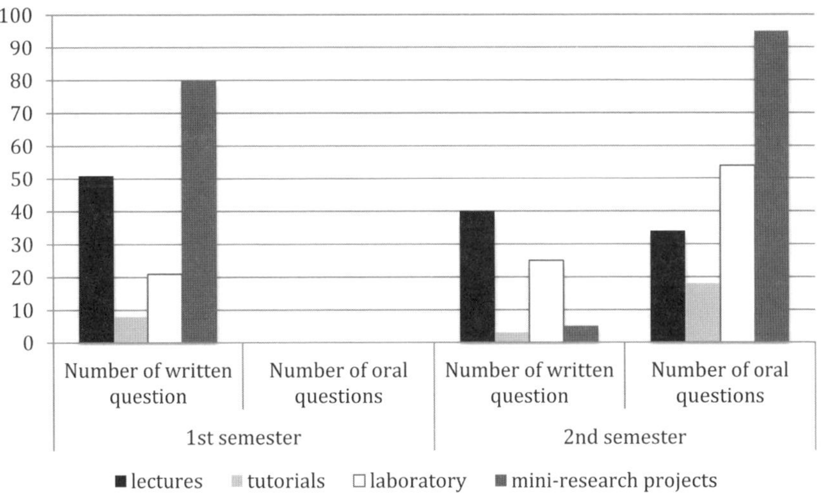

Figure 1: Number of student questions asked during the academic year

Drawn from our project, the following are instances of written questions raised during the first semester:

"How does heavy water form? What is it useful for? Where can we find it?"

"How might one confirm that cathodic protection prevents corrosion?"

During the second semester the number of questions increased to 274; these were mainly asked during mini-research projects sessions, laboratory classes and lectures. It is important to bear in mind that mini-research projects were only run this semester and were the strategy that stimulated more questions, with almost all of them being asked orally (see Figure 1). Drawn from our project, some instances of questions raised during the second semester are:

"Is fluoridric acid a weak or a strong acid?"

"Would lithium and fuel cells stand, in the future, on equal footing to generate electric energy?"

During interviews at the end of the first semester, some students explained that they had not felt comfortable raising oral questions at the beginning of the year because they did not know their peers and the teacher:

"I did not participate more because I did not know the teacher and my colleagues. Lately, it is different, because I already know them better. Now I also feel more confident to answer to the teachers' questions and to explain him my reasoning."

(Marco)

"I don't ask because I don't feel very comfortable with my colleagues."

(Ana)

Even when students already knew their colleagues and the teacher, they still failed to raise oral questions and some students pointed to this situation during interviews:

"If I have a doubt, first I try to solve it by myself. I look at the notes from the class; I look in the book… If I can't solve it, I ask my friends. If they don't know the answer too, well… I must ask the teacher! But I can't ask everything that crosses my mind. I can't ask something that has an obvious answer. What would the teacher think?!"

(Maria)

Nevertheless, during the second semester, students started to ask also oral questions. Furthermore, during this semester, students asked many more oral then written questions (Figure 1).

It seems that the irregular distribution of students' questions is mainly related to the nature of the lesson. Teaching approaches or lessons that are less expositive, more student-centred and that involve a smaller group of students tend to generate a higher number of oral questions. On the other hand, classes with a large number of students, such as lectures, promote a higher number of written questions. The teaching approach that led to the highest number of questions was the mini-research projects. From the 100 questions raised during the mini-research project sessions, only 5 were written questions, with the remaining 95 being asked orally.

During interviews at the end of the second semester, some students mentioned some reasons that might explain the high number of oral questions raised during mini-research project sessions:

i.   The reduced number of students that were present during mini-research project sessions:

"We were just a few students. I think it has to do with that, we feel much more comfortable when we are just a few!"

(Ana)

ii.   The urgency and need to clarify their doubts:

"Those meetings were to tackle doubts, and we wanted to get on with the project. So, we had to ask! It was the only time we had to clarify our doubts with the teacher!"

(Filipe)

iii.   The questioning environment that was created in the course of the mini-research project meetings:

"In the first meeting I was kind of shy, but then my colleagues started to ask questions, and I felt more comfortable to ask too."

(Alexandre)

This last aspect was referred to by several students. Students did not felt comfortable in doing something that was not usual for them: asking the teacher questions. Nevertheless, when this behaviour was adopted by some students, it started to become 'normal' and other students also felt comfortable asking – a clear example of what we have called the snowball effect of the modelling effect of vicarious learning.

There are some other reasons that were not mentioned by the students during the interviews to explain the higher number of oral questions raised during the mini-research project sessions but that must be considered:

i.   Mini-research projects were carried out during second semester, when the students already knew each other, allowing a wider and better interaction between peers and also between the students and the teacher

ii. Mini-research projects were developed in small groups, which incites dialogue and questioning between the elements of the group and between these and the teacher

iii. The topics of the mini-research projects had visibility and practical application, which facilitated the formulation of questions at the initial stage of students' work.

It is also important to emphasise that the habit of questioning, created throughout the development of mini-research projects, also had effects on other lessons, such as lectures and tutorials (see Figure 1) – another example of the snowball effect. Working in small groups with the teacher made the students feel more confident and more able to ask questions during mini-research projects sessions and also during the other classes.

> *"I think it is related to confidence. With the mini-projects I felt more comfortable with the teacher. I think I felt closer to the teacher! I don't feel so 'small' and this way it is easier to ask questions during classes, even during lectures!"*
>
> (Joana)

The relation of proximity established during mini-research-project sessions spread to the other classes and made the students feel more comfortable asking questions.

It is important to notice that only 40 of the 100 students of the chemistry class participated in mini-research projects. But the students involved in the mini-research projects performed an essential role in the development of a questioning behaviour among the other students through the snowball effect.

> *"If everyone is quiet I will not ask too. But if others ask it becomes normal to raise questions! And then I can also question!"*
>
> (Marco)

> *"I don't feel very comfortable asking questions. If you notice I am never the first one to raise a question during a tutorial… I just can't! I don't know why, but if others start to question, then I am just another one in the middle of all the others! Does this makes any sense to you?"*
>
> (Jorge)

These students express how they felt impelled to ask oral questions during classes, since this became a normal behaviour in all chemistry classes (and not only during mini-research projects sessions). However, it is important to underline that the mini-research projects were the seed of oral questioning, which later spread to the other types of classes.

Conclusions

This work confirms what we have presented elsewhere (Pedrosa de Jesus, Teixeira-Dias & Watts, 2003; Albergaria Almeida & Teixeira-Dias, 2011a). It is possible to create a questioning environment where asking questions becomes an integral part of everyday transactions between teachers and students.

When given the opportunity to ask written and oral questions, students tend to ask more oral questions in lessons with a small class which are student centred. On the other hand, students ask more written questions about lessons that have big classes and are more teacher centred.

Mini-research project sessions were a marked success, particularly in terms of increasing the number of questions in the sessions with the teacher, during poster preparation, and of encouraging peer questioning in the final poster presentation session. But mini-research project sessions also had an impact on the questioning behaviour of students during other lessons, such as tutorials and lectures.

Students' questions raised orally throughout the development of mini-research projects have performed two different functions. They:

i. Stimulated other students to ask questions during the mini-research project sessions, and

ii. Inspired other students to ask questions during other lessons, such as lectures and tutorials, performing what we have called the snowball effect of vicarious learning.

It is also important to notice that students who asked more oral questions were the key elements for the vicarious learning. These students also asked better questions, performed better on mini-research projects and had better final marks. At this stage, further research ought to explore how the snowball effect impacts the quality of students' learning. Previous studies (Albergaria Almeida *et al.*, 2008) have shown that written questions usually are higher-level questions than oral ones. Because vicarious learning promoted oral questioning and induced a decrease in written questions, it is important to investigate the quality of students' questions in both semesters.

Implications

Our goal is to enhance the asking of questions within classrooms, in this case within science classes at higher-education level. Our belief is that a climate of inquiry is a significant feature of education and, in this case, of higher education. Most of the strategies we have adopted and evaluated so far have been at a curricular-structural level involving a university department in the revision of their work and the provision of alternative shapes to teaching. This has required new approaches by teachers and students alike. The essence of this research, however, highlights the need for more attention at the level of classroom interactions and social relationships. In our view, this includes:

i. Tutorials in the nature of questioning and the criteria for designing and asking quality questions within the discipline under consideration

ii. Further facilitation of classroom questioning through, for example, small-group work, mini-project research tasks or e-based systems

iii. Requiring peer work so that a 'lead student' can model question-asking in a positive and receptive environment, thus giving other students the opportunity to learn and to 'slip-stream' their questioning in the wake of 'model' question-askers.

The construction, implementation and evaluation of these approaches form the next steps of our work.

Acknowledgments

The authors acknowledge the support of the Research Centre for Didactics and Technology in Teacher Education (CIDTFF) and the support of the Portuguese Foundation for Science and Technology (FCT).

About the authors

Patrícia Albergaria Almeida is a researcher at the Research Centre for Didactics and Technology in Teacher Education, Department of Education, University of Aveiro, Portugal. She can be contacted at this email: patriciaalmeida@ua.pt

José Teixeira-Dias is a Full Professor of Chemistry at the Department of Chemistry, University of Aveiro, Portugal. He can be contacted at this email: teixeiradias@ua.pt

Chapter 3
Social-media Learning Environments

Christine Lenstrup

Introduction

The purpose of this chapter is to discuss the importance of new ways of teaching and learning in higher education through the use of social-media learning environments, in order for the new generation of 'digitally native' students to become more engaged and motivated and to create a meaningful learning experience.

A social-media learning environment is a web-2.0-based environment in which teachers and students can work and learn together as creators or co-creators of user-generated content, in contrast to websites where users are limited to the passive viewing of content that was created for them. Contrary to web-1.0-based environments which focus on the distribution of information, a social-media learning environment promotes interaction and information sharing between its users (see Figure 1 below). This interaction and information sharing can be as simple as asking for the students' comments on a subject, or as complex as asking the students to reflect on their learning via learning journals. The students can log in via their laptops, iPads, etc. to participate in a classroom environment in which they can view lecture slides, post and view comments, and upload questions, assignments and tasks. The teacher can comment on these assignments, questions and tasks, thereby interacting with the students; and the students can also interact by commenting on each other's assignments.

Figure 1: The main characteristics of web 1.0 and web 2.0

Today's students in higher education have spent their lives surrounded by technological tools (computers, mobiles, online games and various console games) which have made it possible to be online constantly. The new 'digitally native' learners are learning in a new environment, one aspect of which is social media. Prensky (2001:n.p.) states that *"today's students think and process information fundamentally differently from their predecessors"*. He argues further that it is essential to teach the students the tools of tomorrow (for example, working in online environments, making video and programming) in order for the students to be prepared for the future (Prensky, 2012). Often, students are constantly online, texting or chatting with their friends or searching on the Internet before, during and after class via their mobile devices, such as smartphones, pads and laptops. This constant interaction with their mobile devices influences language creation and perception in that interaction and collaboration become an integral part of their lives.

The increasing use of information technology makes students dependent on the web for searching information and engaging with others (Mondahl *et al.*, 2011). The content of learning is aggregated by the students using their own personal RSS reader or similar application. From there, it is remixed and repurposed, the finished product being fed forward to become fodder for some other student's reading, project or use (Dirckinck-Holmfeld, 2010).

The wave of technological innovations and changing expectations from new generations of students necessitates educators and researchers in higher education to make use of new ways to teach and interact with the students (Garrison & Vaughan, 2008) in order to enhance the overall learning experience. In the 1970s, computer-based training emerged with a lot of stand-alone stationary computers taking over much of the traditional teaching from teachers. The students worked independently and at their own speed. Ten years later, we experienced a shift towards exploration and construction through games and modelling, then in the 1990s, computer-supported collaborative learning began both in the classroom and at a distance. At the beginning of the 2000s, online learning environments were implemented and, some years later, social-media platforms (such as Facebook and Twitter) saw the light of the day. In 2010, the transition from physical environments to online personalised environments took place (Dirckinck-Holmfeld, 2010). In the years to come, a continued and even increased use of web 2.0 technology in education seems very likely as the development of cheaper and smaller mobile devices might make it natural for everybody to interact (Jee, 2011).

Modern technology has changed many people's reading and writing patterns in the past decade and a new type of literacy, known as 'e-literacy', has arisen. E-literacy refers to *the ability to find, select, organize and make use of information, as well as to read and write in the new medium*" (Warschauer & Shetzer, 2000:172, cited in Jee, 2011). This makes teachers and researchers in higher education engage in new ways of teaching and learning in order for students to be involved in the learning experience, because meaningful learning is best obtained by actively motivated learners.

With the adoption of social-media learning environments, the role of the teacher is changing. The teacher is no longer a traditional teacher but is functioning as a facilitator, continuously engaging with the students in online forums, online blogging and suchlike. The question then is how we can facilitate an appropriate dialogue between teacher and students when using ICT (Information and Communications Technology) for teaching in order to obtain a deep learning experience (Biggs, 2003). A deep learning experience arises when the students reflect on their own learning, trying to understand the underlying subject(s) and then *see learning as an enjoyable process*" (Mitsis & Foley, 2010:36); and when students become interested in the subject itself, the outcome might be increased interaction and improved learning. The discussion is to what extent we can make use of social-media learning environments in teaching. Data from the Sprogkernen Project at Copenhagen Business School, which analysed the application of various ICT tools in second-language acquisition, point towards the importance of proper instruction by the teacher of ICT in order to engage the students in an active and successful way (Sprogkernen, 2011). The data further revealed a number of obstacles in connection with the adoption of the various ICT tools in second-language acquisition, one of which is that the new generation of learners may still experience difficulties when trying to interact with computer-supported learning environments. The Sprogkernen Project resulted in a number of recommendations, including how to enhance the students' learning experience.

The learning experience

Second-language acquisition is often seen as an individual process (Svendsen, 2012; Sprogkernen, 2012). Viewed through the lens of social constructivism, however, social interaction plays an important part during the learning process. Different teaching environments (traditional class teaching, web-based forums, etc.) offer different kinds of possibilities for learning but good teaching requires a social system such as a group in which communication and collaboration can take place. We need face-to-face interaction and/or a web-based forum in order to activate learning.

Motivation is also an important issue to address because it is unlikely that students learn without being motivated. In this connection, it is important to talk about different approaches to learning in order to improve the overall learning experience. Biggs (2003) describes two approaches to learning: the surface approach and the deep approach to learning. The surface approach is *to get the task out of the way with minimum trouble* (Biggs, 2003:14), meaning that the students do not see learning as relevant. Students try because they are interested in the results of the outcome and not in the process. This correlates with extrinsic motivation because here students perform a task because the outcome is important (Biggs, 2003:61). The students mainly perform in order to obtain a grade that will allow them to pass the course and are not interested in obtaining a good grade. This is also referred to as the strategic approach by Entwistle *et al.* (2001), for example, and is used by surface-approach students who wish to obtain a positive outcome (passing the course).

The deep approach is built upon *"the need to engage the task appropriately and meaningfully"* (Biggs, 2003:16). Here, students interact vigorously and try to understand the underlying meaning of the subject. Students try to focus on the details but some sort of prior knowledge from the students is required in order to get the total picture. This correlates with intrinsic motivation and here the students learn because they are interested in the subject itself, not because they are required to. The result is often a more meaningful learning experience with motivated, interested and engaged students (Biggs, 2003:62) thereby creating a more fruitful learning climate for both the students and the teacher. The adoption of a deep approach to learning depends on the teacher and on the strategies he/she uses but it mainly depends on the students. The same teacher might use one strategy and some students will adopt a deep approach while others will adopt a surface approach.

Communication plays a vital role in teaching and learning. Consequently, it is of vital importance that the teacher articulates the connection between what the students are going to do (the activity), the situation in which they will do it (the educational context), the reason why they are going to do it (the outcome/the learning objectives) and the tools they are going to apply in order to perform the task. The application of ICT might move the students' motivation from being extrinsic to intrinsic in that ICT often promotes collaboration and group work, thus making the students engage actively in the teaching. Extrinsic motivation is a result of external rewards, such as getting a good grade or avoiding a low grade and its negative consequences (for example, a low average compared with the entry grade point average of a desired university place). The increased motivation might be a direct consequence of the application of ICT because ICT creates variation in second-language acquisition and makes it more fun by encouraging the creativity of the individual students. Intrinsic motivation is a result of the task and the related positive associations and emotions (Deci *et al.*, 2001). In the beginning, students may be indifferent to the content of the task and only think that the ICT part is fun; yet it may well be that the positive associations thus created can influence the content of the task. In other words, ICT has an indirect effect on the students' intrinsic motivation to learn languages.

Social-media learning environments

Within our globalised world, many of the businesses that hire graduates are using social media in their internal and their external communication. By including social media in higher-education classrooms, we enable our students to hone their competences within social-media environments (Mondahl *et al.*, 2011).

According to Jee (2011), web 2.0 technology provides new kinds of learning and teaching with technology in second- and foreign-language instruction because web 2.0 technologies have user-created content, which enhances the users' participation. Moreover, the basic concepts of social-media learning environments are knowledge sharing and collaboration, and so their use makes it easier for learners to connect and collaborate with other learners. Web 2.0 technologies have free or low-cost access and knowledge sharing and collaboration without limitations are obtainable. One could argue that, in most learning situations in which students are required to collaborate to reach a result, social media or other web-2.0-based e-learning tools will facilitate the students' learning processes and thereby be a contributing factor in transforming their learning from surface learning to deep learning (Biggs, 2003).

Social-media learning environments offer a number of possibilities in language learning classes. Firstly, students might experience increased autonomy and independence because social-media learning environments promote collaboration and group work, thus making the students engage actively in the teaching. Secondly, the passive learning structure will be limited or perhaps even absent. The students go from being passive recipients of information to active co-creators of knowledge. Due to the didactic triangle being reversed, the students are allowed to explore the substance itself actively, in collaboration with other students (Sprogkernen, 2012).

The new generation of students' constant interaction with their mobile devices (smartphones, pads, laptops) influences language creation and perception in that knowledge sharing and collaboration become an integral part of their lives. The new generation of students is accustomed to finding, selecting, organising and making use of information on the Internet, and to reading and writing in several online media. Social media have created new openings for both teachers and students to engage, interact and collaborate in learning tasks that enhance learning processes and the overall learning experience (Benson, 2008; Prensky, 2012).

When using web 2.0 technology in the classroom, however, teachers are faced with some obstacles. Firstly, even though today's learners are seen as 'digitally native', some might still experience difficulties when trying to interact with social-media learning environments. Secondly, one might observe resistance from some teachers towards the application of web 2.0 technology in the classroom. Some teachers might even experience insecurity over the use of web 2.0 tools and how to handle the teachers' changing role in the classroom. Further, differing expectations between students and teacher on the frequency of being online might also be a hindrance. Thirdly, many universities are not well-enough equipped to cater for the increasing use of various digital aids (having, for example, insufficient plug-ins for laptops, an insufficiently functioning and stable Internet connection, etc.).

From our study in Sprogkernen II, we found that the role of the teacher changes from lecturing expert to consultant with a mentoring role (Sprogkernen, 2012). This means that the teacher is no longer the 'authoritarian' teacher in class, the result being that the typical old-fashioned 'top-down' and very asymmetric learning structure is significantly restricted. The students feel more autonomous and independent which might lead to, among other things, a sense of self responsibility and a higher degree of motivation. When present on social media, the teacher might activate students between lessons to obtain enhanced student preparation and rewarding/fruitful appearance in the classroom environment (Andersen, 2004) and support collaboration in learning. When it comes to second-language acquisition, collaborative learning not only stimulates student interest and participation but is further supported by the use of social media (Mondahl *et al.*, 2011).

Teacher identity and teacher impact are key to much student motivation and interaction (Borg, 2003). The teachers' instruction of their students in the use of web 2.0 tools and also its purpose is vital. Many students like to see a clear link between the suitability, the employment, and the purpose and goal of using a particular ICT tool. According to Borg (2003), contextual factors play a pivotal role in the extent to which teachers are able to disclose information/instruction consistent with their cognition and data collected in the Sprogkernen Project at CBS supports this (Sprogkernen, 2011).

The Sprogkernen Project

'Sprogkernen' can be loosely translated as the basic and most important part ('kernen') of language ('sprog'). The project began in 2010 as 'Sprogkernen I' and involved a co-operation between a research group, the 'UFO Group' (which translates as 'the educational research group'), from Copenhagen Business School, Copenhagen University, DEA (the Danish Research Academy) and a number of Danish 'gymnasium' schools. The Danish 'gymnasium' offers a three-year, general, academically oriented, upper-secondary programme which builds on the ninth or tenth form of the primary and lower secondary school. On graduating from the 'gymnasium', a student is qualified for admission to higher education. The overriding purpose of the second part of Sprogkernen, 'Sprogkernen II', which began in 2011 and is still running, is to pinpoint which educational tools can be applied in order to enhance students' language competences. The underlying purpose is how to create a higher degree of motivation and interaction in the classroom with increased outcome as a result. In continuation hereof, Sprogkernen II focuses on the implementation of a number of sub-projects, all of which involve the application of various forms of ICT in the teaching of foreign languages. The key assumption from the research group involved in Sprogkernen is that the use of various forms of ICT in the teaching and the use of cases can help increase students' motivation and engagement, thereby achieving interaction and collaboration and deep learning among the students. The different forms of ICT in the sub-projects were photo story, moviemaker, voki, e-books and social-media tools such as wikis, blogs and chats. In the Sprogkernen Project, we investigated and interviewed teachers and students from two different Danish 'gymnasium' classes at two different schools in which the students were to apply ICT in their German lessons. We initiated qualitative research by way of focus group interviews with teachers and students from the two chosen 'gymnasiums'. We carried out the interviews at the chosen 'gymnasiums' and at Copenhagen Business School, and we also made classroom observations of the teaching.

Sprogkernen findings

The Sprogkernen Project revealed that the way in which the teacher believes he/she articulates the purpose or goal of using various web-based tools in foreign language acquisition to the students plays a vital role for the students' perception of learning. This is supported by statements made from audio-recorded group interviews with some of the students in the Sprogkernen Project:

"[ICT] is relevant if you have received proper introduction first…"

(Student 1)

"We don't really know why we are going to use it [ICT]."

(Student 2)

All student statements in this paragraph have been taken from Sprogkernen 2012. The project also revealed that many students preferred the use of web-based learning environments in the second-language acquisition classes to traditional classroom instruction (Sprogkernen, 2012). This is also supported by statements from some of the students in the Sprogkernen Project:

"ICT-based teaching is more exciting than traditional teaching…"

(Student 3)

"I want to learn languages"

(Student 4)

"ICT provides variation and makes me more motivated…"

(Student 5)

"I become more creative and I look forward to participating in the lessons…"

(Student 6)

These data correspond with data from another UFO Group project, with second-year BA students in International Business Communication at Copenhagen Business School, in which a social-media learning environment called Podio was utilised as our joint learning environment (UFO Group, 2010). Podio resembles Facebook in many ways, possessing the possibility of creating your own apps, blogs, wikis and so on within the platform. Blogs were used as learning journals to support reflection and learning (see Stupans in this volume) thereby creating the basis of personalised feedback to the students on the individual tasks. The students had access to two forums, a joint classroom forum and a group forum. Group forums were created in the joint classroom forum in order for the students to work collaboratively on the cases in relation to the course, thereby facilitating reflection and deep learning. In the electronic group forum, the students had the opportunity to track their own learning by writing learning journals. At the same time, the teacher could follow the students' development by reading their journals and then make one or more comments. This means that learning in a social-media learning environment can be an individual process with personalised feedback, well suited to the generations of students with whom we are familiar today. But social-media learning environments also accentuate collaboration.

The use of social media

So in what ways can we use social media in a teaching environment? Social media have created new openings both for students and teachers because, through their use, individual and group creativity can be unfolded, also enhancing collaborative learning processes (Svendsen & Mondahl, 2011). Through a web-based environment, such as a social-media learning environment, students might learn individually by creating and using new apps in their own personal forums, but also collectively because social-media learning environments facilitate knowledge sharing and collective problem solving in the group.

Social-media learning environments contribute to enhancing the students' communication skills when presenting in the classroom, thereby adding new knowledge and leading to positive learning outcomes for the entire class (Svendsen & Mondahl, 2011). Because social-media learning environments support individual and group creativity (for example, by the creation of new apps in the students' group forums), new means of knowledge sharing are invented in the learning process and this might increase student motivation. Learning through a social-media learning environment might even be perceived as less 'instructive' by some students and therefore more appealing. In other words, we see a shift away from traditional top-down teaching from teacher to students to collaborative teaching where students interact with each other. A teaching situation can be described in terms of its three components: teacher, students and content. These components and their interactions can be described in a didactic triangle. In a didactic situation, students approach the subject through the teacher's curriculum design, choice of literature, teaching methods, assessment methods, connection of theory to practice, etc. When applying social media, the didactic triangle is turned upside down and the students start to investigate by themselves reflecting on their own input and on input from fellow students (see Stupans in this volume). In this way, the students act as each other's sparring partner and the teacher acts as a facilitator. Being able to go into dialogue with fellow students and teachers might enhance motivation from the students, thereby resulting in a deep learning experience.

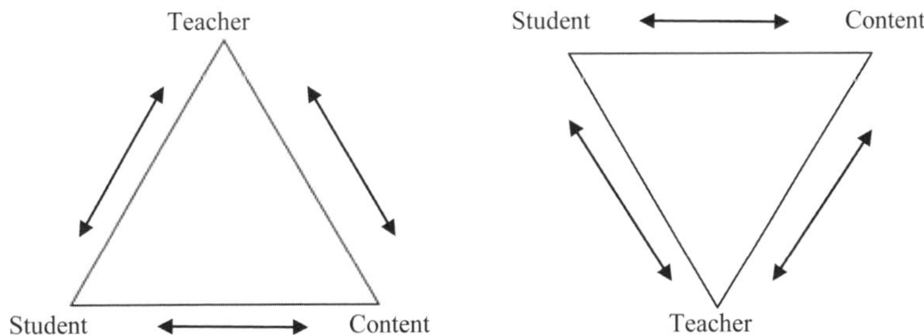

Figure 2: The classical didactic triangle and the reversed didactic triangle
Adapted from Kansanen (1999)

Teachers can view, preserve and comment on the details of the students' interactions during group activities, making these available for the students as tools for reflection (Dirckinck-Holmfeld, 2010). Web-based learning environments such as social media can increase student collaboration and interaction in the classroom, and the recognition of being able to collaborate with others is increasingly being seen as a *"core interpersonal skill required for employment in the twenty-first century"* (Ernest *et al.*, 2011:3) by many employers.

The level of motivation plays a significant role for students' construction of knowledge from a learning encounter. Apart from promoting collaboration in the classroom, social-media learning environments might actively engage students. Being able to go into dialogue with their teachers and peers might sharpen and elaborate the students' understanding, thereby promoting deep learning (Biggs, 2003).

When adopting web 2.0 tools, we also need to discuss the occurrence of negative aspects both for the students and for the teachers. Even though today's students are often perceived as 'digital natives', they might still experience difficulties and obstacles when interacting in social-media learning environments. This also necessitates a clear link from the teachers between the application of the specific web 2.0 tools and the specific learning context (Biggs, 2003). In other words, the teacher also needs to consider if the choice of web 2.0 tools suits the particular course. Social-media learning environments promote collaboration and group work when solving a learning task. However, for some students, group work is not seen as preferable and they might not want to join a group. This is of course detrimental to the group work process. There is the possibility that not all group members share the same amount of knowledge and have the same level of skills, although this does not necessarily need to be a downside. In such a scenario, the difference in knowledge and skills among the students might foster more collaboration and promote co-operative writing, because the students might then share with each other.

The adoption of social-media learning environments makes it possible to socialise and collaborate anywhere and at any time. This constant interaction, however, might put strings on the expectations between students and the teacher and between the individual students as to when they are expected to be online. Here, it is important to have a clear dialogue between teacher and students in order to avoid any possible misunderstandings.

The role of the teacher

In contrast to the traditional classroom teacher role of expert deciding the curriculum, the role of the teacher in a social-media learning environment could be one of a facilitator for the students. When teachers engage in the use of social-media learning environments, they experience a change in role from lecturer to facilitator. The ways in which instructional practice and mutual cognition are informing also change (Borg, 2003). The changing role/identity is not constrained by the context of the classroom but by the content of a social-media learning environment (Danielsen & Nielsen, 2010). In other words, the challenge is thus to establish a web-based learning platform with content, making it possible for the new digital generation of students to engage actively and collaborate in the learning process.

The traditional classroom teacher is one who instructs, decides on curriculum and is perceived to be expert on a specific subject. This form of teaching is especially seen within textbook discussions and written communication of papers giving feedback and good advice. In a web-based learning environment, the teacher acts as facilitator and is expected to be even more flexible and sensitive in relation to the needs of the students, perhaps even making the social-media teacher a mediator, or what Danielsen & Nielsen call *"almost a therapist"* (Danielsen & Nielsen, 2010:5).

The occurrence of fast-growing possibilities with smartphones, tablets and the like has begun to make the idea of education occurring at anytime, anyplace and anywhere seem more feasible. This is also a contributing factor to the expectation of flexibility. The challenge here is to manage the expectations of students for teachers always to be flexible and online.

In an OECD report on cross-cultural teacher beliefs and teacher practices, it was concluded that many teachers, specifically in Scandinavia, tend to regard students as active participants in the learning process rather than merely seeing the students as receivers of the 'correct answer' (OECD, 2009). This ties in with the occurrence of web-based learning platforms in which active participation is a pre-requisite for successful outcome. Not only are the students supposed to upload group assignments, for example, but they are also expected to take active part in the evaluation of other groups' assignments in the form of peer evaluation.

The result is a dialogue between teacher and the students and a dialogue amongst the students, with the teacher functioning as facilitator.

The question then is how we can facilitate an appropriate dialogue between teacher and students when adopting ICT in the classroom. It is significant that the students are introduced to the suitability of ICT (the *what*), the employment of ICT (the *how*) and the purpose and goal of using ICT (the *why*). Data from the Sprogkernen Project point towards the importance of proper instruction by the teacher of ICT in order to engage the students in an active and successful way (Sprogkernen, 2011). In order to nudge the students from only acquiring surface learning to acquiring deep learning, it is of utmost importance that the students receive a proper introduction from their teacher.

In the Sprogkernen Project, the responses from the students in both classes on their perception of the use of ICT in the classroom differed quite a lot. In one of the classes, in which the teacher had given clear instruction on the what, the how and the why, the majority of the students were in favour of applying ICT. They thought that ICT was a motivating factor to learn German through increased variation, creativity, active learning and engagement, and also increased responsibility and autonomy. The teacher of the first class explained that she was very much aware of the importance of proper instruction in ICT and she also used time to explain the purpose and goal both before and after the lessons. Here, we observed symmetry between form and content and the students felt confident and experienced meaningful learning. In the second class, in which the students had received only a little instruction as to the what, the how and the why from their teacher, the students were, in general, more sceptical with regard to the application of ICT. They did not quite understand the purpose and goal of ICT and some students thought that ICT was too technical. Some students preferred the variation just for the sake of variation and not the fact that ICT was used. On the other hand, the teacher of this class thought that he had given the students enough instruction on ICT. In other words, here we discovered asymmetry between form and content. Further, we also observed the importance of clear communication from the teacher to the students.

Communication from the teacher is vital and it is thus important that the teacher explains the *what*, the *how* and the *why*. If the students do not receive proper instruction to ICT, it might be perceived as not serious enough, too childish and irrelevant, and too technical. The students, therefore, will not understand the purpose of using ICT. First, ICT must be adapted and integrated to the teaching, because asymmetry between form and content might prevent the teaching from being challenging enough, thereby not engaging the students actively and nudging them towards deep learning. Second, proper instruction is vital. The teacher must explain to the students the relevance of applying ICT. This can be done via constant introduction and iteration of very clear learning targets. Third, if the students feel certain that the application of ICT is relevant, they might become more motivated. Last, active and explicit feedback from the teacher is important as a follow-up on the what, the how and the why.

Conclusion

The need for new ways to advance learning in order to engage a new generation of 'digitally native' students has become increasingly more important because much interaction across multinational organisations takes place via social-media learning environments or Internet sites. In addition, many of the enterprises that hire higher-education graduates are using social media in their internal and their external communication. Social-media learning environments have created new ways for students and teachers to engage and collaborate in a fruitful and rewarding way. Social-media learning environments can both support individual learning through the creation of new apps in the students' own personal forums and foster collaborative learning through collective knowledge-sharing and problem solving among the group. The challenge is to design a web-based learning environment suitable for the new generation of 'digitally native' students in order to increase student collaboration and engagement in their own teaching. This can also create dynamics in class and create students with increased collaborative skills, increasingly requested as a core competence by many businesses (Ernest *et al.*, 2011).

When working as a group or a team, students learn to collaborate, spar, brainstorm and problem-solve. Through a web-based environment, such as those provided by social media, students might learn individually but also collectively because social-media learning environments facilitate knowledge sharing and collective problem solving in the group. This might foster the students not only to think of the outcome but also to think of the process of learning, thereby creating a deep learning experience. The students move from surface learning to deep learning and the outcome is students who are more actively engaged and motivated. According to Biggs (2003), students create knowledge via teaching activities and the students' own attitudes to learning. The result of the learning process thus depends on the extent to which the students 'only' want to pass a course or subject by repeating facts (surface learning) or actively want to reflect, interpret and investigate (deep learning). In other words, teacher identity and teacher impact are key to much student motivation and interaction, and so the way in which instructional practice and mutual cognition are informing one another (Borg, 2003) is vital. Teachers, therefore, also need to recognise the importance of how they articulate the use of ICT and for which purposes. When students feel more motivated and engaged, they are more likely to participate and, in this way, the teacher can obtain enhanced student preparation and rewarding and fruitful appearance in the classroom environment (Andersen, 2004) to support increased collaboration in learning (Ernest *et al.*, 2011). The changing role of the teacher from traditional classroom instructor to facilitator might pose difficulties or even produce resistance from some teachers but, with the prospects of enhanced student participation and thereby enhanced learning outcomes, most teachers would presumably welcome more web-based learning environments.

Clear communication between teacher and students is important. Likewise, it is important that the teacher explains the what, the how and the why of ICT. In this way, symmetry between form and content is achieved, motivating students to engage not only in the outcome but also in the learning process. In doing so, students will try to focus on the details of the subject; however, it also requires some sort of pre-knowledge from the students in order to get the total picture. This correlates with intrinsic motivation. Here the students learn because they are interested in the subject itself, not because they are required to. The result is motivated and actively engaged learners.

About the author

Christine Lenstrup is Assistant Professor at IBC (International Business Communication) at Copenhagen Business School, Denmark. She can be contacted at this email: cl.ibc@cbs.dk

Developing Student Contemporary Leadership Capacity through Teamwork

Ieva Stupans

Introduction

Because a highly skilled population is necessary for economic success, universities have a critical and growing social and economic role. Transferable skills associated with employability, such as critical thinking, life-long learning, cultural awareness, teamwork, communication and leadership, are included in a suite of attributes which, as Barrie (2006) has described, many universities aspire to develop within their graduates. Aside from employability, there are also imperatives for universities to develop skills so that graduates may confront what has been described by Barnett (2000:257) as "supercomplexity", "*a world where nothing can be taken for granted, where no frame of understanding or of action can be entertained with any security*" (see Su, in this volume).

This is the case across individual disciplines and also in an interdisciplinary context. For example, health professionals will need to face a plethora of new challenges such as those described by Christobal *et al.* (2009) – for instance, the emergence of new diseases, a growing pandemic of non-communicable disorders, largely due to inappropriate lifestyles and social and educational changes as well as global information technology in a consumerist environment. Introducing the innovations and influencing the processes, irrespective of whether this is in a global or local context, necessitates building leadership capacity. In this context, leadership is seen as central, enabling a response to these challenges and thus improving healthcare. Leadership is an imperative for graduates of health and other programs; however, curriculum design to support development of leadership capacity in our graduates has to date been a neglected area of theoretical and empirical research.

This chapter begins by exploring the various representations of contemporary leadership and argues for the central role of collaborative teams. Examples of literature which suggest a relationship between group work, teamwork and leadership development are then used to illustrate the need to provide scaffolding which includes definitions of leadership and the development of explicit guidelines for students. The discussion of the model commences by describing the significance of specifying learning outcomes, features of the affective learning domain and the internalisation of leadership. The curriculum consequences of the relationship between learning outcomes and assessment are then considered. I argue that learning outcomes and learning opportunities with a focus on teams and assessment which recognise the team as the unit of analysis are central to the model. A framework is presented for scaffolding and providing supportive teaching strategies for the development of leadership.

In this chapter, I propose a model in which teamwork is pivotal and assert that it will lead to development of contemporary leadership capacity alongside discipline knowledge.

Representations of leadership

There are diverse representations of leadership. The following definition emphasising process has been used to support the discussion in this chapter *"Leadership may be considered as the process (act) of influencing the activities of an organized group in its efforts towards goal setting and goal achievement."*(Stogdill, 1950:3). However, rather than being associated with process, much of the discourse and popular representations around leadership are associated with a heroic or leader-centric paradigm of individual intellectual stimulation, charisma and individualised consideration, with a sharp distinction between leaders and followers. In this traditional model, influencing activities and efforts and goal achievement is the focus of "leaders". Given the challenges of influencing change in a supercomplex world, focussing only on a heroic-leader model of leadership risks placing great import on the leader and ignoring the greater majority of the workforce. The focus is now shifting from an individual "leader" toward the collective act of "leadership" (Day, 2000).

Contemporary leadership development therefore looks beyond the development of single individuals as leaders to the process of leadership. Leadership, for the purposes of this chapter, is conceptualised as a process of *"influencing the activities of an organized group in its efforts towards goal setting and goal achievement"* (Stogdill, 1950:3) and, of particular relevance to contemporary leadership, as something all individuals have the capability to develop and engage in, whether or not they hold a formal leadership position. I argue that leadership capacity – that is, the ability to participate in contemporary leadership processes – may be developed through the collaborative interactions between individuals, such as through learning opportunities which focus on pedagogically sound teamwork.

Within the complexity of leadership there is also its overlap with management. The terms "leadership" and "management" and their meanings are often used interchangeably (Kotterman, 2006). As described by Kouzes and Posner (2002), leadership is a process of influence leading to the achievement of desired purposes; management involves effective maintenance of current activities. It has been proposed by Bolden (2004) that the outcome of leadership is positive and on occasion leads to significant changes, whereas management on the other hand produces order, consistency and predictability.

There are a number of representations of contemporary leadership which shift the focus from individual leaders to a more systemic perspective, conceived as a collective or collaborative social process. These are "distributed", "shared", "collective", "collaborative", "emergent", "democratic" leadership and "co-leadership". Woods *et al.* (2004) propose that there are a number of features associated with these representations. First, leadership is an emergent property of a group or network of interacting individuals; second, there is openness to the boundaries of leadership; and third, there is distribution of varieties of expertise across the many. A key attribute of this is what Gronn (2002:432) describes as "concertive action" – a complex web of conjoint activity in which the members of the *"unit(s)... synchronise their action by having regard to their own plans, those of their peers and their sense of unit membership".* The outcome of the process is significantly more than the sum of its parts. Bolden (2011) and Currie and Lockett (2011) have considered the similarities and differences between these representations of leadership. Briefly, there are differences in how and where these concepts are utilised within the literature and as to how they may be viewed with respect to concertive and conjoint action (Bolden, 2011; Currie and Lockett, 2011).

The contemporary view of leadership emphasises the role of collaborative teams. A review of literature which reports a relationship between group work, teamwork and leadership is now presented to provide insight into currently proffered approaches for development of leadership capacity alongside discipline knowledge. In particular, this section of the chapter concentrates on the evidence for effectiveness of team, group and collaborative work and development of leadership capacity and the clarity and detail provided to students as regards leadership. This second point is of particular relevance when considering the diverse representations of leadership.

Learning from the academic literature: group and teamwork in relation to leadership

There is a body of literature, in which individual studies may be contextualised in disciplines, which professes the notion that using group work, teamwork or co-operative learning supports the development of students' leadership skills. In these reports (Hassanien, 2007; Dyball *et al.*, 2007), in which students work together in small groups to achieve a specified goal, it is suggested that leadership capacity is developed amongst a number of other generic skills such as organisation, negotiations, delegation, conflict resolution and time management. From this body of literature a number of insights can be drawn.

- Group, co-operative and teamwork in the literature are generally associated with performance by students of some type of project activity.

- In much of the literature, the terms "co-operative", "team" and "group" are used interchangeably, although it is acknowledged that students in groups do not necessarily work co-operatively (Ballantine and McCourt Larres, 2007).

- With respect to Kirkpatrick's four levels of evaluation (1994), students' learning around teamwork, if discussed, is self-reported and thus evaluation of the initiatives is at the lower levels. Briefly, Kirkpatrick's four levels of evaluation have been adopted when evaluating changes to learning opportunity design or execution, for example, the evaluation of an inter-professional intervention in health sciences as described by Miers *et al.* (2007). The first level involves evaluating the reaction of students; the second determining students' learning; the third level is the measure of behaviour change. The fourth level evaluates effects on students' or graduates' performance in the work environment.

- Reference is made to leadership without definition of the term "leadership". One of the recommendations made within this chapter with respect to scaffolding of leadership development attends specifically to this point.

A number of studies are now presented in greater depth to illustrate the above findings. A qualitative study reported by Hassanien (2007), which elicited the views of sport, performing arts and leisure students about group work, commented on the role of group work in developing leadership skills and reported a number of quotations particularly pertinent to this discussion. *"[S]ome group members just don't like to be told by others. On such occasions, I felt we needed a formal leader who could motivate individuals and facilitate the process"* (Hassanien, 2007:142). A second quotation from a different student is also illuminating: *"I found it very time-consuming to arrange a meeting, to get people together, to split the activity into different tasks, to convince each group member about his/her bit, to sort out conflicts between group members, to satisfy different people, and to get the job done in time"* (Hassanien, 2007:142). Students in this work are reporting a heroic, leader-centric understanding of "leaders"; the authors do not define the term.

Accounting students' views on the impact of co-operative learning on generic skill development have been reported by Ballantine and McCourt Larres (2007). Students self-reported benefits across a range of generic skills including verbal communication, negotiating and leadership skills. Although leadership skills were surveyed, a definition of leadership skills was not provided in the paper.

Baker and Clark (2010) have proposed a model to help lecturers set up successful co-operative learning programs with ethnically and linguistically diverse classes, which includes training for academics around group roles including leadership. The model also includes student groups determining their own group processes such as deciding on their preferred "leadership system". Elaboration on leadership styles was not provided.

Electronic media (see Lenstrup, in this volume) have also been utilised in developing students' perceptions of developing transferable skills such as teamwork, whereby online discussion boards have been used to evidence interactions in the learning of anatomy (Choudhury and Gouldsborough, 2012). In this example, formal heroic leadership of the team is considered, although again not defined, with leaders awarding grades to team members.

Thus the literature, although making assumptions, suggests that teamwork in the execution of projects is a learning opportunity for the development of leadership capability.

Learning outcomes, learning opportunities and their relationship to leadership development

The traditional approach to curriculum design was to start from the content of the course. The shift from a teacher-centred to a student-centred approach to teaching has led to contemporary curriculum design based on learning outcomes. Moon (2002:17) has defined learning outcomes as *"a statement of what a learner is expected to know, understand and be able to do at the end of a period of learning and of how that learning is to be demonstrated"*. Subject or program learning outcomes describe what learners are supposed to know or be able to do after having completed that subject or program of study. With respect to developing student contemporary leadership capacity, appropriate learning outcomes need to be formulated. In curriculum models that use learning outcomes, clear statements of such outcomes serve as the foundation on which to develop learning opportunities and also the assessment of those outcomes. Of relevance to this chapter is the design of learning opportunities and assessment of the leadership-related learning outcomes.

The writing of learning outcomes is frequently underpinned by the hierarchies within Bloom's taxonomy (Anderson *et al.*, 2001) as described by Kennedy *et al.* (no date). The three domains of learning – knowledge, skills and attitude – correspond to the cognitive, psychomotor and affective domains of Bloom's taxonomy (Anderson *et al.*, 2001). Each level within the hierarchies depends on the student's ability to perform at the level or the levels that are below it.

The affective domain includes supporting relationships with others and the larger professional domain relating to personal affect, integrity and worthiness, self-awareness, and a willingness to contribute, lead or participate constructively. With respect to leadership, Bloom's taxonomy in the affective domain represents a "continuum of internalisation". The process of internalisation begins when attention is captured by some phenomenon; the phenomenon is valued and responded to, eventually almost automatically. Finally the values are interrelated in a structure or view of the world. This process has been subdivided into five major areas, which include *receiving, responding, valuing, organisation* and *characterisation* (Anderson *et al.*, 2001).

Leadership development may also be viewed through a leadership identity development model as described by Komives *et al.* (2009) which comprises the key categories for understanding how individual students develop a social identity as leaders. This model proposes stages of awareness, exploration/engagement, leadership identification, leadership differentiation, a commitment to developing leadership in others and integration/synthesis. The leadership identity development model (Komives *et al.*, 2009) developed through a grounded-theory methodology aligns with the extensive body of literature which argues that leadership is in fact a distributed activity – *"leadership is everyone's business"*, as argued by Kouzes and Posner (2002:383).

It is important to note that, within the leadership identity development framework, transition stages, parallel to those developed for learning within the affective domain, are also described. A framework for students' leadership capacity development can be constructed through alignment of Komives *et al.*'s (2009) leadership identity model and the hierarchy of Bloom's affective domain as outlined by Krathwohl *et al.* (1964). The framework highlights the importance of a number of aspects which include emphasising leadership as a concept and, more importantly, the critical role that teamwork plays in the internalisation of leadership capacity (Stupans, 2012). The role of active learning approaches such as teamwork in the conduct of a project, to facilitate development of students' leadership capacity, rather than instructor-centred approaches such as lectures, also aligns with our understanding of instructional approaches regarded appropriate for learning in the affective domain (Weston and Cranton, 1986).

There are distinctions between teams and groups which are of significance when discussing the development of leadership. An analysis of the concept of teamwork undertaken by Xyrichis and Ream (2008) examining a number of definitions of teams has identified the critical characteristic that a team consists of a group which collaborates in its work. Characteristics of teamwork include *"recurring cycles of mutually dependent interaction"* (Morgeson *et al.*, 2010:3), thus aligning with the conjoint activity of leadership (Gronn, 2002). Phases can be divided into first, evaluation or planning, and second, an action phase of work activities. Informal, internal team leadership is associated with functions within the transition phase and action phase. When considering the development of students' learning around leadership, these stages need to be elaborated. Functions associated with the transition phase are composing the team, defining the mission, establishing expectations and goals, structuring and planning, training and developing the team, sense making and providing feedback. Functions associated with the action phase are monitoring the team, managing team boundaries, challenging the team, performing the team tasks, solving problems, providing resources, encouraging team self-management and supporting the team climate (Morgeson *et al.*, 2010).

Assessment of teamwork

Learning outcomes also provide a framework for the form and detail of assessment of learning opportunities – for example, a project which needs to be completed by a number of individuals working together. Assessment as outlined by Yorke (2003) is recognised as having two main purposes which may in fact be interlinked: certification of learning; and aiding learning, as in formative assessment. Self-assessment is a process of formative assessment during which students reflect on the quality of their work, judge the degree to which it reflects explicitly stated goals or criteria, and revise accordingly. Students may also plan for future learning (see Enomoto and Warner, in this volume). Rubrics – explicit criteria with indications of levels of achievement – may also be useful in helping to guide students in their self-assessment of a piece of work (Andrade and Valtcheva, 2008).

In the case of criteria or standards-based assessment, there are two aspects to assessment of a piece of work completed by a team: product and process. The first of these is the 'quality' of the piece of work itself, the product, which is assessed and awarded grades. With regard to the second of these aspects, the process (as outlined by Hughes & Jones, 2011), learning outcomes which refer to teamwork necessitate the awarding of grades which reflect teamwork, reflect assessment of the students' processes of working together and which refer to the team's performance as a whole and to its collective success. The team is the unit of analysis, not individual students.

There are a number of papers which report on approaches to awarding assessment grades which incorporate peer grades for individual team members' contributions to team projects, – for example, Oakley *et al.* (2004). However, more recently, the view that allocation of grades for assessments for co-operative learning situations should be different from allocations for individual assessments (Albon and Jewels, 2009; Hughes and Jones, 2011) has been espoused. Regarding this view, a team grade – i.e. the same grade awarded to all students for the process – (with some allowance for the student's stage of program) and the product is proposed. Thus allocation of individual grades for individual contribution and effort in team assessments is not appropriate. The awarding of a team grade is consistent with assessment which aligns with learning outcomes which specify teamwork. The awarding and scaling of a grade for individual contribution and effort does not align with a teamwork-associated learning outcome.

Acknowledging the formative as well as summative role of assessment, it is important to revisit the importance of reflective practice in student learning. Formative assessment helps to inform the teacher and the students as to how the students are progressing. Similarly, students' reflection on the quality of their work assists students to plan for their own future learning. Assessment of students' reflections and self-assessment of their own individual performance against a rubric, which defines assessment criteria by describing performance at different points on a rating scale, may provide students with an opportunity for learning.

Potentially affective outcomes are slowly attained (Krathwohl *et al.*, 1964) and there is argument that their development should permeate the whole curriculum rather than be isolated in a single or specialised course (Scoufis, 2000). Therefore I propose a model, presented in Figure 1, in which some allowance within the process grade can be made, such that student learning is acknowledged. The process grade incorporates grades from student self-assessment (individual student grades) and grades for collective student success (all members of group working together receive the same grade). Early in the students' program of study, less emphasis is placed on the team grade; as students learn, less emphasis is placed on the process of reflective self-assessment. The product is awarded a grade based on its "quality".

Many of the available rubrics that describe performance criteria and standards around teamwork include peer assessment of team members. In my view, the team is the unit of analysis for learning outcomes associated with teamwork – peer assessment in this context is inappropriate. I propose that clear expectations for students would be provided through a rubric which guides students through the processes of teamwork as described by Morgeson *et al.* (2010). These are:

- The transition phase: composing the team, defining the mission, establishing expectations and goals, structuring and planning, training and developing the team, sense making and providing feedback; and

- The action phase: monitoring the team, managing team boundaries, challenging the team, performing the team tasks, solving problems, providing resources, encouraging team self-management and supporting the team climate – and thus facilitating student learning.

As shown in Figure 1, evidence for individuals and of the teamwork process could be captured through reflective writing and through wiki or blog online technology respectively.

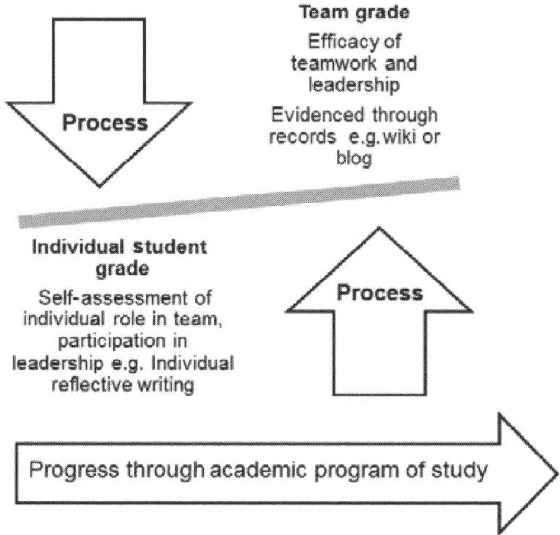

Figure 1: Proposed model for incorporating individual and team grades for the assessment of the "process" of teamwork

This model aligns with teamwork-appropriate learning outcomes whilst recognising students' learning trajectories for the affective domain. The presented model focusses on assessment. The next section of the chapter discusses other considerations for supporting the development of students' leadership capacity.

Scaffolding for leadership

The term 'scaffolding' has been widely used to describe supportive teaching strategies. Scaffolding necessitates students being enabled to carry out a task which they would not have been able to carry out on their own, with the guided steps eventually enabling them to complete the task as evidenced by learner achievement (Verenikina, 2008). There are numerous, very diverse examples of scaffolding in the literature including the use of worksheets in problem-based learning (Choo *et al.*, 2011) and the provision of skills practice in a higher-education setting prior to skills application in a work-based placement (Stupans *et al.*, 2010). However, no research could be located regarding the role of academics in scaffolding student learning of attributes such as leadership.

Although not referring specifically to the notion of leadership, guidelines to facilitate effective team, as distinct from group, structure (Oakley *et al.*, 2004) include developing student expectations and evaluation of both progress and team members. These approaches align with functions associated with the transition phase in teamwork as described by Morgeson *et al.* (2010). The guidelines also include the suggestion that members of the student groups allocate among themselves the roles of facilitator, coordinator, recorder and monitor. In such a team structure, the role of a leader as such is not articulated, aligning with the concept that leadership is distributed throughout the team.

It has been proposed that group, team and co-operative learning opportunities are provided to students to decrease the marking load on academics (Morris and Hayes, 1997). However, it is apparent that pedagogically sound teamwork contributes to scaffolding for the development of leadership. Regarding scaffolding, it has been shown that clarity and explicit communication regarding definitions, benefits, expectations and processes enhance the quality of students' learning experiences, as evidenced through assessment (Stupans *et al.*, in press). Detail of the expectations (standards) provided through rubrics provides students both individually and in their teams opportunity to self-assess their processes and develop improvement strategies.

Table 1 provides a framework which academics may adopt in order to scaffold student development of leadership. This development may occur in concert with discipline cognitive knowledge or psychomotor skills through the use of teamwork-based learning opportunities and assessment.

The way forward

In this chapter, I set out to provide a model which would develop contemporary leadership capacity in students alongside the learning of discipline knowledge. In providing this model, I have raised a number of points. First, teamwork in the higher-education environment, critical to the contemporary leadership development trajectory, needs to be structured such that it facilitates all students to identify with leadership. Second, alignment of learning outcomes, learning opportunities and assessment around teamwork provides a framework for conceptualisation of the development of students' leadership capacities. Third, the scaffolding of student learning through clarity and explicit communication regarding definitions, benefits, expectations and processes is critical.

Steps	Strategies
Planning	Setting of learning outcomes which specify teamwork
Contextualisation within the discipline	Clear articulation to students of why leadership development is pertinent to their discipline
	Clear explanation to students of "leadership" as opposed to "leaders" and as opposed to "management"
Learning opportunity	Setting of learning opportunity which specifies teamwork as the approach to be used by students (generally some type of project work)
	Explicit guidelines for students for processes of teamwork, explaining:
	• The transition phase (composing the team, defining the mission, establishing expectations and goals, structuring and planning, training and developing the team, sense making and providing feedback) and
	• The action phase (monitoring the team, managing team boundaries, challenging the team, performing the team tasks, solving problems, providing resources, encouraging team self-management and supporting the team climate – and thus facilitating student learning)
Assessment	Grade is awarded on the basis of process and product:
	• Process grade awarded on basis of individual self-assessment and assessment of team processes (see Figure 1)
	• Product grade based on "quality" of product
	The team is the unit of analysis as regards team grades i.e. all team members receive the same team grade

Table 1: Framework of scaffolding for student contemporary leadership capacity development through teamwork

However, there are tensions for academics wanting to include teamwork in their approaches to teaching and learning design in that team assessment may determine a student's overall subject grade and therefore a student's progress through a degree. Undergraduates may be competing with each other for various awards, prizes and scholarships. With respect to graduates, they will be expected to perform individually in some areas of future employment and in some cases individual accountability – for example, in terms of professional registration and maintenance of competence – is important. Group/teamwork is also not uniformly regarded positively by students, which may in turn affect its inclusion in academic programs for a number of reasons. Student satisfaction and their evaluation of their courses and teachers are measures that drive significant activity in universities. Student satisfaction is used as a measure of the quality of the teaching and learning at an institution, and is subsequently tied to student choices of university as well as to funding incentives and rewards. Within universities, student feedback is used as evidence in teaching awards and academic promotion.

It is critical that academics and academic institutions support pedagogically sound teamwork which is structured such that it facilitates all students to identify with contemporary leadership capacity thus positioning graduates to participate in future leadership processes, influencing change.

Acknowledgements

This work has been funded by an Australian Learning Teaching Council fellowship.

About the author

Ieva Stupans is Professor of Pharmacy at the University of New England, N.S.W. Australia. She can be contacted as this email: ieva.stupans@une.edu.au

Learning Design and Transdisciplinary Pedagogical Templates (TPTs)

Eva Dobozy, James Dalziel and Bronwen Dalziel

Introduction

An ongoing challenge in higher education is the support of educators in their development of effective pedagogies. Innovative teaching and learning strategies are intended to immerse students in deeply engaging learning experiences and, in turn, lead to more desired learning outcomes. This is especially true because many university educators have limited pedagogical training and have, as students, often been exposed to traditional transmission pedagogies. Indeed, research reports and anecdotal evidence (Aoki, 2011; Conole, 2011) suggest that many university students and educators in established, new and emerging democracies are still comfortable with traditional transmission pedagogies, such as lecturing and requiring students to fill out worksheets to test their understanding of foundational knowledge. In this chapter, we refer to these traditional pedagogies as the classical 'knowledge telling' approach to education.

Learning Design (LD) is a relatively new field in education, created to describe the pedagogy (or precise account of teaching processes that are generally classed as non-traditional methods) of different educational topics, themes or disciplinary subjects. The simplest example is that of a teacher writing up a lesson plan of activities that they intend to use to explore a particular topic. For the purposes of this chapter, the field of LD is further conceptualised as the strategic process of creating a *"framework to describe a sequence of educational activities"* in an online environment (Dalziel, 2008:3). This description of a sequence of educational activities can also be referred to as a pedagogical 'template'. Once captured, the template can then be transferred to new teaching situations and topics. In other words, the pedagogical template can become a transdisciplinary teaching tool, which we refer to here as a transdisciplinary pedagogical template (or TPT). Effectively used, these TPTs can transform teaching and learning practices by introducing new pedagogies into educational disciplines that have historically used classical knowledge-telling approaches.

The field of LD and, specifically, the subfield of the design and utility of transdisciplinary pedagogical templates (TPTs) can provide a way for higher-education institutions to support those educators seeking to modernise their teaching and learning approaches. Hence, LD can assist educators embrace what Löfvall and Nygaard (in this volume) call a "partnership model", where they refrain from knowledge-telling approaches in favour of more social-constructivist learning and teaching provisions.

This chapter provides a rationale for the use of LD in transforming teaching and learning practices in an online environment. It includes the introduction of LD principles, outlining some initial ways in which higher-education institutions are supporting educators in the implementation of LD across disciplinary boundaries. It begins by introducing the new field of Learning Design and then discusses the creation of LD templates for deep learning. We refer to them as TPTs (transdisciplinary pedagogical templates), which are designed to enable more interactive learning experiences that promote deep thinking and knowledge creation. The chapter continues with a discussion of practitioner experiences with TPTs, which were constructed using LD principles. Specifically, the use of the Learning Activity Management System (LAMS), developed by Macquarie University (Dalziel, 2003), is discussed in detail, as its use is one method of capturing and transferring TPTs in an online environment. We argue that LAMS lends itself particularly well to transferring TPTs to new subject areas and across disciplinary boundaries. Finally, some obstacles and challenges to the use of TPTs are noted and the need for further research is emphasised.

Learning Design: a new field in education

The new field of Learning Design (LD) has evolved through researching ways that online learning can go beyond delivery of content to include different pedagogical approaches and to take into account the different learners that increasingly populate the higher-education landscape (Sims, 2006). It has crystallised into a more formal pursuit of accurately describing the sequencing of educational activities in online learning environments (Dalziel, 2008). LD as an emerging field of education aims to guide educators to incorporate current understandings of good pedagogy, built on social-constructivist learning theory. The concept of sequence should be understood broadly to mean any collection of activities, for example, predict–observe–explain, problem-based learning, role play (Dalziel, 2010), and structured controversy (Dobozy, 2008) that have some form of structure over time. The phrase *"a learning design"* is also sometimes used to describe a specific instance of a sequence of activities (Dobozy, 2012:42). This sequence of activities can be used to inform the design of a future set of activities. In other words, a specific LD sequence can be a template for future learning environments. Therefore, LD describes the development, implementation and adaption of "learning designs", created in various contexts and for multiple purposes (see also Conole, 2012).

The move away from traditional university teaching methods based on teacher-centric and content-driven transmission education strategies in higher education is what is of particular interest to LD researchers. All forms of constructivist theories, for example Piagetian or Vygotskyan, emphasise active and independent engagement with information with the aim of developing academically mature university graduates, which Schmidt (2010:6) refers to as *"cognitively autonomous individuals"*. Through active engagement, discussion, debate and social participation in learning, the (meta)cognitive skills of collaborative and creative problem solving are developed, enhanced and co-produced through communication and interaction in an attempt to solve the cognitive challenge at hand through scenario-based, inquiry or problem-based learning designs (see Dalziel, 2010 and Dobozy, 2008, 2012 for illustrative examples).

Hence, LD principles can be used to produce a set of problem-based teaching and learning activities, which together form a sequence (or template) of practical steps for university educators and their students to follow. These professionally developed LD templates are authentic and based on a particular teaching strategy, such as problem-based and inquiry-based learning, role play or scenario-based learning. Student and teacher activities may vary but, importantly, they are generally underpinned by contemporary learning theories and depart from classical knowledge-telling approaches to teaching and learning.

The shift away from technical issues and towards professional development of university educators and innovation in course development marks an important step towards the broader impact of LD on education (Dalziel, 2005, 2009). Learning Design is sometimes also mentioned in the context of discussions of "instructional design" (Chu & Kennedy, 2011), especially in the US educational literature, or "curriculum design" (Ferrell, 2011) and "educational design" (Goodyear & Ellis, 2010) in Europe and Australia. In the education psychology literature, it has been linked to the concepts of TPACK, or "technological pedagogical content knowledge" (Juang *et al.*, 2008). Nevertheless, the term 'Learning Design' (LD) seems already to have gained prominence in Australia and Europe.

LD has most recently been conceptualised by Dobozy (2012:45) as a way of *"making explicit epistemological and technological integration attempts by the designer of a particular learning sequence or series of learning sequences"*. In other words, LD research seeks to describe, share and re-use effective pedagogical strategies in higher education. It has been recognised as having the potential to assist educators modernise their pedagogical practices and reconceptualise their approaches to teaching and learning (see Dalziel, 2003, 2005, 2009; Laurillard, 2009; Conole *et al.*, 2008).

Introducing LAMS

Since its launch in Australia and the UK almost a decade ago (Dalziel, 2003) as an open-source learning platform, the Learning Activity Management System (LAMS) has gained international recognition as an innovative software program. LAMS can be described as a pedagogical tool rather than a management system (Dobozy *et al.*, 2011). For example, one distinct feature of LAMS is the ability to represent visually the teaching and learning sequence as a meta-representation of various links and relationships between activities, resources and desired learning outcomes.

In the field of LD, the LAMS learning platform can be used both to create a sequence of online activities populated with content, using the visual layout of the authoring tool (see Figure 1), and to run that set of activities for learners in a separate learner window (Figure 2). Most importantly, the sequence of activities, or LD template, can be packaged into a file and exported from the LAMS platform where it was created and imported onto the authoring space of a different LAMS platform. The sequence can then be edited, adapted and reused for different learners and further shared with other educators through educational communities such as LAMScommunity.org, or simply by emailing the file if desired. This is but one feature that sets LAMS apart from conventional Learning Management Systems (LMSs), such as Blackboard, Moodle or Desire2Learn (Dalziel, 2005; Dobozy *et al.*, 2011). The designs created in LAMS are easy to share and adapt, which makes LAMS, so we argue, ideal for the actualisation of Learning Design. LAMS is mainly used for online and blended learning and teaching purposes, encouraging and enabling teacher-to-student and peer-to-peer collaboration through formal Learning Design features and structures, which make extensive use of web 2.0 applications and mashup environments.

LAMS is flexible enough to allow designers to develop information-focused and collaborative learning activities, requiring case reviews, discussion, debate and questioning/testing of preconceived assumptions. These designs can rapidly be adopted by university educators and/or adapted to suit specific contexts. These sequences can be short, designed to introduce a topic or issue or highlight a dilemma, or they can be complex and require much time and effort from students. Figures 1 and 2 provide illustrative examples of this concept. Whereas Figure 1 shows the author view of the complete sequence, Figure 2 shows the learner view. Designers drag the chosen activity from the activities toolkit (on the left-hand side) to the authoring screen and develop the sequence (see Figure 1).

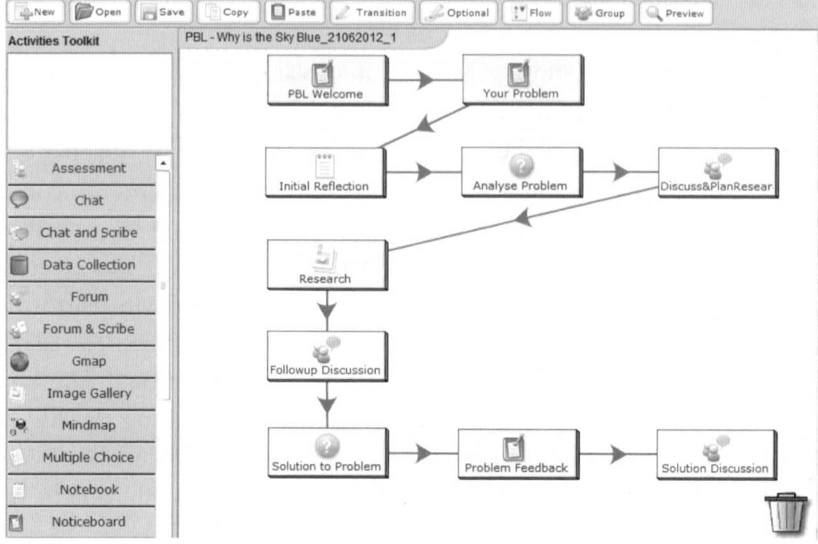

Figure 1: Example of problem-based learning sequence in LAMS (author view)

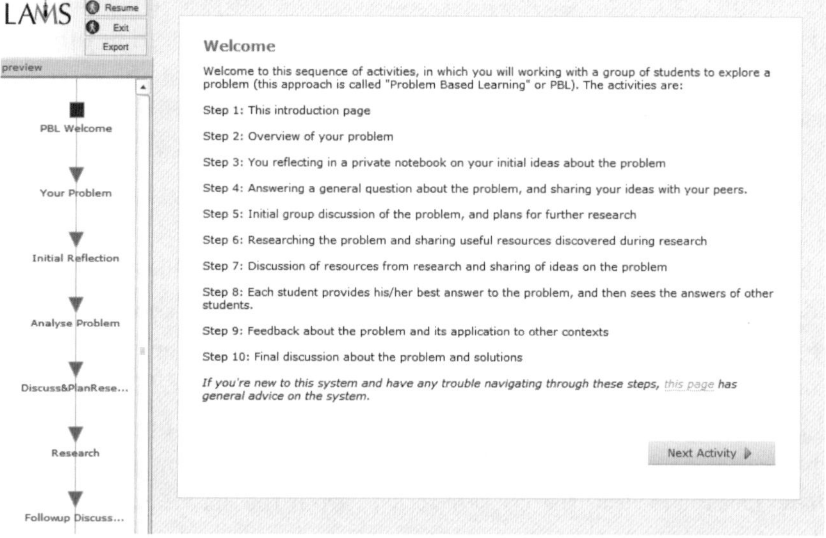

Figure 2: Example of problem-based learning sequence in LAMS (learner view)

Educators who choose the sequence (template) called "PBL – Why is the sky blue?" are able to edit further and/or populate the design with content by double clicking the icon. The next figure (see Figure 2 below) provides the learner view of the same sequence as a "swim-lane" on the left-hand side and the particular "window", in this case, the introduction or "PBL Welcome" page. Therewith, students have an overview of the complete sequence and are cognisant of the stage of their activity and its relationship to the complete teaching and learning sequence.

Later in this chapter, we show how LAMS has been used for the creation and the dissemination of TPTs within higher education focusing on the sharing of LD templates across disciplines. LAMS, as an LD platform, has been independently evaluated and has been recognised as having the potential to transform higher education (Laurillard, 2008).

Creating Learning Design templates for deep learning

We argue that all higher-education disciplines need to move towards the development of interactive learning experiences that promote deep thinking through a culture of knowledge sharing, reflection and collaborative problem solving, similar to Löfvall and Nygaard (this volume). This change in higher-education teaching and learning practice can occur through the creation of Learning Design templates. These LD templates typically include a range of activities to enable deep thinking and collaborative knowledge creation, in a broad range of topics and across multiple subject disciplines, which can be as diverse as teacher education and medical education. Here we refer to them as transdisciplinary pedagogical templates (TPTs).

Table 1 depicts the aim of the Learning Design strategies described above. The table is an adaption of Dobozy's (2012) conceptualisation of the various levels of learning engagement, learning activities and student actions, and illustrates that deep learning requires students to engage actively with the learning material and each other, with the goal of arriving at evidence-based position taking and purposeful decision making. This requires that students are active, interactive and drawing on a multiplicity of knowledge sources in the quest to engage deeply with the learning activity. Deep learning engagement is contrasted with shallow and surface learning engagement, which mainly require memorisation of facts and figures to demonstrate meaning-making and/or simple problem solving, typically after the university educator 'taught' the 'correct' steps to follow to arrive at the 'correct' answer through knowledge-telling approaches.

Level of learning and engagement		Learning Design		Learning impact (Personal knowledge-transfer)
Bennet & Bennet (2008)	Bloom (1956)	*Learning activity*	*Student action*	
Surface	1–2	Traditional knowledge telling	Memorising, remembering, acting	Near transfer of knowledge and skills; students are able to act in a predictable way in similar situations
Shallow	2–3	Traditional knowledge telling and some formalised structures to encourage knowledge sharing and simple problem solving	Explaining, acting, applying knowledge	Near transfer of knowledge and skills; students are able to act in a predictable way in similar situations and explain their actions accurately
Deep	4–6	Inquiry-based or problem-based learning provision that demands effortful problem solving, meaning making of contradictory and partial information; the learning is immersive and the issues or problems to be solved are drawn from real-world events	Position taking using evidence, purposeful decision-making and acting	Far transfer of knowledge and skills; students develop resilience and a willingness to share ideas and construct various possible solutions in collaboration; students are able to pool resources and solve unfamiliar problems; they are able to explain why they made particular choices and how these were seen as preferable to alternative solutions

Table 1: Depth of knowledge and action

The (re)production of foundational technical knowledge by students within a discipline is important. However, it can be relatively simple when contrasted with the production of deep and integrated knowledge. The latter requires that the knowledge producer is able to draw on a multitude of information sources and interpersonal experiences, which represent interplay between disciplinary (technical) and generic (multi or transdisciplinary) knowledge. As Table 1 illustrates, surpassing the "student-consumer" stage (Dobozy, 2011) requires that the learning design makes possible the acquisition and refinement of generic knowledge in new and unfamiliar situations, for example, working through real-world scenarios, inquiry-based and/or problem-based learning. This form of learning is referred to by Costa and Silva (2010:403) as an "*immersion-centric*" learning experience (see also Newman, in this volume, who discusses challenge-based learning designs).

Local designs versus generic designs (TPTs)

As LD templates are created and shared among educators in popular online repositories (see, for example, the LAMS community, www.lamscommunity.org), a difference in designs has been noted and investigated by Dalziel *et al.* (2009:66). Dalziel *et al.* categorise these as "*local designs*" and "*generic designs*". The primary difference between local and generic learning designs has been found to concern the role of discipline-specific content. A "local design" is one which combines discipline-specific content and pedagogical decision-making and action on the part of the educator and student, resulting in a learning design "ready to be used" by a colleague from the same "local" discipline area.

A "generic design" (or transdisciplinary pedagogical template – TPT) might contain specific information (content) related to the pedagogical decision-making and instruction to students. However, by definition, it does not incorporate discipline-specific content. Rather, as depicted in Table 2 below, the generic design is structured in a way that encourages educators to insert their relevant discipline-specific content into a generic pedagogical template, designed to elicit deep engagement from students with the content, based on principles of social-constructivist learning theories.

	Local design	**Generic design (transdisciplinary pedagogical templates – TPTs)**
Detailed description	A local LD contains specific information related to (a) pedagogical decision-making, including requirements of individual and collective student action and (b) discipline-specific curriculum content to be learned by students	A generic LD contains specific information related to pedagogical decision-making, including requirements of individual and collective student action, but does not include discipline-specific curriculum content; instead, it is populated with simple 'place holder data', providing advice to educators about how to insert discipline-specific content
Characteristics	Combines (a) discipline-specific content with pedagogical decision-making and instruction to students	Contains carefully designed and sequenced learning activities, devoid of specific content; pedagogically sound learning sequences are made available with placeholder data, ready to be adapted and transformed into local, contextualised designs for specific use
Primary usage	A discipline-specific LD can be used by an educator from a particular discipline background teaching a set topic without the need to make changes	A pedagogical LD template can be used for multiple topics within a single discipline, or ideally across multiple disciplines, but it requires discipline specialists to insert specific discipline-related content; each template can be applicable across many different disciplines
Advantage	Ready to be deployed to students, complete with content, no additional content or modification needed	Pedagogically sound learning design, ready to be adapted to local, contextualised use; multiple applications in various disciplinary contexts; it draws attention to the re-usable nature of the underlying pedagogical approach and the specific learning design used (i.e. role play)
Disadvantage	Only applicable to the "local" discipline context, hence limiting the potential for re-use and wider impact	The need to replace placeholder data with actual and relevant discipline-specific content

Table 2: Local learning designs versus generic learning designs

Learning design templates are used by educators who are proficient in their discipline content but wish to employ alternative strategies to their current teaching approaches. They may lack pedagogical content knowledge or the time to invest in upskilling to acquire the required knowledge base to create scenario-based, inquiry and/or problem-based learning sequences, enabling deep learning. Dalziel (2007) reports that some university educators seem to prefer "local designs" over learning design templates (generic designs) due to the lack of discipline content familiarity. Some educators have commented that generic templates can feel "lifeless" or otherwise uninspiring due to a lack of compelling, embedded discipline content. Nevertheless, it is the generic designs that are of greater value to higher education (due to their broader potential impact), despite the fact that they can prove to be harder to implement.

In the next section, we offer examples of how carefully constructed TPTs can provide a means for shifting mindsets of university administrators and educators. The TPTs make it easier for them to adopt contemporary learning designs, which are purposely constructed to equip future knowledge workers with the necessary knowledge, skills and attitudes to tackle increased and as yet unimaginable challenges. The designs test learners' willingness and ability to explore and employ strategies that are new and untested. Contemporary learning designs demand novel and innovative mindsets from educators and learners that need to move beyond classical transmission approaches as discussed above.

Transdisciplinary pedagogical templates: helping educators modernise their teaching

TPTs are designs that can contain rich resources that provide contradictory, partial and partisan views, highlighting the importance of the multiplicity of ways of knowing (Bennet & Bennet, 2008; Giannikis & Daskalopulu, 2009), or contain no resources, rather focusing on the types of activities that might be used, relying on the educator to provide the resources most suitable. Most importantly, these templates demand that university educators refrain from easy compartmentalisation of 'bite-size' provisions of information to a simplified consumable version and instead support a "student-producer" version of learning (see Dobozy, 2011).

There is clear and mounting evidence that student-centric teaching and learning approaches that focus on deep learning (see Table 1) have a number of benefits – such as improved retention rates, more engaged learners, increased intrinsic motivation, increased academic performance and resilience – leading to better prospects of postgraduate study (Brew, 2010; Healey & Jenkins, 2009). However, the literature also points to attitudinal barriers to increased adoption of more student-centric teaching practices in universities. These obstacles to reform in teaching and learning are likely to persist as long as the achievement of a critical mass in the adoption of inquiry-based, problem-based and/or challenge-based teaching and learning approaches is not attained. An increase in the adoption of more student-centric teaching practices would, so we argue, enable sustained system-wide trialling of new and innovative pedagogical practices, such as the use of local and generic TPTs.

Enabling policies and mechanisms for greater adoption and dissemination of initiatives, such as carefully constructed TPTs, based on Learning Design principles, means opening an avenue for shifting mindsets of university administrators and educators. As we move into the second decade of the twenty-first century, future knowledge workers need to be equipped to tackle increased and new, as-yet-unimaginable challenges, which demand novel and innovative mindsets ready to explore strategies that are new and untested. University educators in Australia and elsewhere can ill afford to be trapped in knowledge-telling practices, which effectively deny students the right to learn twenty-first-century skills and knowledge, preferably in transdisciplinary and heterogeneous learning environments that are infused with and mediated by web 2.0 applications.

In terms of practical application, two recent projects in teacher education and medical education (Dalziel & Dalziel, 2011) provide indications of how TPTs can be applied to assist educators, and potential challenges to adoption. In both cases, these projects explored how best to structure templates for adoption by educators, including accompanying advice on how to edit templates to incorporate discipline content.

One of the lessons from the teacher education project was that although a given constructivist pedagogical strategy, for example, scenario-based learning or role play, could be instantiated in many different ways for a "ready-to-run" template, such as different templates for 2/3/4+ roles, different templates for synchronous use over 1–2 hours versus asynchronous use of

2–4 weeks, educators who attempted to work with many slightly different implementation versions of a teaching strategy found the number of variations overwhelming. Instead, an educator considering a novel teaching strategy generally preferred to explore one "classic" implementation of the pedagogical strategy – and while many different variations might be needed to suit different constraints of practical implementation, these variations were not helpful in the initial period of template exploration.

Related to this problem of "cognitive overload" during exploration of novel, student-centric pedagogical strategies, educators felt that seeing a "worked example" of a template, such as an example of the generic LD template including embedded content from a specific discipline area, was helpful in aiding understanding of potential usefulness of the generic LD template for the educator. Although ideally an educator would see a worked example using his/her own discipline area (hence requiring many different worked examples to suit different disciplines), even a worked example from a different discipline was often felt to be more useful than a template with no discipline content.

The combination of these two findings informed an approach in which each given constructivist teaching strategy, such as role play, PBL, structured controversy and so on, was presented in two formats – a "classic" example of the format including embedded content, followed by the same "classic" example as a generic pedagogical template, without the discipline content. This approach has been implemented for three constructivist teaching strategies (see www.practicaleteachingstratcgics.com) with detailed advice about each strategy provide in Dalziel (2010). Figure 3a provides an example of the author's view of a generic LD template based on a role-play pedagogy. The template is devoid of content but still shows the teaching strategy behind a role-play sequence (TPT), including four phases, with each line representing a different phase:

Phase 1:   Background and preparation ("Role play overview", "Scenario", "Task structure", "Role groups")

Phase 2:   Role allocation, research and debate preparation ("Grouping for roles" and "Branching")

Phase 3:   Role play – the acting out of the role ("Forum – Everyone")

Phase 4:   Post-role-play debriefing and reflection ("Voting", "Journal", "Final Q+A")

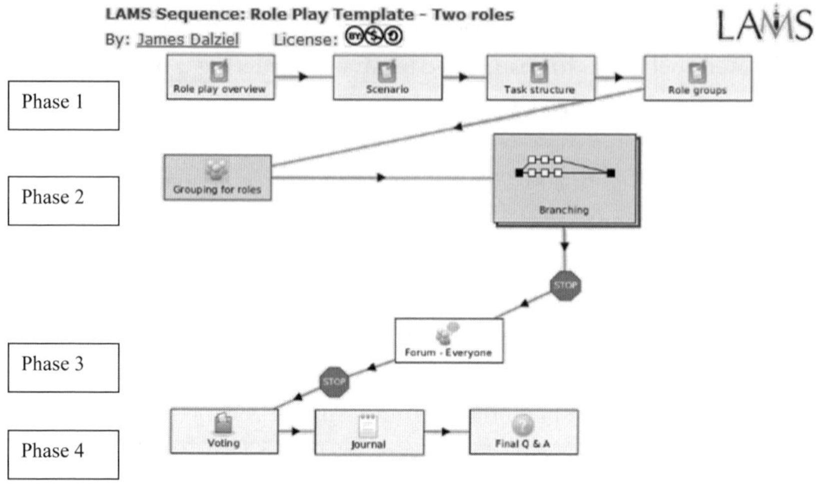

Figure 3a: LAMS role-play generic template

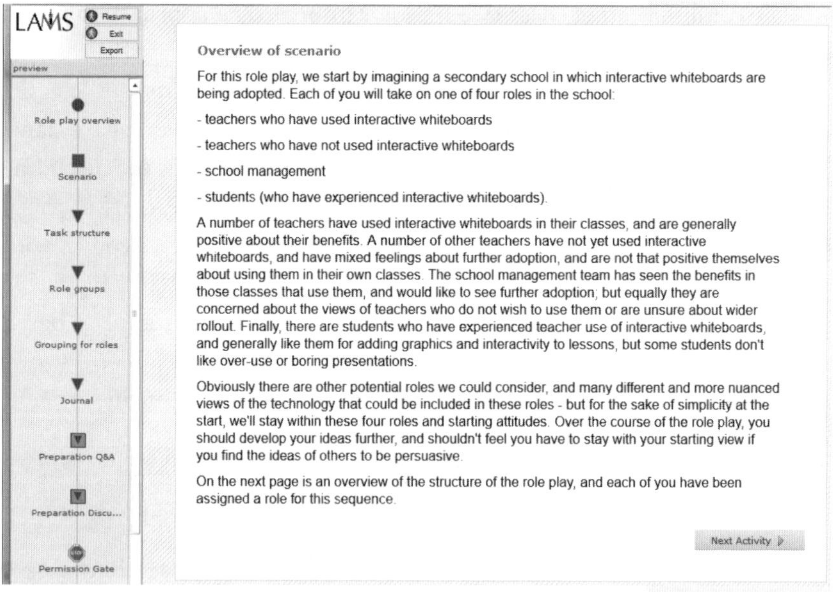

Figure 3b: In this figure, the LAMS role-play template has been edited with course-specific content on the topic of "The (dis)advantage of interactive whiteboards in primary school classrooms". (Learner view of the template, showing the second noticeboard activity – Scenario)

When an educator wishes to use the generic template in their own teaching, each task in the LAMS role-play generic template can be opened and edited to put in course-specific content while the underlying structure of the template, and hence the role-play pedagogy, is maintained (Figure 3b).

A different set of issues arose in the medical education context. In this case, a problem-based learning (PBL) pedagogical strategy was already widely understood and adopted within the relevant medical education course. This PBL approach was used when developing online activities for later-year students on the scientific basis of medicine. However, despite the provision of a PBL template to medical educators (similar to Figure 2) in order to assist with the creation of different sub-discipline topics, in practice medical educators did not use the TPT but rather built sequences "from scratch".

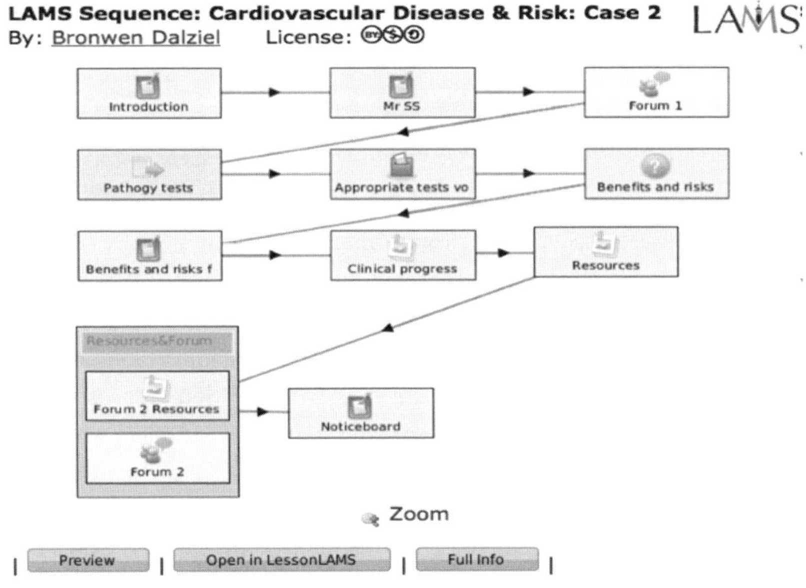

Figure 4: LAMS PBL-style sequence example for medical education (in the sub-discipline of cardiovascular systems)

Further discussion with the medical educators indicated that the PBL template had not been ignored – rather, it had functioned as a more general "inspirational" guide to medical educators when building their own set of activities. In this context, the PBL-style learning design (see Figure 4) acted more like a conceptual "meta-template" for the implementation of a variety of medical sub-discipline teaching and learning activities, in the sense that all sequences were informed by social-constructivist learning theories and used the general framework of PBL; but these medical educators did not directly edit and re-use the PBL template provided. An example of a sequence is provided in Figure 4, which was developed for the medical project described above.

In both projects, the TPTs were found to be valuable in assisting educators in considering the application of novel pedagogical strategies that are informed by contemporary learning theories. Nevertheless, in each case there were important contextual factors that had an impact on the way in which these templates where perceived and adopted by educators. There is a great deal of research yet to be done on how different kinds of TPTs are adopted across different disciplines.

TPTs and functional fixedness

A number of factors can hinder educational reforms designed to include more student-centric learning provisions and a clear departure from classical knowledge-telling approaches in higher education. These factors include cognitive rigidity or inflexibility in thinking.

University educators and students are often comfortable with and expect or demand traditional transmission education approaches (see Dobozy, 2011). Hence, it is not surprising that many students who expect traditional modes of education are likely to experience great difficulty in classrooms that use pedagogical practices more clearly aligned with social-constructivist principles, such as LD sequences in LAMS. However, a carefully constructed and scaffolded generic learning environment (see Figure 3) may be able to assist university educators and students embrace new pedagogical strategies which enable deep learning experiences.

Nevertheless, individuals who have been socialised in particular ways of acting and resist necessary changes in behaviour may experience functional fixedness, a specific kind of cognitive rigidity. They are unable to consider alternative processes or uses for particular objects. For example, imagine a group of university educators who are asked to imagine how to implement inquiry or problem-based learning experiences using one of the pedagogical templates described above. If some of them have a tendency towards functional fixedness, they might not consider alternatives to local designs that generally include required pedagogical and discipline-specific curriculum content. By contrast, some of the more cognitively flexible educators might be more willing and able to take the initiative, experiment with LD templates and choose a particular TPT based on the above examples, such as role play or PBL (see figures 3 and 4). Then, together with some discipline colleagues, they may populate the TPT with the required curriculum content.

Conclusion

Demands for deep learning provisions in higher education are intensifying. In this chapter we introduced the field of Learning Design (LD) and explored some of the possibilities that TPTs (transdisciplinary pedagogical templates) provide for university educators. These templates are based on LD principles and were built in LAMS, an online learning platform that focuses on pedagogy rather than on management and should, therefore, not be equated with traditional learning management systems, such as Blackboard, Moodle, Desire2Learn and others. The LAMS system enables the building and sharing of sequenced activities. Hence it is seen as an ideal platform for the construction, adoption and adaption of TPTs, some of which were described here as "local designs" and others as "generic designs". These TPTs have the potential to surpass the "student-consumer" stage through design decisions, demanding that students share their ideas and struggles to arrive at decisions and solutions to problems that are complex and unfamiliar. Thus we argued that our model has the potential to assist a wide range of educational practitioners in higher education, who are experts in their field but may need assistance in modernising their pedagogical practices, to move away from traditional transmission education methods of teaching and learning. Finally, we highlighted some obstacles to education reform, such as functional fixedness, which can hinder the adoption of innovative educational strategies in higher education.

Despite the barriers identified to the adoption of more student-centric pedagogical practices in higher education, it is clear that TPTs are perceived as valuable by university educators from various disciplinary backgrounds. As we seek to understand better how to support university educators through the development of TPTs, we begin to understand that too many variations and options "overwhelm" educators. There is a need to continue the research on how TPTs are utilised and how they can support both university educators and students in embracing new pedagogies designed for deep learning. If the conceptual foundations of this chapter are appropriate then they provide a framework for a broad-ranging practical interdisciplinary and global research program.

About the authors

Eva Dobozy is a Senior Lecturer in the School of Education at Curtin University, Australia. She can be contacted at this email: Eva.Dobozy@curtin.edu.au

James Dalziel is a Professor in Education and Director of the Macquarie eLearning Centre of Excellence (MELCOE) at Macquarie University, Australia. He can be contacted at this email: James.Dalziel@mq.edu.au

Bronwen Dalziel is a Senior Lecturer in the School of Medicine at the University of Western Sydney, Australia. She can be contacted at this email: B.Dalziel@uws.edu.au

Designing a Learning-centred Degree: Challenging to Learn and Learning to Challenge

David R. Newman

Introduction

A new department in an old university is starting a new postgraduate degree. On 20 September 2012, 30 ambitious students arrive in Oxford to learn how to become better policy-makers, during a one-year Master of Public Policy degree. The aim is to cultivate potential leaders in public policy.

Many of the skills required in policy work are not developed in traditional university education. There are tensions between the desire to expose students to the material that is needed to understand different aspects of public policy (an instructivist perspective) and the need for students to learn in ways that enable them to develop the professional skills they will need after graduating (a constructivist perspective). Consequently, people involved in curriculum design need to transform a degree that was initially designed around content into one that is centred on learning processes and outcomes, and the learners' needs.

This chapter shows how a degree designed on transmission of content could be, over time, transformed into challenge-based learning. I have written it based on six months of action research that began when I started work as the learning technologist for the degree and ended with the discussions with other chapter authors at the LIHE symposium, applying their theories and practical experience to this case.

In this chapter, we will look at the degree objectives, the requirements and constraints set by different stakeholders, discuss alternative theory-based pedagogies and then set out some appropriate combinations of pedagogy and technology that will best support student learning in this new degree.

The department and the degree: time and context

Since this chapter concerns a case that is ongoing, it helps to keep track of events in the past and future, as shown in the timeline (Table 1).

Date	Action
2010 Sep. 20	Blavatnik School of Government launched
2011 Apr.	Content curriculum designed and approved
2011 Nov.	Author joins BSG as learning technologist
2011 Dec.	Course co-ordinator interviews
2012 Feb.	Dean makes explicit the degree goals and professional skills needed in interview
2012 Mar.	Teaching and Learning Committee brainstorms student learning activities to develop relevant professional skills
2011 Apr.	Curriculum day, in which course directors shared how they were thinking of teaching
2012 May	Visits to learn from other universities using iPads
2012 Jun.	LIHE Symposium
2012 Aug.	Equip teaching building
2012 Sep. 20	30 Master of Public Policy students arrive
2013 Jan.–Mar.	Review first term and revise curriculum for 2013–14
2013 Sept.	60 students start
2014 Sept.	75 students start
2015	Move into brand new building; 120 students start

Table 1: Timeline

The Blavatnik School of Government was launched on 20 September 2010, with a £75 million donation to Oxford University by American philanthropist Leonard Blavatnik. Both the donor and the Dean,

Professor Ngaire Woods, were keen that it should start out, not with a research degree, but with a professional degree aimed at creating the next generation of public-policy leaders. That is the Master of Public Policy. The first students arrive on 20 September 2012.

It is a professional master's degree, akin to an MBA but aimed at potential senior policy-makers. They may be working in government or doing policy-related work in NGOs, private companies, consultancies or think tanks. It is multidisciplinary, with courses aimed at getting policy-makers to be able to think like economists, scientists, philosophers, not just becoming policy analysts. It is intensive as all this is learned in one year.

Students are coming from around the world, with 0 to 10 years' experience after their first degrees. Given their professional background, they will have high expectations for the quality of the teaching staff and the learning environment. Every student will get an iPad for use throughout the course and to keep, free with their £30,000 fees.

Teaching staff are leading academics in their fields, supplemented by professionals in national and international government. Every guest lecture will be captured. The degree is starting in an old building with a small cohort of 30 students. This will grow in subsequent years to 60, then 90, and finally 120 in the new building currently being designed.

Action research into the degree design

I started work in the Blavatnik School of Government in November 2011. My job as learning technologist is centred on the interactions between learning and technology, so I set out to investigate what kind of learning activities in the degree might be supported or enhanced by technology.

The degree had already been approved by university committees, so curriculum and programme specification documents already existed. These had been written based upon the content that would be taught to the students, identifying the aspects of public policy that students should hear about in an intensive year. This was in line with the content stream of curriculum design (Nygaard & Bramming, 2008), as shown in Figure 2 in Löfvall and Nygaard's chapter (in this volume). Unlike Löfvall and Nygaard, I do not see these approaches to curriculum design as an either/

or choice. Rather, a good designer should consider both the content and processes as necessary to achieving the degree goals.

I set out to research the intended learning outcomes as well as the learning and teaching processes that were being considered for the degree and its component courses. I interviewed every course co-ordinator, asking four questions:

> What change would there be in the students after completing the course?

> What would the students do (activities and tasks)?

> What resources would the students need?

> What technology did the teacher use?

From these interviews I derived the teacher requirements.

In a professional degree, it is important that students develop the skills needed in professional practice. To elicit these employment requirements, I interviewed the Dean about the degree aims and the skills students will need, and ran a focus group at the UK Govcamp in March 2012.

Although we do not know the specific needs, expectations and skills of the students starting in September 2012, we do know what to avoid, thanks to a series of focus groups run by the Oxford University Student Union (Medland & Evans, 2011).

So much research, what about action? In action research, it is normal to carry out cycles of design, intervention and reflection. It is not yet possible to test the effects of design changes on students, as the first cohort starts in September 2012. However, it was possible to get reactions of teaching staff when I presented reports on my findings to the course director and the teaching and learning committee. I even ran an electronic brainstorming session in which course co-ordinators came up with ideas for student activities in which they can develop the required professional skills.

Finally, I discussed possible ideas for redesign of this degree with other chapter authors during the LIHE Symposium in June 2011. This chapter presents the outcome of this process of research and reflection: a discussion on how to transform a degree from transmission learning to challenge-based learning.

Degree objectives and outcomes

The overall aim of the degree is to equip graduates with the skills needed to work in public policy and grow into public-policy leaders, be it in government, NGOs or private companies. From my interviews with the Dean and the course co-ordinators, it was possible to identify objectives and skills of this professional degree that differed from those of the normal Oxford University postgraduate degree.

Degree objectives	Student skills
By the end of the course, students should have a manifest improvement in all of the following:	To reach these objectives, they have to develop the following skills:
1. Sharper analysis.	1. An outstanding and differentiated writing ability, particularly in putting together a one-page brief, a four-page policy brief or a policy report.
2. Closer attention to evidence.	
3. Outstanding communication and interaction skills.	2. An ability to present verbally whatever answer they have in a clear and memorable way.
4. A really strong peer group.	
Course objectives	3. An ability to work in groups and to best harness the different strengths in the group.
Each course is giving the students one or more of the following:	4. An increased ability to absorb new information in unfamiliar surroundings. In particular, to avoid using their simplified prior assumptions to filter their understanding of the situation.
1. An ability to think like people in a particular discipline and/or become better consumers of the products of that discipline.	
2. Some subject-specific skills useful in policy work.	These are skills that alumni wished they had been taught. This is in addition to the skills normally addressed in university assessment and teaching, such as:
3. Practice in analysing a policy issue or solving a problem.	1. Sharper powers of analysis.
4. A critical appreciation of public policy.	2. Being more careful with evidence.
	3. Being aware of assumptions and how the assumptions shape the analysis.

Table 2: Master of Public Policy degree objectives and skills

Now, given these objectives, how should the students learn? When and where can they practise and develop the skills needed for policy work and achieve the learning objectives for both the whole degree and each course? Is covering a lot of content in one year sufficient? Contrast:

Content curricula	Issue-based learning
1. Divide degree into courses by discipline	1. Start with an issue or problem (the big idea)
2. Divide course into weeks by topics	2. Set a challenge for students (solve a problem, investigate a situation, analyse an issue)
3. Choose readings and speakers for topic	3. Student teams decide on guiding questions to investigate
4. Present chosen material in week	4. Student teams direct their own learning activities, facilitated by staff and drawing on resources
5. Students memorise material	5. Students develop and critically assess solutions
6. Students are assessed on their memory	6. Students present, document and publish solutions

Table 3: Content vs. issue-based learning

On the left, we can teach a lot in a one-year M.Sc.; but on the right, students are practising the skills of absorbing information in new surroundings, critically evaluating it, synthesising the knowledge they create into reports and policy briefs, and presenting this clearly (as they have to do in policy work). So how can we incorporate such an issue-based approach into the curriculum and into teaching on this degree? That is the problem to be solved.

Challenging to learn

The student learning outcomes emphasise the skills students will develop that will help them perform as public-policy professionals; but the curriculum is designed around giving them a breadth-first understanding of public-policy issues (as in many one-year M.Sc. programmes). What alternative pedagogic approaches might be tried to develop students' skills as policy professionals without omitting important public-policy issues, concepts and techniques?

Nygaard and Bramming (2008) considered how to develop a learning-centred curriculum for a Master of Public Administration (MPA). The competence profile of an MPA graduate is different from that identified for our MPP students. However, in both cases, the graduates need to make competent analyses of contextually bound empirical situations. Learning the tools is not sufficient; they need to be able to choose and apply them when working at speed in unfamiliar circumstances. They need to learn how to learn, through experiencing enquiry-based approaches to learning such as case-based learning (Erskine *et al.*, 1998; Mauffette-Leenders *et al.*, 1999), problem-based learning (Boud & Felleti, 1998; Savin-Baden & Major, 2004) or project-based learning (DeFillippi, 2001).

All these enquiry-based approaches have two things in common: students explore a problem; and the enquiry is student-led, with the teacher facilitating the process. The problems, issues or cases are sufficiently complex that there are alternative lines to explore.

In policy-making, a professional will go through a problem-solving sequence, similar to those explored in problem-based learning or explicitly used as a model for learning in Garrison's Theory of Critical Thinking (Garrison, 1991, 1992; Newman *et al.*, 1997). For the policy professional, the stages might be as follows:

1. A triggering event brings a private problem into the sphere of public issues that might require intervention. This is often done by external stakeholders, people with knowledge and experience that are unfamiliar to the policy worker.

2. As stakeholders start to explore the problem, the policy professional has quickly to gather evidence in a completely unfamiliar environment, from people who speak different disciplinary languages.

3. In assessing this evidence, the policy professional has to apply critical-thinking skills to make judgements, while avoiding preconceptions that bias judgement.

4. The issues and possible solutions are then synthesised in reports and then summarised into two-page policy briefs.

5. In acting on this knowledge, the policy professional has to make short (10–15 minute) oral presentations to senior policy-makers and other stakeholders who know almost nothing about the situation.

Similar stages in public problem solving have been identified in the deliberative democracy literature, in relation to public consultation and mediation processes (Morison & Newman, 2001).

Given the competence requirements of problem solving and critical thinking among policy workers, we should look at pedagogical approaches that challenge such students to solve problems. One that combines problem-based learning and project-based learning is challenge-based learning.

Challenge-based learning

This is a development of problem-based learning. Instead of being given a small problem to solve, students are given a major challenge, something as big as "find something to do about climate change". Student teams not only investigate the problem but decide on a project to do something about it.

> *"Challenge based learning is a collaborative learning experience in which teachers and students work together to learn about compelling issues, propose solutions to real problems, and take action. The approach asks students to reflect on their learning and the impact of their actions, and publish their solutions to a worldwide audience."*
>
> (Apple, 2009:1)

The simplest and clearest explanations are found in the key elements and process tabs of the challenge-based learning website, at http://www.challengebasedlearning.org/pages/about-cbl.

The students start by thinking about a big idea. Each student team then decides on one essential question the group will answer. The instructors help the team turn this question into a concrete challenge to create a specific solution. As in problem-based learning, students then work out a set of questions to guide their learning, identifying the resources they need to answer them. But having mastered those resources, they must then go on to work out an actionable solution and at least partially implement it in a real-life setting. Furthermore, they have to evaluate the solutions according to criteria they designed with the teachers at the beginning of the process. Throughout all the stages they reflect on their experiences and continually document both their work and their reflections. There are some important differences from problem-based learning:

1. Students have to implement a solution. That is a feature of project-based but not of problem-based learning.

2. There is more documentation, of both the work output and the learning process.

3. There is more emphasis on personal reflection.

4. There is explicit student evaluation of their solutions.

5. Last, but not least, students feel from the beginning that they are working on important problems, not just a teacher-set exercise.

Challenge-based learning clearly takes quite some work to organise. Is it worth the effort? Some evaluations have been published. Roselli and Brophy (2006) set out to measure the impact of challenge-based versus taxonomy-based instruction in biomechanics on one of the least promising measures: performance on knowledge-based questions. I would not expect challenge-based learning to help people memorise facts. However, they found that students in the CBL classes performed significantly better on the more difficult questions, whereas the control classes did better on the simpler questions. So even in a memory-related task, it seems that the skill of understanding and interpreting the questions is improved by challenge-based learning: surface learning is not sufficient.

The New Media Consortium carried out an evaluation of a challenge-based learning in 19 institutions from primary to graduate level, involving 65 teachers and 1,239 students (Johnson & Adams, 2011). Of their findings, those on group working most directly bear on the objectives of this degree:

> *"Interestingly, 80% of students felt that they did most of the work in their group, supporting the finding of strong engagement among the students around the group activities. The most compelling finding related to the student experience was the strong shift that occurred in students'*

perceptions of how they might contribute to a group project over the term of the project. Fewer than 15% saw themselves in a role such as leader, creative contributor, or strategist before the project began, but by the end, most students listed all these and several other ways in which they contributed to the work of their groups. 95% agreed with 'I usually contribute by sharing ideas and strategies'."

(Johnson & Adams, 2011:13)

After completing the project, students on average like group working less than before. This varied greatly according to their experiences of their own groups. In the post-project survey, over 80% found group work more exciting and more fun, 94% reckoned that group work developed new skills and 95% thought that when a group works well, members help each other to do the best work, but 79% agreed that in most groups one or two people end up doing most of the work.

Furthermore, 90% of the teachers reported that the 12 key twenty-first-century skills improved significantly, including leadership, creativity, media literacy, problem solving, critical thinking, flexibility and adaptability. Over three-quarters of students, across every age group, felt that they had learned more than what was required of them, were part of solving a big problem and worked harder than they normally would.

Given those findings, could challenge-based learning be applicable to the Master of Public Policy? The project-based learning component appears to develop group working skills, the social aspect of the group work can help develop a strong peer group and the practice in problem solving can help sharpen analytical skills. But how can the practice of implementing a solution be applied to policy work? Well, it turns out the solution need not be a new business or a mobile phone app. At Miami University in Oxford, Ohio:

"Several of the teams created printed materials as part of the solutions to the challenge. … One team created a visual mapping system to show how liberal education classes relate to one another. Another team created a brochure that identified different aspects of the many student organizations on campus. Another team created a promo piece for the Career Services Office."

(Johnson & Adams, 2011:26)

One could imagine that the output might be a written policy briefing presented to a retired minister like Peter Mandelson while the reflection on learning could be presented as a video.

I would expect our professional, experienced and engaged students to rise to such challenges. Imagine a curriculum designed around a number of challenge-based learning exercises. A small challenge near the beginning would introduce students to this way of working and help them to discover their own strengths. In the current curriculum, the students start with a small challenge: working out what to do about the resource curse (the way economies are distorted by abundant natural resources like oil) in three days. A big challenge at the end would allow them to apply all the skills and knowledge they had learned to a big policy problem. Each course in the degree would be centred around a set of policy issues. When studying an issue, students would be encouraged to view it from different perspectives, using the tools of more than one discipline. In a discussion, they might move from a banker's perspective on returns on investment to a farmer's perspective on soil erosion. Such multi-perspective discussions develop critical thinking skills and deep learning (Johnson, 1997).

Learning to challenge

If students are going to be challenged to learn, how do they learn to challenge? How can students learn the skills and attitudes needed to benefit from challenge-based learning? How can teachers learn to design and facilitate learning challenges?

There has been a debate in *Educational Psychologist* on the effectiveness of inquiry-based learning. Kirschner *et al.* (2006) wrote an article entitled 'Why Minimal Guidance During Instruction Does Not Work: An Analysis of the Failure of Constructivist, Discovery, Problem-Based, Experiential, and Inquiry-Based Teaching'. They claimed that evidence from empirical studies indicates that minimally guided instruction is less effective and less efficient than instructional approaches that place a strong emphasis on guidance of the student learning process. The advantage of guidance begins to recede only when learners have sufficiently high prior knowledge to provide "internal" guidance. They were particularly concerned about overloading working memory during free exploration of complex environments. Nor did they consider that studying simulations of how experts worked was necessarily the way to start to learn.

In two rebuttal articles published in *Educational Psychologist*, it was argued that problem-based learning and enquiry learning are not minimally guided instruction and that Kirschner *et al.* (2006) were wrong to lump them together. These approaches first train the students in the individual enquiry and group working techniques needed, then provide scaffolding to help students make sense of the problem and its environment. These reduce cognitive load, provide expert guidance and help students acquire disciplinary ways of thinking (Hmelo-Silver *et al.*, 2007; Schmidt *et al.*, 2007).

They also pointed out meta-analyses of research into problem-based learning that did find positive effects, contradicting the meta-analyses cited by Kirschner *et al.* (2006). A meta-synthesis of meta-analyses found that PBL was superior when it comes to long-term retention, skill development and satisfaction of students and teachers, while traditional approaches were more effective for short-term retention as measured by standardised board exams (Strobel & van Barneveld, 2009).

Given those findings, curriculum designers and teachers need to find ways to help students learn to challenge. What techniques can they use? A number are described in this volume. I will take them in the order of the problem-solving stages set out by Garrison.

As students start to define a problem and explore it, they have to think of questions to answer. This is one of the first steps in challenge-based learning. Albergaria Almeida and Teixeira-Dias (in this volume) show how effective student-generated questions are in getting students to think more critically about what they read and hear. This is similar to the techniques often used in flip teaching (November & Mull, 2012). Rather than just listen to a lecture and take notes, students view videos of mini-lectures, five-to-ten minutes long, in the style of the Khan Academy, before the classroom session. They each have to come up with three questions about the video, perhaps about something they don't understand or some possible application elsewhere, before they attend the class. They can often start discussion online. When they come to the class, instead of lecturing, the teacher becomes a facilitator, answering their questions to remove misunderstandings, leading discussions on implications of what they have learned and supporting students as they do exercises on the topic. Albergaria Almeida and Teixeira-Dias found that the example set by students who asked good questions was emulated by other students, who then started to think more deeply about the readings (an example of vicarious learning). As teachers pick up on particular powerful questions (Vogt *et al.*, 2003), students start searching for other questions that catalyse insight and innovation.

Once students have come up with questions to guide their learning, they get feedback from teachers in challenge-based learning. They need to learn how to make use of feedback to plan how to explore the problem. Enomoto and Warner (in this volume) explain a technique for getting students to reflect on their learning. Every time students get feedback on a task, they complete a study action plan, selecting learning methods and strategies to do better next time. Later they write personal reflections on how well each strategy worked, prompted by searching questions designed to get them thinking deeply about their learning experience. This seems an ideal approach to use in a degree where many students have been out of education for some years but are quite familiar with designing action plans and evaluating performance against them.

The next stages of problem exploration and problem evaluation require students to develop good group communication skills, with guidance on appropriate discussion processes at each stage of the challenge. Communication skills are practised and developed (with increasing student engagement) in social-media learning environments, as discussed by Lenstrup (in this volume) and used in the Master's in Strategic Marketing at Imperial College London. But communication is not sufficient. It is necessary to get the students to work effectively in groups and to find, in the words of the Dean, "how to best harness the different strengths in the group". That requires an understanding of leadership styles and skills, as discussed by Stupans (in this volume).

One form of scaffolding that helps students to manage approaches such as challenge-based learning is a range of knowledge representations suitable for the context and the disciplines used to understand it. As student teams work on a challenge, knowledge emerges from their discussions (Newman & Holtham, 2008); but it often needs to be transformed from informal notes into more structured representations, such as concept and mind maps. Hager (in this volume) found that students used ePortfolios and blogs not just to present their final project pieces but also changes over time, making it possible for them to share and view each other's work and aggregate and reflect on their own work. More complex representations are found in simulations and games in which students can interact dynamically with the simulations, getting an experiential understanding of the problem environment and the models used by experts to understand it.

Throughout all the stages of challenge-based learning, students can use technology to organise their work, curate their emergent knowledge and reduce their cognitive load. The meta-analyses cited by Kirschner *et al.* (2006) were from 1993, in the days before Google searches, shared bibliographies, wikiwiki editing, the semantic web or the tablet computers that students carry everywhere, documenting every stage of their learning. In the next few years, I expect the development of more flexible technologies to support group work and pedagogies that make more effective use of technology to challenge students to learn.

In the meantime, how can students be prepared for the processes and techniques used in challenge-based learning? Currently, the plan is to arrange skills training separate from the degree courses. However, Benzie (in this volume) shows how the mismatch between general preparatory courses and each particular degree often leads to a failure to transfer skills from one context to another. It would be better to design the CBL skills training into the first challenge. More generally, the development of student skills in learning to challenge could be included in pedagogical templates of the type explained by Dobozy *et al.* (in this volume). The Learning Design Support Environment project in the UK is developing a web application to provide guidance on learning design, teaching and technology for academic staff (Balch *et al.*, 2012).

Future challenges

This is an account of the early stages of action research aiming to redesign a degree. What comes next? How might we get from a well-designed but content-focused curriculum to a degree that continually challenges students to learn?

It is a long-term project to design a whole degree around challenge-based learning: perhaps something for the new building in four years' time.

Meanwhile, it is possible to gradually introduce new approaches to learning, starting with the design of student tasks and activities that get them to practise the skills needed for policy work within the current curriculum. Many of the specific techniques discussed, such as student-generated questions and study action plans, can be used initially in traditional teaching. Then new tasks can be designed to increase active learning. Alongside that, there is a great potential for the use of technology to support reflective learning, starting with student iPads being filled with everything they note and observe during the year.

About the author

David Newman is the Learning Technologist at the Blavatnik School of Government, University of Oxford. He can be contacted at this email: drdrnewman@gmail.com

Strategies for Augmenting Students' Attention in Higher Education

Barbara Hong and Catheryn J. Weitman

Introduction

One of the most important goals of higher education is to cultivate the mind. The film *Dead Poets Society* reminds us how difficult this can be. Unlocking this reality causes one to pause and rethink the teaching–learning connection as it relates to the dynamics of attention. If the goal is to engage the mind critically, contemporary dialogues about learning in higher education must include an understanding about human cognition and attention sustainability so that authentic learning can occur. While a plethora of information, resources, approaches and rationales has been written about student engagement in higher education (Barkley, 2010; Harper & Quale, 2009; Schlechty, 2011; Wehlburg, 2006; Weimer, 2002, 2010), we contend that the missing piece is a focus on how human cognition works. Thus, our chapter links three dynamics of cognitive functions to learner-centred teaching and shows how they each affect attentiveness, deep thinking and sustain memory.

Before students can engage their minds and construct knowledge, they must be motivated. The condition to induce motivation is to bring learners from a passive state to an active state (Thorne & Thomas, no date). The former is unintended, allowing one to discount stimuli almost unconsciously. The latter is deliberate, arousing active attentiveness to the intended stimuli. What this means is that students need to actively 'attend' to the learning act and participate in processing information in order to remember it. Without being attentive, learning cannot occur.

In reflecting on his teaching, the infamous basketball coach John Wooden stated that *"students must become interested in the subject"* (Nater & Gallimore, 2006:115). Wooden went on to note that he had other teachers *"who simply threw the material at us and expected us to learn. Generally, their reasons for that style, especially the college professors, was [sic] they believed college students don't need interest generated. They said students should be interested because they are in college to graduate. I don't agree. Students of all ages learn better when interest is generated."* (Nater & Gallimore, 2006:115) Yet, in order to cultivate interest, students must attend to their learning purposefully and consciously in order to *draw* the information into their cognition.

This chapter addresses the dynamics of attention as a means toward improving the teaching approaches of faculty members and the learning behaviours of students in higher education. By focusing on how cognition functions, we hope faculty members will be cognisant about designing contextually sensitive curricula that involve familiarising themselves with the students' attentional capacity and asking complex questions that activate thinking at a deeper level.

Attentiveness and psychological satisfaction

Huba and Freed (2000:3) noted that in order *"to focus on learning rather than teaching, we must challenge our basic assumptions about how people learn and what the roles of an instructor should be"* in higher education. One of these basic assumptions is challenged by uncovering how attention impacts learning. While learning and attention are different cognitive functions, they are intertwined and dependent upon each other (Miller, 2005). Motivation is an innate prerequisite for students to engage their minds for learning. When motivation is induced, a learner's position changes from one of passivity to one of activity. What this means is that students actively 'attend' to the learning act; take an interest in learning; and become increasingly motivated in expanding and strengthening their consumption of that knowledge.

Miller (2005) pointed out that there is a co-dependency between attention and learning even though they are comprised of different cognitive functions. The difference between attention and learning is that one is a condition reliant upon the other. Simplistically, attention is the process of selecting information and deciding which items are to be acted upon (Miller, 2005). While much more information is ignored than illuminated, the brain seeks out those stimuli that it notices among the sea of millions of others. Once these dominant stimuli are designated, the mind determines to which it ought to attend, much like the way a beacon of light from a lighthouse focuses on a ship in the ocean.

Learning, on the other hand, acts upon those dominant stimuli that were found among the thousands of other stimuli available. As the brain acts upon the selected stimulus, it stores information for later retrieval when needed. Learning, then, is like the culmination of stimuli that were selected, stored and used in some capacity later on. In short, learning is dependent upon one's attention, particularly at the initial learning stage when one encounters new information for the first time.

Attention impacts all facets of learning – from arousing interest and cultivating motivation to being actively engaged. Students who are interested in what they are learning *"concentrate more, are focused, apply themselves willingly, share ideas, productively use time, question, and often are proud of their work"* (Silver, 2007:7). In essence, interested students are attentive and responsive. As a recursive process, attention is sustained through interest and motivation while, simultaneously, attentiveness must be unrelenting to perpetuate and maintain interest and motivation. By being attentive, one displays cognitive presence whereby the mind is intentionally occupied, explicitly mindful and thoughtfully aware of what is being attended to. Thus, there is a blending or convergence of what is *"cognize[d], know[n], [thought], and [seen]"* (Naft, 2010).

Attention is sustained through interest and motivation. Alluring interest and arousing motivation are key for procuring attentiveness. Barkley (2010) suggested that motivation is the result of expectancy times value (motivation = expectancy x value). Expectancy can be either external or internal, with internal being more critical than external. Expectancy is the belief that one can succeed. Externally, this entails professors designing actively challenging assignments or tasks so that students can be successful at completing them given the necessary level of background knowledge. Internally, students must feel that they can be equally successful. Knowing that one can do something is psychologically self-empowering and immensely motivating. Having the confidence and trust that the task can be completed satisfactorily is paramount for expectancy, which in turn impacts one's attentive behaviours.

The other half of Barkley's motivation equation is value. Value connotes the worthiness of the task or assignment to the learner. Wiggins and McTighe (1998) also attested that tasks must be worth doing – they must be relevant, meaningful and purposeful, especially to retain attentiveness. The value or merit that is placed upon completing a task determines how motivated, interested and ultimately attentive one becomes to seeing it through to fruition. If students see the worthiness in learning the material or completing the assignment, they will be more likely to place high value on it. In essence, they are more inclined to be internally involved in learning and decidedly more attracted to the task. Consequently, they are more attentive and psychologically satisfied.

Attentiveness and active learning

The establishment of keen interest and motivation is embedded into active learning, once attentional processes are triggered. Barkley (2010) defined active learning as that which engenders the mind to be engaged. Fink (2003:104) suggested that active learning consists of first-hand experiences, such as *"doing and observing"*, coupled with metacognitive or reflective experiences (see Enomoto and Warner's chapter in this volume). In her chapter in this volume, Su proposes that we develop the notion of "learning to be" – that is, learning skills applied first-handily by doing or through some intentional undertaking. Supporting this contention, Huba and Freed (2000:153) pointed out that *"the rationale for active learning is that students learn more and better when they explore a topic rather than when they watch and listen."* Finally, Danielson (2002:23) noted that *"active mental processing (e.g. creating appropriate metaphors and predicting outcomes)"* is needed for mindful engagement when preceded by attentiveness. As such, learners are greatly attuned to the learning context when they are actively involved.

When attention is at its prime, students are engaged. Such high levels of engagement allow for rudimentary knowledge to be challenged, expanded and intensified at the pace of the learners. Such an approach also enables students to integrate various genres of knowledge using multiple senses and stimuli, transcending across disciplines. Hence, as dynamic attenders in the learning act, students' minds become energised and invigorated. For this reason, designing learning activities that sustain attention, interest and motivation intentionally tend to engage the mind and challenge the learner more than traditional instruction. Such engaging conditions create opportunities for active and deep thinking to thrive. For instance, strategies such as problem-based learning deliberately motivate, activate and stimulate the mind to strengthen students' learning and elevate higher-order thinking in relevant applications.

Closely related to active learning is the concept of high-impact activities. Attention, interest and motivation are furthered through the deliberate implementation of high-impact activities. Research shows that high-impact activities have a strong correlation to active learning and result in more profound thinking when the level of attentiveness is greatest (Kuh, 2008). For example, in the United States, such activities involve service-learning projects, study abroad programs, student–faculty research, internships and capstone experiences.

Attention and critical thinking

Why is it that students can sometimes think critically in one situation and not in another? Why is it that students sometimes find it challenging to see issues from another or a different perspective? We know that thinking critically, constructing one's own knowledge and using metacognition are important aspects of engaged learners. Why, then, are critical-thinking skills so difficult to teach? Part of the answer lies in the construct of critical thinking. Garrison *et al.* (2004:2–3) noted that thinking critically *"is both a process and an outcome. As an outcome, it is best understood from an individual perspective – that is, the acquisition of deep and meaningful understanding as well as content-specific critical inquiry abilities, skills, and dispositions."* Stassen *et al.* (2011) also delineated 12 types of critical thinking, each requiring differing or overlapping processes. However, critical thinking is implicitly observed: that is, the ability to think critically is displayed through the application of the processes (abilities, skills and dispositions) innately developed. For example, students may demonstrate their critical thinking by displaying their ability to judge, synthesise, evaluate, draw conclusions and so forth. The two key ingredients in the development of critical thinking are the selectivity of dominant stimuli, which is attentiveness, and the relevance of background or domain knowledge. The thinking process here entails paying attention to the needful information in order to arouse one to ask questions, to think deeper, to provoke and to challenge beyond the surface structure of the problem presented.

Huba and Freed (2000) proposed that advanced cognitive skills are dependent upon different types of knowledge and on their interaction and interdependence with one another. Two of the more basic types of knowledge are declarative and procedural knowledge. Declarative knowledge (i.e. that grounded in basic facts) establishes a foundation for procedural knowledge (i.e. knowledge of the processes of asking questions, communicating effectively and so forth). Substantial background and experience in these are needed so that both contextual (i.e. where and when declarative and procedural knowledge are applied) and metacognitive knowledge (i.e. self-regulation and critical reflection) are developed. (See Albergaria Almeida and Teixeira-Dias's chapter in this volume.) Because of the interdependence and interaction between and among differing knowledge types, attention behaviours need to be overtly and explicitly selective, allowing advanced cognitive skills to evolve and progress. Ultimately, critical thinking entails generating a wealth of knowledge-based processes so that the mind is attentive and engaged in order for learners to construct their own knowledge. For example, project-based, problem-based or inquiry-based learning compels students to approach thinking intuitively from their own contextual background with differing perceptions and differentiated ways of application.

Two constructs of critical thinking

Exploring two constructs pertinent to critical thinking provides insights into what to consider when cultivating and designing advanced thinking abilities. First, as noted above, critical thinking is reliant on procedural knowledge, not necessarily on declarative knowledge. Such knowledge includes: (a) understanding and implementing inquiry techniques; (b) generating higher-level questions that cause one to dig deeper; (c) embracing declarative knowledge while identify gaps and reconstituting prior knowledge; (d) being adept with multiple and varied resources; (e) communicating needs, expectations, and outcomes; (f) knowing how to reason, make judgments, evaluate, negotiate content and merge similar and different constructs; and finally (g) propose sound and new solutions. Accordingly, faculty members must allow for development and scaffolding of these skills across multiple venues in order to keep students from losing the internal expectancy needed for successful completion and transferability. In some cases, the required dominant stimuli may be initially ignored or overlooked. In many cases, stimuli are only attended to after multiple exposures and re-teaching as a way to emphasise and capture the dominant stimuli for future need. One way to insure recursive exposure to dominant stimuli is to use interdisciplinary and transdisciplinary instructional design (see Dobozy *et al.* in this volume).

Often, faculty members on face value presume that students possess complex critical-thinking skills when they come to college. This leads faculty members to assume that because students were perhaps exposed to the application of critical-thinking skills, they ought to be readily able to apply these same skills in any setting. However, students' levels of attentiveness might not have been as high as they should have been when first exposed to the information, so they may be confused or unfamiliar with how to apply that knowledge in another setting. Conceivably then, because of misguided attentive dynamics, students are often unable to complete advanced thinking skills or view an issue from different perspectives. However, with intentional practice and retrieval of relevant knowledge, faculty members can assist students through the process of deep learning by asking deep questions that stimulate the mind as it relates to that issue.

The second construct pertinent to critical thinking is that of problem solving. Problem solving employs what is called deep structure. What this means is that the mind engages multiple sets of skills collectively, interactively and simultaneously in order to respond to stimuli involving advanced thinking skills. This is true regardless of the situation or setting. Hence, while the outward or surface structure differs, the deep structural processes are often the same. As an example, the surface structures encountered when switching from an automatic to a standard transmission in a vehicle may be different but the deep structure of operating a vehicle is more or less the same. In other words, if students can use their logical reasoning to analyse a certain mathematical algorithm, then they can probably apply the same thinking process to understand a plot in a piece of literature. Similarly, once familiar with certain word-processing software on a computer, another word processor, even if it is in a different language, is generally recognisable because the deep structures of the programs are similar. Often times, however, students neglect to see that the deep structure of thinking processes is the same and can be easily transferred to another context. This is again where expectancy – the belief that one can be successful – comes into play and it is the role of the faculty member to help students identify these similar structures.

Strategies commonly used to aid students in attending to and recognising deep structures include asking different levels of questions about the same types of problem, asking the same level of questions across different types of problems and using facets of learning that involve perspective and empathy as ways to demonstrate learning (McTighe & Wiggins, 1999). An example of combining all three elements of inquiry would be to pose a higher-level or inquiry-based question to students so that they are driven to understand the information from a different perspective and at a deeper level. For example, ask students to consider how the Germans might have felt during World War II. Would their feelings change during the course of the war? Then, to gauge carefully whether or not students have attained an enhanced level of thinking, invite them to formulate their own questions at a different level and restructure their outlook on the same issue.

Influences from cognitive science on attention

Thus far, we presented information that emphasised some issues surrounding attention as linked to psychological satisfaction, active learning and critical thinking. We turn more to the dynamics of attention by addressing the brain capacity, attention pools and sustainability, so that faculty members might consider these as they impact the teaching–learning interaction.

Brain capacity

Attending is difficult; and it becomes more difficult with all the distractions inundating the world. Distractions implode the ability to pay attention. Simply removing distractions might (only slightly) increase attentiveness. As we uncovered, attentiveness is a much more complex and multifaceted dynamic impacting interest and motivation. One of the most fundamental research findings concerns brain capacity.

The brain can only hold limited pieces of information. Danielson (2002) noted that information is filtered in the sensory stage before it is stored as working memory or knowledge. As the brain takes in more information each time, it has limitations on how much newly acquired detail can be stored. This is exemplified with the feeling of being overwhelmed. Logically, then, if faculty members need students to take in more information, they must first help students make room in their primary (working) memory by relieving some of burden of being overloaded by shifting the information from the primary locale to the secondary locale. Because information decomposes or slips away after only 20 to 30 seconds, each piece of information must be processed into the secondary storage almost concomitantly (Barrouillet & Gaillard, 2011).

Faculty members can help students to process information in many ways. For example, faculty members can organise and present information in more manageable chunks for students in a given context and/or transfer information into meaningful connections based on students' prior knowledge. In a biology class, for instance, students are asked to remember the seven parts of a cell. If each part of the cell is associated with its functionality and critical presence to the other parts, learning the parts of the cell would be easier than trying to memorise all the parts in isolation without any connections. Hence, when retrieving a term for one part of a cell, the brain will tend to trigger the associate term as well to the other parts of the cell. Thus, learning the seven parts of the cell will be more relevant, parallel and meaningful. By successfully binding these related synapses in the brain, linking old with new information, the nerves in the brain are strengthened and the placement of that information in the brain becomes more permanent (Barrouillet & Gaillard, 2011).

In order to enhance memory for storage and retrieval of any information, students need to learn material accurately the first time it is introduced. Students must continuously remain active partners in making connections to their prior learning by keeping their attention intact and averting distractions. Otherwise, students may slip into a state of disequilibrium between what they think they heard, understood and learned, and what was actually intended. Disequilibrium results because of the disparity between what was apparently understood (learned) and what students thought they learned or when dominant stimuli were expected to be stored and were not. When disequilibrium emerges, a randomisation of fragmented knowledge within the brain's capacity occurs. Thus, when students employ metacognitive skills (as they do with deep learning and the application of deep structures), knowledge is fused and stored continuously in the brain.

Attentional pools

Multitasking has seemingly become a valued aptitude, although cognitively non-existent. Concentrating on multiple tasks simultaneously with the same level of quality (i.e. multitasking) is difficult. When more than one task is attempted simultaneously, attention is divided so that corresponding functions occur and compete with each other. Depending upon the task at hand, corresponding functions fall into three types: dual, continuous and discrete (Willingham, 2004). Each one of these corresponding functions impacts attention and the degree of concentration given to each of the competing stimuli. With dual-type tasks, attention needed for the easier task is much less than that needed for the more complex task. For example, an individual might be able to cook a routine breakfast and chat on the phone simultaneously. The concentration may be higher for the conversation on the phone than for the cooking because the latter is performed procedurally on autopilot. For continuous-type tasks, attention is endlessly routine. These are tasks that have been internalised and require little attention or thought to perform. For example, using a keyboard could be a continuous type task for someone who is very familiar with the placement of the keys and subliminally attends to the act of word processing, per se. In the classroom setting, students take notes furiously and habitually and might not necessarily pay attention to what they are writing or hearing – they just write. The last type of task demanding attention simultaneously is called a discrete task, in which both competing tasks have finite parameters. For example, imagine you're watching a favourite TV show and someone calls on the telephone. Because both tasks have a fixed time limit needing attention, one is often competing with the other. Students display this type of situation when they are distracted by some conversations in the class while instructions for an assignment are being given. Therefore, essentially, faculty members must acquire the ability to identify and assess combinations of the types of tasks that induce the most optimal attention behaviours of students before choosing and assigning them.

The notion that the brain can give the same level of focus to every task all at the same time is implausible. According to Poldrack (2007), our brains are not wired for multitasking, even though it appears that we are more "efficient" when managing more than one thing at a time. The quality of the finished product is often short changed because of our competing attentions with conflicting demands. Notice the difficulties in maintaining dexterity during the following exercise:

> *"While sitting, lift your right leg off the ground and rotate your foot clockwise. Now, with your right hand, draw the number six (6) in the air."*

The reason that this seems awkward, even unnatural, is that our cognitive processes do not enable us to conduct ourselves simultaneously with contrasting behaviours. Attention is limited, selective and focused. As such, the mind picks up the signals of dominant stimuli in order to select which ones to keep and which ones to filter out. Because there are opposing attentional pools in our cognition (Pinker, 2009), only one of the tasks that we are most familiar with will be performed better or at a faster rate. (In the exercise above, was the more familiar motion that of rotating your foot or drawing the numeral? Which was performed fastest?)

Two types of attentional pools exist: those that can be combined, such as with auditory and visual pools, and those that must remain separated, as with vocal and spatial pools (Willingham, 2010). For example, most individuals can drive a vehicle (a visual act) and listen to music (an auditory act) at the same time. However, if there is an accident on the road, explicit concentration on driving is needed. The radio, MP3 player or iPod might be lowered, even turned off, as a means of redirecting one's own attentiveness in order to drive more carefully with deliberate concentrated effort. Such explicit concentration is evident when an announcement such as this is made in class: "This material will be on the exam!" Suddenly, students redirect their focus and pay more careful attention. Often, they start composing notes and may even ask to have the information repeated so as to be certain they heard it – unequivocally.

In contrast, tasks involving vocal and visual attention pools are more difficult to combine. For example, to sing a pop song (vocal) while simultaneously watching a thriller movie (visual) and enjoying both would be hard. Likewise, students cannot write a research paper while talking to a friend. More often than not, one of these tasks (usually the more complex one) will be compromised and thus careless errors are often introduced.

Barrouillet and Gaillard (2011) explained that our cognition is simply not designed to function with competing pools, at least not in an effective manner. As much as we would like to drive and text at the same time, the splitting of opposing attentional pools, even for a second, is not possible and could even be deadly. Small and Vorgan (2009) explain that, if students are checking their social media (e.g. Facebook, twitter, emails, etc.) while instruction is occurring, they will most likely miss part of the information, despite their best efforts to stay focused and pay attention. Only stimuli that are attended to fully and unilaterally will enter our thinking processes (Pinker, 2009). Thus, faculty members in higher education must consider competing attentional pools when employing activities to engage students.

Sustainability

Finally, maintaining attention is challenging. The mind is constantly thinking and wandering. This occurs regularly regardless of how motivating or interesting the stimulus might be (Pinker, 2009). Typically, one's concentration is limited to between 10 and 15 minutes before attention drifts to other stimuli – perhaps thinking about what to eat for dinner, calling someone, watching TV tonight and checking Facebook or emails.

Similarly, in the classroom setting, students' attention will routinely wander even in the midst of an engaging discourse. The brain wanders because it is constantly seeking different stimuli to rekindle itself (Pinker, 2009). While there are some students who are exceptionally self-regulated in controlling which stimulus to yield to and which to ignore or resist (Willingham, 2010), those students are few. Many individuals find it extremely difficult to sustain attention for long durations of time and to keep from thinking about other things. (How often did your mind drift or wander to unrelated things as you were reading this chapter?)

That being said, students can sustain their attention in 15-to-20-minute clusters because of their natural cognitive reflex to pull themselves back to the current stimulus. Faculty members would benefit greatly from utilising strategies that encourage peek attention through instructional blocks comprised of short teaching intervals. When designing instructional activities, faculty members can maximise sustainability by planning for and implementing multiple activities during one teaching–learning occurrence. For example, a series of activities might include shifting questions, involving students in discussions, presenting conflicting examples and so forth. Additionally, being aware of students' body language can help to monitor their attention.

Sustainability also happens in a very different mode as well. The 'feeling' of knowing can sometimes give one a false sense of confidence. Frequently, students respond to a question by claiming "I know it but I can't explain it!" Such pseudo-learning emerges when students are listening to instruction or studying on their own (Schacter, 2002). When students hear or read familiar text, their minds often mislead them into thinking that they have grasped the concept and have understood the material, when in fact they have not. This false confidence disengages the student from the learning act, which then lessens their attention.

The pseudo-learning phenomenon occurs during re-reading of textbooks or reviewing notes over and over again in preparation for an exam, or when editing papers for classes. This feeling of 'knowing' is deceptive and gives students a false sense of knowledge – misguiding them on what they actually know versus what they do not know. As Schacter (2002) explains, the tendency to misjudge one's "feeling of knowing" as understanding is not uncommon. Faculty members in higher education would need to ensure that students actually understand the information by assessing their knowledge in applicable contexts and asking them to reconstruct that knowledge by teaching it to their classmates.

Strategies for augmenting students' attention

Throughout this chapter strategies have been embedded to improve attention and ultimately deep thinking. We explored these dynamics of attention to understand better how they intersect with the learning act in higher-education settings. Recognition of these dynamics is foremost in moving students towards deeper thinking. Strategies for augmenting attention to empower students to thrive as actively engaged learners and critical thinkers can be employed using the findings from cognitive science. Thus, through awareness of attention behaviours, faculty members can restructure teaching so that students pay attention to what they are learning (metacognition). We conclude with additional thoughts to consider when providing teaching–learning interactions to maximise attentional behaviours.

In order to sustain students' attention for long periods of time, faculty members must to be cognisant of the length of their discourse (i.e. the amount of teacher talk), the pacing of their delivery (i.e. fast or slow), the challenge level presented for students (i.e. lower level or higher level), the organisation of the materials and the flow of their presentation. All of these elements impact the interchange between and among the dynamics of attention and the teaching–learning exchange. Strategies used in active learning should focus on problem solving, analysing, thinking critically, conversing and constructing one's own knowledge – building bridges from prior knowledge to newer knowledge, in essence, transforming knowledge. At the higher-education level, active learning is composed of multiple responses to inquiries, multiple representations of ideas and multiple ways to engage.

Weimer (2002) cautions that faculty members, perhaps unknowingly, employ strategies that are often counterintuitive to kindling active learning. For example, faculty members might think the "prime time" of learning is during the middle part of class whereas the "down time" is at the beginning and end of class. However, researchers ascertained that the optimal "prime time" for most attentive learning is at the beginning and toward the end of class, whereas the "down time" happens during the middle period (Fisher & Frey, 2007; Sousa, 2006). The implications of these findings for faculty members suggest radical changes in how we design instruction for beginnings and closures. If we want to bring attentiveness to the forefront, activities that do so must begin the lesson rather than come in the middle of the learning event. Therefore, if faculty members want to instil attentive behaviours that lead to modes of higher learning involvement with their students, they ought to reallocate how time is spent.

As referenced previously, this entails that a faculty member divide the class period into 15-minute segments. A simple way to use the first 15 minutes is to arouse students with thought-provoking questions. Invite them to contribute to the conversation as active participants and involve them in implicit knowledge constructions and making connections to surface concepts with deep structural learning from previous instruction. This introductory time is used as an anticipatory, proactive convention to prepare students' minds to be attentive and aroused in the proceeding instruction. This way, faculty members prepare students to retrieve the necessary prior knowledge so that they can connect their new learning and develop relevant schemas for organising their information. As the instruction proceeds, students now have a concept map or agenda for what to expect. Then toward the end of class, faculty members review with students, for example, by having them write down the three most essential components which they gathered during that class and explain each one to a classmate. Further, students might reflect on their expected outcomes and justify their attainment of that knowledge to assess their own understanding. This closing time is best used to correct any misunderstandings, reinforce intended knowledge and close the gap for any lingering questions which students might have. Students ought always to leave the class with accurate information (grounded declarative and procedural knowledge), a sense of closure (cognitive equilibrium) and psychological satisfaction (self-regulation, motivation and self-empowerment).

Another effective strategy is constantly to regroup the class by actively involving the students through personalising experiences, provoking questions and generating spontaneous dialoguing among students. Research found that when students become part of the instruction as attentive learners, they are better able to process and relate materials to their previous learning (Willingham, 2010). Providing prompts and time for students to converse with each other during the teaching–learning act reinforces attentiveness and sustains long-term memory of what was just learned.

Further, as a means to lessen the effects of pseudo-learning, faculty members can facilitate learning by framing questions that 'target' the application of core knowledge. Likewise, to help with reviews, faculty members can pose questions that demand different levels of challenges (beyond surface levels) so that students are driven to look at the same materials from divergent angles and at new depths, thus creating opportunities to experience the critical thinking processes. Wiggins and McTighe (1998) suggest incorporating questions focused on differing perspectives, empathy and self-knowledge or efficacy to accomplish this.

Finally, several methods to augment attentiveness are discussed in this volume. All of the following techniques provide students with a means to capture their attention so that they can interact with content and become highly involved in the learning act. Examples of ways to arouse attention include:

- Developing questioning strategies (see Albergaria Almeida and Teixeria-Dias' chapter in this volume)

- Using social-media strategies (see Lenstrup's chapter in this volume), and

- Implementing case studies, simulations and gaming strategies.

Conclusion

Learning is a complex synergy between the brain and the instruction. Each component of the brain has its own capacity for sifting through and selecting stimuli, storing them for later retrieval and memory. Retaining and constructing new knowledge, based on the original dominant selectivity processes embedded with attentive behaviours is foremost. Every dominant piece of information is intertwined with background knowledge and experiences.

As faculty members become cognisant of how learning can be optimised through understanding the dynamics of attention, they will hopefully become reflective of how teaching – and more importantly, learning – can be internalised, especially through instructional strategies that embed these constructs. We brought to light the contemporary issue of attentional factors as they impact learning. We focused on three areas of attention – brain capacity, attentional pools and sustainability – so that faculty members could be more aware of their teaching on student learning. Strategies were provided to augment students' attention in higher education for more effective and deeper thinking to occur. The synergistic outcome of effective teaching can bring about the holistic, germane and coherent acquisition of functional knowledge that is needed to be attentive, think critically, solve problems and develop complex reasoning skills – to be actively engaged in the learning process. Thus, in this manner, attentive students develop into consumers of learning rather than mere consumers of knowledge.

About the authors

Barbara Hong is an Associate Professor of Special Education at the Pennsylvania State University Altoona College and a Research Associate for the Partnership for Applied Research and Training in Novel Educational and Related Services (PARTNERS). She may be contacted at this email: bsh15@psu.edu

Catheryn J. Weitman is Dean and Professor of the College of Education at Texas A&M International University. She may be contacted at this email: catheryn.weitman@tamiu.edu

Universal Design for Learning in Higher Education

John Branch and Alyssa Martina

Introduction

According to the National Center for Learning Disabilities (NCLD), more than 2.4 million elementary- and secondary-school students in the United States have been diagnosed with a learning disability. With a school population of close to 64 million, this means that about one in every 27 American children receives some type of special educational service. It is no surprise, therefore, that the issue of learning disabilities is a major concern to a wide variety of stakeholders, including educators, policy-makers, administrators, parents and, of course, students themselves.

Learning disabilities, however, are not limited to elementary and secondary schools. Indeed, the number of students with learning disabilities who now attend institutions of higher education has grown in recent years. The population of students in higher education in the United Kingdom with known learning disabilities, for example, increased from 27,465 in 2007–8 to 34,095 in 2010–11 (www.hesa.ac.uk). Overall numbers are still relatively low, but society has undoubtedly begun *"another evolutionary stage of development in the provision of services to [students] with learning disabilities"* (Gajar, 1992:508), that which Grigal *et al.* (2010) called the *"next frontier"*.

Institutions of higher education – often through a special centre or department – and now also several private not-for-profit organisations (see www.experiencecle.com, for example.), typically serve students with learning disabilities in two ways. First, they provide technological learning tools and a variety of services, such as counselling, coaching and advocacy, all of which are intended to ensure that students stay and graduate (Mull *et al.*, 2001). Second, they also work with students and their instructors to develop appropriate accommodations (sometimes called adjustments) for their learning disabilities – extra time for preparing an assignment, for example, or an isolated room for sitting an examination.

The notion of accommodations is premised on a sort of binary logic that there is a dichotomy between abled and disabled. Abled are the norm, disabled are the deviants; abled are the majority, disabled are the marginalised. Consequently, the standard approach in education has been one of dualism. Universities and colleges focus on the abled and accommodate the disabled. Classroom exercises, for example, are designed with the abled in mind; students with learning disabilities are an afterthought.

An alternative approach – one which embraces plurality – has recently been gaining popularity in education. Called 'universal design for learning' (or sometimes 'universal design of instruction'), it is an *"approach to teaching that consists of the proactive design and use of inclusive instructional strategies that would benefit a broad range of learners, including those with cognitive disabilities"* (Scott & McGuire, 2005:121). It draws on the principles of the more general idea of universal design which arose in architecture and recognises the 'neurodiversity' (Pollack, 2009) which is inherent in the human species.

The purpose of this chapter is to explore universal design for learning in higher education. It reviews the history and principles of universal design. It then surveys universal design in education, with a view towards higher education. To begin, however, the chapter traces the history of learning disabilities in American higher education.

Learning disabilities in American higher education

Gallaudet University, the world's first and only university to focus its programmes and services exclusively on the deaf and hard of hearing, was founded in 1864 by an act of the US Congress, with Abraham Lincoln serving as one of the University's charter signatories (www.gallaudet.

edu). It was not until the 1960s and 1970s, however, that mainstream American colleges and universities began to welcome students with disabilities (Mangrum & Strichart, 1988). This opening of higher education to students with disabilities paralleled the broader inclusion movement which was spreading at the time (Stainback *et al.*, 1989), not only in the United States but also in Canada, the United Kingdom (for example, see Barnes, 2007) and elsewhere.

Subsequently, colleges and universities in the United States also began to provide for students with learning disabilities. As a result, starting in the 1980s, more and more students with learning disabilities began pursuing higher education (Patton, 2005). Prior to that time, it was often assumed that students with learning disabilities were incapable of succeeding in higher education. Today, higher education is even an option for students with intellectual disabilities, including Down's syndrome (Calefati, 2009).

The reasons

But inclusion was not the only reason for colleges and universities to provide for students with learning disabilities. There has been increasing pressure from the government to find an alternative to what is often a seven-year secondary school diploma. By law, students with learning disabilities can receive special education services until the age of 21 (26 in the State of Michigan). As part of the Individuals with Disabilities Education Act of 2004, schools are also mandated to plan 'transitions' for students with learning disabilities; the Office of Special Education Programs of the US Department of Education holds them accountable through annual data reporting (www.nsttac.org).

Of course, the dream of many parents is for their children to attend college or university; and this dream is no less prevalent when their children have learning disabilities. Students with learning disabilities now also see higher education as a viable goal. They are also eager to progress with their age peers who are graduating and leaving for college or university.

With chronic budget issues challenging higher education, many college and university presidents see students with learning disabilities as another source of revenue (Mangrum & Strichart, 1988). Some presidents also recognise the benefits of a diverse student population;

recruiting students with learning disabilities, therefore, is part of their philosophical commitment to diversity (NJCLD, 1999).

Finally, pundits continually suggest that, for the United States to retain its leadership position in the global economy, the youth of America – including those with learning disabilities – must be well-educated. At a more modest level, Gilson (1996) noted that students with learning disabilities who hold a college or university diploma are simply more likely to secure meaningful employment.

The numbers

Despite the provision for students with learning disabilities in higher education, the numbers remain relatively low. According to the National Center for Learning Disabilities (NCLD), approximately 10% of students on American college and university campuses are disabled. Of these, 42% are classified as having learning disabilities, attention deficit disorder (ADD), mental illness or depression.

There is large variance from campus to campus, however. Indeed, 10% of secondary school students with learning disabilities go on to four-year higher education, 22% study at two-year institutions and 5% attend vocational/technical colleges (www.NCLD.org). As reported by the Office of Services for Students with Disabilities at the University of Michigan, only 4% of students have a learning disability. But all these numbers are probably low because in American higher education, by law, learning disabilities are self-reported.

The law

Children with learning disabilities in the United States are covered by the Individuals with Disabilities Education Act (IDEA). According to this legislation, children who have been diagnosed with a learning disability, using a multi-factor evaluation, are entitled to a 'free and appropriate public education' or FAPE. As part of the FAPE, each child with a learning disability receives an individualised education plan, which outlines the child's current performance, their annual goals and the services which are recommended for achieving these goals. The individualised education plan continues until it is no longer required or, as mentioned before, the child 'ages out' of the system.

An individualised education plan often prescribes special services such as one-on-one instruction or learning aids. It also allows for accommodations for time, process or product – 'product' here refers to curricular content or even required student output. And in many cases, an individualised education plan will provide an alternative classroom situation to a child with a learning disability. This could be a homebound 'school', for example, or a resource centre which is located apart from the regular general education classroom.

In American higher education, however, students with learning disabilities are covered by two civil rights laws: Section 504 of the Rehabilitation Act which prohibits discrimination on the basis of disability in all programmes or activities which receive Federal financial assistance; and the Americans with Disabilities Act which prohibits discrimination on the basis of disability by public entities. As such, it makes learning disabilities more about discrimination than 'action'. Indeed, under these two laws, the protection of and services to students with learning disabilities are guaranteed. Curricular standards, however, are not required to be lowered and services are limited to accommodations. Additionally, neither law mandates individualised educational plans. And perhaps most notably, accommodations are dependent on self-disclosure by the student with a learning disability.

Learning disabilities

According to IDEA, a learning disability is:

> *"a disorder in 1 or more of the basic psychological processes involved in understanding or in using language, spoken or written, which disorder may manifest itself in the imperfect ability to listen, think, speak, read, write, spell, or do mathematical calculations."*
>
> (20 U.S.C. § 1401 [30])

The psychological processes to which this refers include perceptual disabilities, brain injury, minimal brain dysfunction, dyslexia and developmental aphasia, but do not include those which can be attributed to:

1. Visual, auditory or motor disabilities

2. Intellectual disabilities

3. Emotional problems

4. Environmental, cultural or economic conditions.

Another common definition suggests that the term 'learning disability' refers to "a heterogeneous group of disorders manifested by significant difficulties in the acquisition and use of listening, speaking, reading, writing, reasoning, or mathematical skills" (NCLD, 1990). Important to this definition is that learning disabilities can coexist with self-regulatory, social perception and social interaction problems but that these themselves are not considered to be learning disabilities. Similarly, learning disabilities can coexist with sensory impairment, mental retardation or emotional problems, or with cultural differences, poor instruction or other environmental factors, but are not the result of them. Learning disabilities are intrinsic to the individual and might endure for the individual's lifetime.

Universal design

It is this idea of the individual and, more importantly, the variation between individuals which stands at the centre of universal design. Known sometimes as *'design for all'* and *'inclusive design'*, universal design rejects the notion of the 'average person' and instead seeks to create environments, objects and systems which can be used by the widest array of people. As such, it makes things more accessible, safer and convenient for everyone (CIDEA).

Universal design recognises diversity in human populations and attempts to embed *"choice for all people in the things which we design"* (www.universaldesign.com). Universal design, therefore, involves flexibility, providing people with a choice of alternative means of use or interface. It aims to serve all people, irrespective of their age, physical or mental abilities, economic status and so on. And it attempts to impact all things in human life, from spaces, to products, to systems.

The term 'universal design' was coined by architect Ronald Mace in the 1970s, who challenged the 'majority world' design philosophy of the time. But the concept of universal design can be traced to earlier critics, including Selwyn Goldsmith, whose book *Designing for the Disabled* (1963) spawned a movement of inclusion for the disabled and whose invention, the dropped curb, is now a standard feature of the built environment. Today, it has widespread appeal among architects, product developers and other design professionals.

The principles of universal design

In 1997, the Center for Universal Design at North Carolina State University published seven principles of universal design (see Connell *et al.*, 1997). The principles were derived from the results of a three-year study funded by the US Department of Education and were meant to *"guide the design process, allow systematic evaluation of designs and assist in educating both designers and consumers about the characteristics of more usable design solutions"* (Story, 2011:4.4).

Each of the seven principles of universal design was further expanded into a series of guidelines which should be followed in any universal design (see Table 1). It was also envisioned that two additional levels would eventually be developed. Level 3, compliance tests, would provide the standards by which a universal design might be evaluated and Level 4, design strategies, would offer designers specific advice on how to meet the guidelines and compliance tests.

Principle 1: Equitable Use

The design is useful and marketable to people with diverse abilities.

Guidelines:

1a. Provide the same means of use for all users: identical whenever possible; equivalent when not.

1b. Avoid segregating or stigmatising any users.

1c. Make provisions for privacy, security and safety equally available to all users.

1d. Make the design appealing to all users.

Principle 2: Flexibility in Use

The design accommodates a wide range of individual preferences and abilities.

Guidelines:

2a. Provide choice in methods.

2b. Accommodate right- or left-handed access and use.

2c. Facilitate the user's accuracy and precision.

2d. Provide adaptability to the user's pace.

Principle 3: Simple and Intuitive Use

Use of the design is easy to understand, regardless of the user's experience, knowledge, language skills or current concentration level.

Guidelines:

3a. Eliminate unnecessary complexity.

3b. Be consistent with user expectations and intuition.

3c. Accommodate a wide range of literacy and language skills.

3d. Arrange information consistently with regard to its importance.

3e. Provide effective prompting and feedback during and after task completion.

Principle 4: Perceptible Information

The design communicates necessary information effectively to the user, regardless of ambient conditions or the user's sensory abilities.

Guidelines:

4a. Use different modes (pictorial, verbal, tactile) for redundant presentation of essential information.

4b. Maximise 'legibility' of essential information.

4c. Differentiate elements in ways that can be described (for example, make it easy to give instructions or directions).

4d. Provide compatibility with a variety of techniques or devices used by people with sensory limitations.

Principle 5: Tolerance for Error

The design minimises hazards and the adverse consequences of accidental or unintended actions.

Guidelines:

5a. Arrange elements to minimise hazards and errors: most-used elements should be most accessible; hazardous elements should be eliminated, isolated or shielded.

5b. Provide warnings of hazards and errors.

5c. Provide fail-safe features.

5d. Discourage unconscious action in tasks that require vigilance.

Principle 6: Low Physical Effort

The design can be used efficiently and comfortably and with a minimum of fatigue.

Guidelines:

6a. Allow user to maintain a neutral body position.

6b. Use reasonable operating forces.

6c. Minimise repetitive actions.

6d. Minimise sustained physical effort.

Principle 7: Size and Space for Approach and Use

Appropriate size and space is provided for approach, reach, manipulation and use regardless of user's body size, posture or mobility.

Guidelines:

7a. Provide a clear line of sight to important elements for any seated or standing position.

7b. Make reach to all components comfortable for any seated or standing user.

7c. Accommodate variations in hand and grip size.

7d. Provide adequate space for the use of assistive devices or personal assistance.

Table 1: The principles of universal design
Connell et al. (1997)

It ought to be emphasised, however, that the seven principles of universal design were not meant to be constraints or boundaries on design. Instead, the authors hoped that the principles would *"articulate the concept of universal design in a comprehensive way"* (Story, 2011:4.4), thereby providing a sort of unifying theory which could be applied to all design disciplines, including architecture, new product development and industrial design.

Examples of universal design

Application of the principles of universal design can be seen every day in seemingly the most mundane of places. A clear example of Principle 1 (Equitable Use) is a refrigerator handle which extends the full height of the door. Indeed, this design is useful to the widest variety of people with different abilities and different heights. Audio-visual systems which have color-coded cables, plugs and jacks illustrate Principle 3 (Simple and Intuitive Use), because anyone, irrespective of their knowledge of electronics, can configure the system.

Figure 1 shows a traditional gate valve on the left, the closing of which requires multiple turns using the wrist. This motion is difficult for many people. The design of the valve also makes it impossible to know if the valve is open or closed from the handle's appearance. The valve on the right, on the contrary, is a ¼-turn ball valve and exemplifies Principle 4 (Perceptible Information) and Principle 6 (Low Physical Effort). Its short handle throw requires minimal movement and can be actuated using the arm instead of the wrist. Quick visual inspection of the handle's position also indicates very clearly if the valve is open or closed.

Equally, it is often very obvious when the principles of universal design have not been applied to a design. Consider, for example, the ubiquitous universal serial bus (USB) which allows electronic devices to communicate. Despite its universal moniker, its design fails Principle 5 (Tolerance for Error) because a USB connector is uni-directional, only fitting in a USB port in the correct face-up position. A better design would have been bi-directional, allowing users to insert a connector face up or face down, not unlike some keys. Similarly, most parking lots today neglect Principle 7 (Size and Space for Approach and Use), with spaces too narrow for easy entry and exit of the vehicle.

Figure 1: Valves

Universal design in education

Although originally developed in architecture as an alternative to the predominant design philosophy of the time, universal design has indeed become a driver in other design disciplines, as suggested by these product development and industrial design examples. But universal design has also worked its way into other less-obvious disciplines, including education.

Mirroring universal design more generally, universal design in education is premised on the foundational belief that there is not an 'average student'. It promotes the design of educational policies, programmes and practices which serve the widest array of students, irrespective of their age, physical or mental abilities, economic status and so on. It ought not to be surprising, given its architectural roots, that universal design was manifest first in the physical spaces of education, including school and residential life buildings, computer and science labs, and libraries. More recently, however, universal design has also been applied to such varying educational activities as software design, registration systems and student services.

As an example, information technology has the potential to level the playing field in educational performance among learners (Burgstahler, 2011). This potential, however, could be squandered if the technology does not reflect the diversity of learners. Consequently, computer manufacturers have begun to re-evaluate their designs with this diversity in mind. Consider the magnetic power cables on all Apple laptop computers which, unlike other cables which require a fixed physical connection, minimise the risk of tripping over the cable and pulling the laptop to the floor.

Erlandson (2002) provides an excellent discussion of other non-information technologies which adopt the principles of universal design. Binoculars, for example, with image stabilisation, serve all students well on science field trips. Portable microphone and speaker systems for class-rooms improve sound quality, even when hearing difficulties are only temporary due to allergies or colds. Incidentally, students in classrooms with audio systems perform better academically than those students in classrooms without these systems (Crandell *et al.*, 1999). And special agile devices can be used in lieu of wheelchairs, which seat physically disabled students at table height and allow them to work directly with their classmates.

A driving force for universal design in education has been the Center for Applied Special Technology (CAST) which was founded in 1984. Originally focused on the development of assistive technologies for students with disabilities, CAST has since turned its attention to the application of universal design to the methods and materials of educa-tion – to universal design for learning (sometimes called universal design of instruction).

Universal design for learning

Universal design for learning aims to improve *"the learning of students with a wide range of characteristics by applying the UD principles to all aspects of instruction"* (Burgstahler, 2007:1). Indeed, it recognises the diversity of learners and their learning styles and abilities and, as such, it *"maximizes learning for all students, minimizes the need for individual accommodations, and eventually benefits every learner by considering different ways that students' minds are activated"* (Hunt and Andreasen, 2011:168).

CAST (2011:3) has an interesting perspective on universal design for learning: *"Because most curricula are unable to adapt to individual learning differences, we have come to recognize that curricula, rather than our students, are disabled."* Consequently, CAST advocates for adaptation of the curriculum, not adaptation by the learner. That is to say, teachers ought to forego the one-size-fits-all mentality, which requires individual students to conform, in favour of a universal approach which serves all students.

According to Burgstahler (2007), adaptation of the curriculum ought to occur in eight different areas:

1. *Class climate*
2. *Interaction*
3. *Physical environments and products*
4. *Delivery methods*
5. *Information resources and technology*
6. *Feedback*
7. *Assessment*
8. *Accommodation.*

For example, classrooms might be configured as a horseshoe, rather than in traditional rows and columns, in order to promote equal interaction among students. Or tests might be computerised in recognition of students whose physical abilities are impacted by paper versions (Rose, 2011). But are there some underlying principles which guide these adaptations of the curriculum?

The principles of universal design for learning

Initially, universal design for learning was guided by two basic principles: access and flexibility (Rose & Meyer, 2002). Access refers to the transformation of education in order to create a more equitable and socially just system (Pliner & Johnson, 2004). Flexibility acknowledges, embraces and nurtures diversity in learning; it represents a departure from the often rigid boundaries of lesson planning, instruction and assessment.

Seeking more specific guidance, however, early advocates of universal design for learning attempted to apply the seven principles of universal design directly to learning. The Center for Postsecondary Education and Disability (CPED) at the University of Connecticut, for example, promoted the following principles of universal design for learning (in addition to access and flexibility):

1. *Simple and intuitive instruction*
2. *Perceptible information*
3. *Tolerance for error*
4. *Low physical effort*
5. *Size and space or approach and use.*

(Bernacchio & Mullen, 2007)

For example, physical education courses which require students to demonstrate fitness with chin ups or bar-hang tests alienate not only students with physical disabilities but anyone whose strength is 'abnormal'.

It must be remembered that the seven principles of universal design were developed originally as a sort of unifying theory for the design disciplines. As such, their direct application to learning often feels forced and has therefore been questioned. More recently, a set of three principles, which together adopt the grand title of Universal Design for Learning (UDL), was introduced by CAST. Not unlike the seven principles of universal design as envisioned by the Center for Universal Design, UDL *"provides a blueprint for creating instructional goals, methods, materials and assessments that work for everyone"* (CAST, 2012b:1). It appears to have widespread appeal, because in a short period of time it has garnered significant attention in education… at least at the elementary and secondary levels.

UDL is premised on the idea that there are three distinguishable but interconnected 'networks' in the brain which are associated with learning. These three networks are referred to as the recognition, strategic and affective networks and, according to CAST, correspond to the three parallel requisites of learning which were identified by Vygotsky (1962): 1. recognition of the information which is to be learned, 2. the use of strategies to process the information and 3. the engagement by the learner (Rose, 2011). Although every learner has all three of these networks, UDL recognises – and even celebrates – that there are indeed differences among learners with respect to their abilities within and across the networks. Consequently, as argued by CAST, these differences ought to be considered and addressed in the design of any educational enterprise, for which the three principles and corresponding guidelines and checkpoints of UDL were created (see Table 2).

As an example, a student who suffers from dysgraphia – a learning disability which affects writing and other spatial activities – might have difficulty recognising exponents in mathematical equations. UDL, and specifically Principle 1 of UDL, proposes the use of multiple means of representation, in order to insure that this student is able to recognise the exponent. In doing so, UDL also helps all other students in the course learn exponents better.

Universal design in higher education

Despite the apparent benefits of UDL for all students, universal design in higher education has been driven almost exclusively by disabled students on college and university campuses themselves. And indeed, as highlighted by Burgstahler (2008), the areas which have to date benefitted most from the application of universal design are student services, information technology and physical spaces. Consider the lower-height counters at college cafeterias, for example, or the text-only versions of university websites (Stahl, 2004).

College and university instructors undoubtedly recognise the increasing diversity of their student populations (Franciosi, 2005; Izzo et al., 2011), but this recognition is often limited to those who have physical disabilities. As a result, despite its promising outcomes, universal design for learning has had limited application in higher education (Smith, 2008). Countless calls for universal design for learning in higher education have been made and numerous process models for its implementation have been offered (Gradel and Edson, 2010). Its use in colleges and universities, however, is still in the exploratory stage (Scott et al., 2003) and examples of successes are relatively rare (Rose et al., 2006).

In 2006, the Association for Higher Education and Disability (AHEAD) promoted a national agenda for adopting universal design for learning as a framework for higher education. But barriers to any sweeping reform remain high in most colleges and universities. As enumerated by

Principle I. Provide Multiple Means of Representation

Guideline 1: Provide options for perception
- Checkpoint 1.1: Offer ways of customizing the display of information
- Checkpoint 1.2: Offer alternatives for auditory information
- Checkpoint 1.3: Offer alternatives for visual information

Guideline 2: Provide options for language, mathematical expressions, and symbols
- Checkpoint 2.1: Clarify vocabulary and symbols
- Checkpoint 2.2: Clarify syntax and structure
- Checkpoint 2.3: Support decoding of text, mathematical notation, and symbols
- Checkpoint 2.4: Promote understanding across languages
- Checkpoint 2.5: Illustrate through multiple media

Guideline 3: Provide options for comprehension
- Checkpoint 3.1: Activate or supply background knowledge
- Checkpoint 3.2: Highlight patterns, critical features, big ideas, and relationships
- Checkpoint 3.3: Guide information processing, visualization, and manipulation
- Checkpoint 3.4: Maximize transfer and generalization

Principle II. Provide Multiple Means of Action and Expression

Guideline 4: Provide options for physical action
- Checkpoint 4.1: Vary the methods for response and navigation
- Checkpoint 4.2: Optimize access to tools and assistive technologies

Guideline 5: Provide options for expression and communication
- Checkpoint 5.1: Use multiple media for communication
- Checkpoint 5.2: Use multiple tools for construction and composition
- Checkpoint 5.3: Build fluencies with graduated levels of support for practice and performance

Guideline 6: Provide options for executive functions
- Checkpoint 6.1: Guide appropriate goal-setting
- Checkpoint 6.2: Support planning and strategy development
- Checkpoint 6.3: Facilitate managing information and resources
- Checkpoint 6.4: Enhance capacity for monitoring progress

Principle III. Provide Multiple Means of Engagement

Guideline 7: Provide options for recruiting interest
- Checkpoint 7.1: Optimize individual choice and autonomy
- Checkpoint 7.2: Optimize relevance, value, and authenticity
- Checkpoint 7.3: Minimize threats and distractions

Guideline 8: Provide options for sustaining effort and persistence
- Checkpoint 8.1: Heighten salience of goals and objectives
- Checkpoint 8.2: Vary demands and resources to optimize challenge
- Checkpoint 8.3: Foster collaboration and community
- Checkpoint 8.4: Increase mastery-oriented feedback

Guideline 9: Provide options for self-regulation
- Checkpoint 9.1: Promote expectations and beliefs that optimize motivation
- Checkpoint 9.2: Facilitate personal coping skills and strategies
- Checkpoint 9.3: Develop self-assessment and reflection

Table 2: The principles of UDL
CAST (2012a:1)

Silver *et al.* (1998), traditions and the momentum to maintain the status quo are strong. Instructors have limited time, are generally not receptive to new teaching strategies and lack formal pedagogical training. Scott *et al.* (2003) came to similar conclusions and added that misperceptions about the costs of universal design for learning, and a lack of awareness about its positive outcomes, persist.

Universal design for learning, however, when implemented in a college or university can have significant impact. McGuire *et al.* (2006) found that the infusion of universal design for learning can create an inclusive environment for all students, can help instructors in re-designing their courses and can aid in professional development. Perhaps more importantly, as underlined by Silver *et al.* (1998), universal design for learning in higher education can make students with learning disabilities no longer feel 'invisible'.

Conclusion

The constitution of the United States begins with *"We hold these truths to be self-evident, that all men are created equal…"*. Of course, Thomas Jefferson's words referred to equality of rights. But when it comes to learning, it is clear that not all men are created equal; indeed, in the United States and elsewhere, a seemingly increasing percentage of the population suffers from some learning disability.

Universal design for learning, which draws on universal design more generally, *"challenges educators to rethink the nature of their curriculum and empowers them with the flexibility to serve a diverse population of learners"* (Izzo *et al.*, 2011:39.1). In so doing, it promises to make education at all levels, including higher education, more accessible and more equitable – something with which Thomas Jefferson would certainly be pleased.

About the authors

John Branch is Lecturer of Marketing at the Stephen M. Ross School of Business and Faculty Associate at the Center for Russian, East European, & Eurasian Studies, both of the University of Michigan, USA. He can be contacted at this email: jdbranch@umich.edu

Alyssa Martina is an Adjunct Professor of Innovative Strategy and Management at the Gabelli Business School at Fordham University, USA and an Adjunct Professor of Entrepreneurship at the University of Michigan Law School, USA. She can be contacted at this email: martialy@umich.edu

Interrelationships between Student Culture, Teaching and Learning in Higher Education

Steffen Löfvall and Claus Nygaard

Introduction

At today's modern universities in Western democracies, slogans like *"the learning university"*, *"from teaching to learning"*, *"beyond transmission"*, *"learning to learn"* and *"life-long learning"* resound in banners on university websites, in documents describing teaching and learning strategies and in brochures marketing university programs. There seems to be a general understanding among policy makers that universities are in a necessary transition from input-based to output-based curricula (Jarvis *et al.*, 1998; Rassow, 1998; Nygaard *et al.*, 2009).

This transition moves beyond purely discipline-oriented education to focus on subject-based education in which interdisciplinary curricula and teaching methods are integrated to link student learning with the knowledge, skills and competencies required in the future job market. Today's university education is not about "giving the right knowledge to students" but about providing students with possibilities to develop the "right" competencies (Nygaard *et al.*, 2009) – "right" meaning transformative and relevant for the job market (Harvey & Knight, 1996; Falconer & Pettigrew, 2003). Overall, this transition from input- to output-based education seems to challenge universities when it comes to aligning the expectations of students, future employers and the universities themselves (personified here for the purpose of clarity by university teachers).

We base this chapter on the argument that, in order to meet such challenges, the university needs to foster the development of a culture in which students are perceived, by curriculum designers and by the students themselves, as collaborative partners in the teaching and learning processes. In this chapter, we will present four archetypes of student culture and discuss their interrelationship with predominant learning and teaching traditions. We will argue that although this relationship is complex, non-linear and involves many variables, there are some commonalities that are important to be aware of when designing higher-education teaching that aims to develop *"the learning university"* in its evolution *"from teaching to learning"*, where teaching goes *"beyond transmission"* and where students are empowered in *"learning to learn"*.

In the light of this anthology, we first present our views on university students' learning. Second, we present four archetypes of student culture at universities. Third, we discuss how student learning and student culture are related to curriculum design and teaching methods. Fourth, we end on a normative note, arguing for ways in which university education may be designed in order to establish a culture of students as collaborative partners.

Key points:

- The current trend in university marketing is to position the university as an environment for "learning" distinct from its traditional role of knowledge transmission.

- Universities are in transition from a purely discipline-oriented to a subject-based education approach that provides students with requirements for the job market.

- The transition toward education as a "product" challenges universities to align the expectations of students, future employers and university teachers.

- In order to meet this challenge, universities need to foster the development of a partnership-like teaching and learning culture.

- A study of four archetypes of student culture and their interrelationships with teaching and learning can provide a basis for designing this new university model.

Learning – a possible definition

In this short section, we briefly present our views of university students' learning. We do this for two reasons: 1) to position our chapter clearly in the very broad and differentiated field of learning theory; and 2) to come to an operational definition of learning which can enable us to present, in a normative way, possible relationships between student culture, teaching and learning at universities.

Our operational definition of learning begins with the body of literature arguing that learning is contextually embedded (Bandura, 1975; Kolb, 1984; Vygotsky, 1987; Ramsden, 1988; Lave & Wenger, 1991; Wenger, 1998; Bruner, 1996; Nygaard *et al.*, 2008; Nygaard & Holtham, 2008; Nygaard *et al.*, 2009). In this view, the product of learning (knowledge, skills and competencies) is subjectively constructed as the learner perceives the situation at hand in relation to past experiences and future expectations. It is through processes such as feedback and feed-forward (Nygaard *et al.*, 2008) that the learner makes sense of the situation at hand. We subscribe to this view of contextual learning from our own experiences as teachers, developers of curricula and researchers. Moreover, there is plenty of empirical evidence from studies of higher education that students engage differently in learning activities and that their engagement is culturally and contextually bound. Some of the more recent studies are Reid & Petocz (2008), Raiker (2009), Dobozy (2011) and Albergaria Almeida and Teixeira-Dias (2011a).

In line with Marton and Säljö (1976) and Ramsden (1988), we divide learning processes into deep learning and surface learning. Student-oriented teaching, in which students are expected to discover differences and similarities between theories and where ideas and suggestions of students are being used in the course, seems to stimulate deep learning (Wierstra *et al.*, 2003). Hence, students with a preference for deep learning try to create a sense of meaning to understand the situation at hand and link it to personal experiences. One could say that the student with a preference for deep learning tries to co-create knowledge while studying by spontaneously using higher-order thinking skills.

Students have a tendency to learn reproductively if the teaching emphasises memorising of facts instead of active involvement in the course (Wierstra *et al.*, 2003). Consequently, the student with a preference for surface learning, when studying, intuitively tries to remember what seems to be factual knowledge in relation to the subject studied, often with the purpose of getting to know what is identified as the canonised knowledge within the discipline.

Inspired by such views on learning, we argue that while learning is contextually bound, it is not solely a social endeavour. Learning is also inspired and driven by individual processes which are closely linked to the identity of the learner. Blumer (1969:5) states: *"the meaning of things is formed in the context of social interaction and is derived by the person from that interaction"*. Identity has been defined as *"the individual's perception of himself as he relates to his environment"* (Hall, 1968:447). It follows that if learning is both a social and a personal endeavour, we may also see identity as both a social and a personal identity. Such a link between identity and learning is also prominent in Su's chapter in this volume.

Personal identity creation is a complex social and individual process developed in relation to and interaction with the context in which we are embedded. According to Goffman (1959, 1961), individuals construct their identities with the purpose of managing impressions during everyday life performances and obtaining strategic resources from their interactions with others. Identity creation is, according to Stone (1962), closely related to appearance, discourse and meaning in the interactions of the individual within society. Identity creation therefore becomes an ongoing, open-ended process of identification, belonging and positioning oneself in different contexts. Seen as a process of social construction, our identity directs the attention we receive from the world and affects our learning, which again affects our identity. We shall therefore argue for the existence of a recursive relationship between identity and learning much the same as the recursive principle presented by Giddens (1984). He argues that social activities are continually recreated by social actors via the very means by which they express themselves as social actors, thereby reproducing through their social activities the very conditions that make possible such social activities. From interviewing groups of students we know that this is the case, since they define their student identities in different ways (Reid & Petocz, 2008; Nygaard & Serrano, 2010).

In summary, we can reach an operational definition of learning by referring to Nygaard and Holtham (2008:13–14), who write of learning that it is:

a. *"never a simple repetition of previous learning. People learn based on their experiences and expectations."*

b. *"both an individual and social process."*

c. *"a contextual process tied to particular situations."*

d. *"a process affected by the identity of the learner."*

e. *"a process affected by the social position of the learner… and by the learners' embeddedness in social collectivities."*

Taking seriously such a definition of learning has implications for higher education. We have to accept that students are different learners. They do not come to university or to the individual class with the same experiences, they do not come with the same expectations and they do not wish to leave either the class or the university with the same experiences and expectations. They are individual learners, embedded in different contexts, pursuing different professional identities. They have different perceptions of themselves, of the purpose of education, of teaching and learning activities, of the teachers' approach to education, of their fellow students, of …, of … and of …

Learning and identity creation are matters of perception and one size doesn't fit all. Students are heterogeneous individuals with heterogeneous identity-creation processes and curriculum designers need to take this into account when they develop the curriculum. We will return to the issues of curriculum development in the chapter.

In the next section, we shall take a look at that heterogeneity of students as we introduce four archetypes of student culture and argue that these will help us understand the limits and possibilities of developing teaching and learning processes in our curricula.

Key points:

*   Learning is contextually embedded and subjectively constructed by the learner through processes such as feedback and feed-forward.

*   Studies show that students engage differently in learning activities and their engagement is culturally and contextually bound.

- Preferences for learning are defined as deep and surface learning.

- The student with a preference for deep learning tries to co-create knowledge while studying by using higher-order thinking skills.

- The student with a preference for surface learning tries to remember factual knowledge in relation to the subject studied.

- Learning is closely linked to the identity of the learner and creation of that identity is a complex social and individual process.

- These views of learning and identity creation have important implications for higher education.

Student culture – four archetypes

The study of student cultures is not new. Even though society and education systems look different today, we can still be inspired by student activism studies from the 1960s and 1970s, current university culture studies in line with national variability studies (Hofstede, 1980, 1986), organisational culture studies (Schein, 1992; Awbrey, 2005) and student role conception studies (Franz, 1998; Bailey, 2000; Cotten & Wilson, 2006; Dobozy, 2011). In line with Clark and Trow (1966) and Long (1976, 1977), we can understand student cultures as archetypes and role descriptions to which students can subscribe. Bolton and Kammeyer (1967) and Kuh (1993) point out that they are role descriptions and not definite determining factors of social behaviour.

Clark and Trow (1966) identify four student archetypes: vocational, collegiate, academic and nonconformist students. Based on this classification, Long (1977) argues that vocational university students see education mainly as a preparation for their future occupation. The student:

> *"is not particularly interested in the social or purely intellectual phases of campus life, although he might participate in these activities on some limited basis. Persons holding this philosophy are usually quite committed to particular fields of study and are in college primarily to obtain careers in their chosen fields."*
>
> (Long, 1977:420)

The collegiate student is quite similar to the vocational student in his perceptions of the benefits of a university education; however, collegiates participate much more in extra-curricular activities. The collegiate student:

> *"is very much concerned with the social and extracurricular phases of campus life. He identifies closely with the college and tries to attend as many campus and athletic events as possible. He is concerned about his education but he feels that the development of his social skills is vital to the cultivation of the well-rounded person. He attempts to 'make grades' but will rarely go out of his way to do extra or non-assigned reading."*
>
> (Long, 1977:421)

On the other hand, the academic student strives for knowledge and understanding, wherever the pursuit may lead. The student:

> *"is seriously involved in course work. He may be fairly active in student government and activities of this sort but, if he is, they have lower priority. He is the kind of person who feels that the social side of college life is not the most important but is certainly significant for his general development."*
>
> (Long, 1977:421)

In Long's empirical study, the nonconformists seem to set very high demands on university teaching and development because of their strong academic and social engagement. The nonconformist student seems very interested in learning about life in general, in ways of his own choosing. He:

> *"is very interested in the things which interest him. For the most part, he would consider himself to be someone who is primarily motivated by intellectual curiosity. Outside the classroom, he would attend lectures, concerts, foreign films, etc. Inside the classroom, when he is interested, he will do extra readings and pursue knowledge and understanding."*
>
> (Long, 1977:421)

The existence of the four archetypes opens the field for a broader view on students' perceptions. Based on an empirical study of students' perceptions of and approach to the teaching and learning environment at Copenhagen Business School, Löfvall (2008) coined the four archetypes of student culture as shown in Figure 1. We use these as the foundation for our discussion of students' approaches to their university education. Although formulated on the basis of an empirical study at Copenhagen Business School, we believe that, as archetypes, they can be used to reflect on student culture in different higher-education contexts.

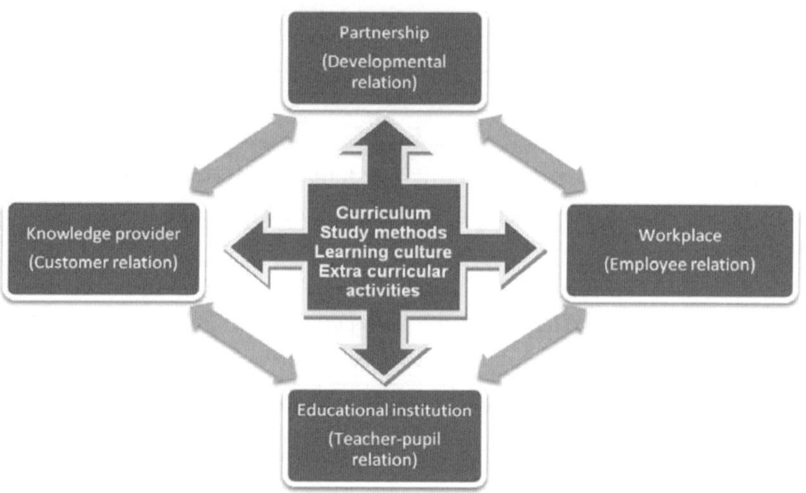

Figure 1: Students' perception of universities
Source: Löfvall (2008)

Below, we take a closer look at the student cultures as presented in Figure 1.

Type 1 students perceive the university as a classical educational institution resembling what they know from their years in school. They think of the university as a hierarchical institution where teachers are in charge. They see themselves as pupils that are guided and directed by teachers who know right from wrong and have the responsibility to plan the curriculum and to teach relevant subjects. When asked to describe their relationship with the university, they focus mainly on the teacher–pupil relationship. To some extent, this student type has beliefs about studying similar to those of the vocational and academic student (Clark & Trow, 1966; Long, 1977).

Type 2 students perceive the university as a knowledge provider. They also think of the university as a hierarchical institution where teachers are in charge. They see themselves as customers who seek to get the best "value for money". They expect to get the best quality, in terms of teachers who are experts within their field and very good at lecturing, and they expect good facilities and administrative support. They think of the university as the place for obtaining knowledge that will increase their future job opportunities. This student type has some characteristics similar to the vocational and academic student (Clark & Trow, 1966; Long, 1977), careerists (Katchadourian & Boli, 1985) and students-as-customers (Franz, 1998; Bailey, 2000; Cotten & Wilson, 2006).

Type 3 students perceive the university as a partnership. They think of the university more like a network for developing learning relations with fellow students and faculty. They see that they must invest time and effort in their own learning process in order to benefit and they believe that learning comes through a strategy of personal integration and responsibility. They seek partnership relations and believe that they can help create an integrative study culture by engaging in curricular and extra-curricular activities. In their view, the university is a collective of like-minded students and staff rather than a school of individual experts. Comparing this with Clark and Trow (1966) and Long (1977), this student type has attributes similar to the collegiate and nonconformist student in relation to active student engagement. This student type has also characteristics similar to strivers and intellectuals (Katchadourian & Boli, 1985; Kuh, 1990) and students-as-producers (Dobozy, 2011).

Type 4 students perceive the university as a workplace. They define their own role as employees and they invest their time and personality in nurturing a workplace feeling and community among fellow students and faculty. For them, studying at the university is a full-time job and not something you do just because you have to get a job after graduation. They live through their studies as employees in a "regular organisation" and they invest their time in organising and developing relationships that improve learning for themselves and fellow students. They also engage in curricular and extracurricular activities. Like Type 3, this student type seems to have behaviours similar to the collegiate and nonconformist student (Clark & Trow, 1966; Long, 1977) and intellectuals (Katchadourian & Boli, 1985; Kuh, 1990).

The existence of these four archetypes opens the field for a more reflective view on students' perceptions and identities. In section 4, we shall look at those aspects in the light of the four archetypes of student culture.

Key points:

- Four student archetypes that define student approaches to university education have been identified: pupils, customers, partners and employees.

- These archetypes influence the relationship of individual students to the learning institution's culture.

- The educational institution culture is a classical hierarchical structure in which pupils are guided by teachers in charge of delivering an "education".

- In the knowledge-provider culture, students use the university as the place for obtaining knowledge to increase their future job opportunities.

- In the partnership culture, students see the university as a collective of like-minded students and teachers and invest time and effort in their own learning process.

- In the workplace culture, students define their role as employees and cultivate a workplace community of fellow students and faculty.

- These different models open the field for a more reflective view on curriculum design and teaching and learning methods.

Curriculum design, teaching and learning methods

Students develop their student identity and perception of student culture partly as a consequence of the curriculum design and teaching-and-learning methods of their university. Based on a desk study of curriculum theory, Nygaard and Bramming (2008) formulated two broad streams of curriculum theory: 1) a content stream and 2) a process stream. In Figure 2 we elaborate on these two streams of curriculum theory.

	Content stream	Process stream
Curriculum	Syllabus / guide for teaching	Learning-centred action plan
Agency	Teacher-driven activities	Student-driven activities
Learning	De-contextual learning	Contextual learning
Orientation	Input orientation	Output orientation
Evaluation method	Summative	Formative / developmental
Main focus points	Curriculum design, syllabus planning, teaching, exams and evaluation	Learning design, process facilitation, supervision and self-/peer assessment

Figure 2: Two broad streams within curriculum theories
Elaboration on Nygaard & Bramming (2008)

Just as we have four archetypes of student culture, we can also think of the two curriculum streams as a dichotomy. We do so for the purpose of proposing some links between student culture and curriculum streams.

Content-stream teaching

Corresponding to Nygaard and Bramming (2008), curriculum designers and teachers subscribing to the content stream as an ideal type think of the curriculum itself as a guide for teaching. This is closely linked to perceiving the syllabus as a product sheet describing the content of the curriculum. They have the idea that students need to learn a conventional and de-contextualised body of theory, which is seen as being highly relevant within the discipline they represent. They see students as a homogeneous group who must learn the same content at the same time. They do not see the context for learning as having a major effect on the learning outcome itself but conceptualise learning as a rather de-contextual process. Good students will learn, bad students will struggle to learn. The key focus points in this view become the course reading lists, the assignments and the exams. Curriculum designers know what the students have to learn, they give students assignments for training purposes and they assess the students' knowledge at exams. The main functions of the curriculum designer and teacher subscribing to the content stream become those of design, development, implementation and evaluation.

This perception of curriculum is pretty much in alignment with the students who perceive the university as a classic educational institution or a knowledge provider (Löfvall, 2008). They expect the teachers to know best and they expect the curriculum to be designed before they enrol in a course. They look for a teaching and learning process that appears professional, smooth and well-prepared and has all the steps in place. In doing so, they conveniently put the responsibility for their learning process in the hands of their teachers who, if they also subscribe to the content stream, are pleased to take on this responsibility. Hence, this view of learning may have the unintended consequence of developing a culture of instructionally oriented teachers and surface learners (Marton & Säljö, 1976; Ramsden, 1988).

Process-stream teaching

Curriculum designers and teachers subscribing to the process stream as an ideal type think of the curriculum itself as a learning-centred action plan, according to Bolhuis (2003) and Nygaard and Bramming (2008). In doing so, they focus on the curricular activities which improve students' learning outcomes. As such, their orientation is toward the processes that lead to a particular educational output rather than the academic content itself. They see students as a heterogeneous group who all engage differently in their studies. In their view, students have different experiences and different aims in studying and the context for learning has a major effect on the learning outcome itself. Students are not good or bad, students are different and they learn through different processes. In this view, the main focus points are the activities and methods facilitating student learning. Curriculum designers know which activities and methods have worked previously and they tailor those to the group of students participating in the course. The main functions of the curriculum designer and teacher subscribing to the process stream are facilitation, coordination, supervision and evaluation.

This perception of curriculum is pretty much in alignment with the views of students who perceive the university as partnership or workplace (Löfvall, 2008). They expect to take part in experiential learning processes that challenge them to learn more. They look for a professional teaching and learning process in which they can engage and learn more through networks of academic and social rigour. In order to do this, they need to take on the responsibility for learning themselves and they do so by interaction with teachers who, if they subscribe to the process stream, are pleased to take on the responsibility for facilitating such learning processes. This may have the consequence of developing a culture of deep learners (Marton & Säljö, 1976; Ramsden, 1988) and a strong supportive institutional behaviour at the university (Tagg, 2003).

Key points:

- Links can be made between student culture and curriculum design.

- Curriculum theory can be broadly identified as either a content stream or a process stream.

- Content-stream adherents see the curriculum itself as a guide for teaching a conventional body of theory within a specific discipline.

- The content-stream approach is in alignment with the students who see the university as an educational institution or a knowledge provider and it may have the consequence of developing a culture of surface learners.

- Process-stream adherents think of the curriculum as a learning-centred action plan leading to a particular educational output rather than the academic content itself.

- The process-stream approach is in alignment with students who see the university as a partnership or workplace and it may have the consequence of developing a culture of deep learners.

Normative implications for university education

According to Scanlon *et al.* (2007), Cotten and Wilson (2006) and McInnis *et al.* (2000), there are several trends in the post-industrial society that undermine a partnership or workplace-like university culture: 1) lecture sizes have increased to the degree that teachers lose intimacy with their students; 2) "lean-and-mean" university pedagogies have restricted staff–student contact hours; 3) marketisation of higher education increases the predominant interpretation of students as consumers;

4) faculty members perceive the university as research institution rather than educational institution; 5) universities often have multiple campus sites; 6) students are spending less time on campus and more time in paid work. These trends have the potential to reduce students' feelings of belonging to the university and incline them toward an identity as pupils or consumers of mass education. The trends also involve a perception of students as recipients of knowledge rather than participants in constructing knowledge.

On the other hand, these trends need not stop our efforts to enhance student learning and prepare students for an engaging career in the post-industrial society. We argue that this can be reached by establishing a new paradigm for curriculum development which is based on students' learning processes. We believe that it is the duty of universities to facilitate the education of students to become active learners able to reflect on the means and ends of their own learning processes. It is our immediate argument that this can be reached through the development of a partnership and workplace-oriented culture. This is not done in the classroom alone and the challenge should be discussed and addressed by multiple stakeholders at different organisational levels.

In this section, we will point out some of the normative implications for university education that arise in developing a student culture of engaged students as partners and/or students as employees. Being normative in our approach, we introduce six different areas which can be clearly addressed and developed within the university and we argue that they have an impact on student culture and, consequently, on teaching and learning: 1) classroom activities; 2) online activities; 3) campus design; 4) teacher training; 5) policy forums; 6) university branding. We are clear that these six areas are not exclusive for development of a partnership or workplace-like student culture and present them as inspirational points for future development of student engagement.

Key points:
- The trends that undermine a partnership or workplace-like university culture are increased lecture sizes, restricted staff–student contact hours, marketisation of higher education, perception of the university as a research institution, multiple campus sites and students working at jobs off-campus.

- These trends tend to incline students toward an educational institution or knowledge provider culture.

- Universities can and should facilitate the education of students to become active learners through the development of a partnership and workplace-oriented culture.

- To support this goal, six areas to address and develop are: classroom activities, online activities, campus design, teacher training, policy forums and university branding.

- These areas are not exclusive but are presented as inspirational points for future development of a culture of student engagement.

Classroom activities

Students are different. They come to university with different expectations and aims in life. They perceive the various academic subjects in different ways. Their learning process is contextually embedded and closely linked to their identity projects. In order to develop successful classroom activities in which students are engaged, it is important to locate the differences in student population and actively use them in shaping the envisioned student culture.

We find it applicable to bring culture into the discussion at the beginning of each course through both course descriptions and oral discussions. Learning contracts which set out a framework for student participation give teachers the ability to calibrate the opinions and expectations of students. This should happen at the initial classroom meeting with students and continue throughout their entire university education. Despite being located in a traditional lecture theatre, the classroom activity itself does not need to be a traditional lecture where the teacher has the responsibility for "broadcasting information" to students.

There are multiple collaborative teaching techniques that are creative in design and might also lead to students developing their own creativity (Nygaard *et al.*, 2010). Game-based teaching exists in many forms, from the use of existing board games (Branch *et al.*, 2011) to the development of original computer games (Warmelink *et al.*, 2012). For a thorough review of how learning games are being and have been used for teaching business skills at business schools, see Henriksen and Löfvall (2012). They explore the game technologies of three historical eras and the institutional organisation at Nordic and American business schools. Furthermore, there are pedagogical approaches, like problem-based learning, which could prepare students for future challenges in contemporary workplaces (Chehore & Scholtz, 2008) and problem-oriented project work, which could bring students closer to an understanding of current workplace practices (Meier & Nygaard, 2008). Recently, the development of the "flipped classroom" teaching concept (Strayer, 2007; Bergmann & Sams, 2012) has resulted in classes where students explore academic problems more independently and with some process support from the teacher. With this change in teacher and student roles, teachers move their focus away from knowledge provision and content-stream teaching to facilitation and process-stream teaching.

Other techniques are more closely linked to the learning process of students and motivate them to assume the responsibility of focusing on their own learning process. One example is the use of portfolios (Papadimitriou, 2009) in which students set personal learning goals and document their learning process. Student questioning is also an effective strategy to enhance active learning, according to Chin and Osborne (2008). Furthermore, the use of student response systems during classes has been shown to provide a better starting point for both students and teachers (Deslauriers *et al.*, 2010). Classroom activities such as this make the students active partners and help them develop a much more reflective approach to the taught curricula and teaching methods. Being engaged in classroom activities through pedagogical approaches that focus on individual learning, and discussing these approaches and their outcomes with the responsible teacher, makes it almost impossible for students to develop a pupil or customer culture.

It is our argument that, by changing classroom activities and systematically using a meta-language to describe and discuss with students the links between the pedagogy and the learning processes facilitated, students are more likely to develop a partnership and/or employee culture and engage in processes of deep learning. If students experience engaging learning and study methods that facilitate student learning, rather than tests and exams, they develop a more comfortable role as partners in their own learning project. Such a culture of student engagement may ultimately lead to students perceiving the university as a place for development or a workplace at which they are employees. This will lead to students defining themselves as community members rather than pupils or customers.

Key points:

- Differences in students should be located and used actively in developing classroom activities that engage them and help shape the envisioned student culture.

- Culture can be introduced into the discussion at the beginning of each course and continue throughout the university education.

- Classroom activities such as game-based teaching, problem-based learning, problem-oriented projects and portfolios make students active partners in their own learning process.

- Teaching concepts such as the "flipped classroom" alter student and teacher roles and influence the learning dynamic.

- Students are more likely to develop a partnership and/or workplace culture and engage in deep learning when classroom activities and discussions systematically link the pedagogy and the learning processes.

Online activities

The increasing use of digital technologies at universities seems to change student cultures and identities. Social media such as blogs, forums and wikis enable students to debate and organise themselves in social groups around the study and subjects (Laurillard, 2009). Used correctly and actively, this can bind students closer to specific disciplines and research communities. It can enhance the communication between students and teachers (Schroeder *et al.*, 2010) and it can create an atmosphere and collegial workplace where teachers, researchers and students share ideas and knowledge with each other (Svendsen, 2011; Lenstrup, in this volume). Nevertheless, many students and teachers still find it difficult to socialise with each other virtually. Even if the motivation for using social platforms in teaching is to encounter students in their social spaces, students often seem not to integrate the academic content. Instead, they treat academic discussions as separate from their social interactions (Bosch, 2009).

Many questions arise when speaking of new media: How can digital technologies improve students' learning processes compared to more traditional teaching methods? How and to what extent should teachers and universities engage themselves in social media? Which student cultures will be most stimulated through dedicated use of social media?

Key point:

- Social media can been used to enhance process-stream university teaching, though academic content is not automatically integrated into the student's social spaces.

Campus design

The physical space has significant importance in the formation of student cultures. Proshansky *et al.* (1983), Scanlon *et al.* (2007) and Cotten and Wilson (2006) argue that the identity of the individual is geographically embedded to some extent. The physical world is manifested in our brains as memories, feelings and values. Successive changes in working conditions during a lecture day at distributed campus facilities can have a great impact on a student's sense of belonging. This raises questions of how the physical environment encourages particular cultures and whether the environment can be redesigned. Which culture does the university seek to promote through its campus design and campus policies? Does the university prefer co-mingling or a physical separation of student, faculty and staff members?

At universities with a significant separation of classrooms, social activities, student housing, group rooms, cafeterias, conference rooms, laboratories and student administration offices, the role of the campus as partnership and workplace is harder to establish than that as knowledge provider. Teachers and students often only meet each other in the classroom and this constitutes a symbolic distance between the two parties. If work resources for students and teachers are grouped more closely, the surroundings shape the students' perceptions and identity in a more workplace-like direction.

Regarding campus design, an increased body of research now deals with learning outside the classroom (Waite *et al.*, 2009) and argues that effective teaching and learning may well take place outside of conventional study environments, even flourishing in an unstructured and spontaneous environment. An example of such an external setting is the concept of "service-learning" which, according to Erickson and Anderson (1997) and NSLC (2012), integrates community service with instruction and reflection to enrich the learning experience. In discussing the development of student culture in the university setting it is therefore important to take a critical review of the physical environment in which students have to study. Traditional architecture at universities has called for identical lecture theatres used for distribution of information across different scientific domains. More contemporary architecture calls for open spaces, informal meeting points, flexible rooms, community design and ownership of the physical space. It is our argument here that by linking together contextualised pedagogical approaches and contemporary architectural design ideas, it is possible to create a physical space for student and staff engagement during formal education hours as well as individual and group study time.

Key points:

- Physical space has significant importance in the formation of student cultures.

- Distributed campus facilities tend to restrict student–teacher interaction and create symbolic distances that make establishing a partnership or workplace culture more difficult.

- Effective teaching and learning may take place in an unstructured and spontaneous environment outside of conventional study environments.

- Discussing the development of student culture requires a critical review of the physical environment.

- It is possible to create physical space that enhances student and staff engagement by linking pedagogical approaches and contemporary architectural design ideas.

Teacher training

Creating a student engagement culture using classroom activities, online activities and the physical space for learning requires teachers who are able actively to design teaching and study methods that improve students' learning outcomes. We argue, in line with Kuh (1993), Wilkerson (1998), Ramsden and Martin (1996) and Bolhuis (2003), that it is important to train and promote instructors who organise their teaching according to process-stream-oriented thinking. Moving away from a traditional input-oriented view of curriculum, where the main focus is on delivering academic content at lectures and marking assignments, often requires inspiration and training. Teachers do not intuitively redesign their curriculum as a learning-centred action plan and start giving the students the responsibility for designing their own learning goals. The role of mentor, facilitator, coordinator, supervisor and assessor of learning processes often requires systematic training. Formal teacher training is therefore an important part of developing a culture of student engagement, which does not originate from the students alone and has to be facilitated by responsible teachers.

Again, there are many issues that should be considered: Is the teacher left alone with the cultural change or can the work be distributed among a larger group of teachers? Which students are disadvantaged if the class contains several mental models and the teacher represents a third perspective?

Key points:

- Creating a student engagement culture requires teachers actively to design the appropriate teaching and study methods.

- Teachers need to be inspired and trained to design learning-centred action plans.

- The role of facilitator, coordinator, supervisor and evaluator of learning processes requires systematic training.

- Formal teacher training is an important part of developing a culture of student engagement.

Policy forums

Culture creation is strengthened when the four student culture metaphors are introduced into governing and coordinating bodies such as study boards and academic councils. These forums define formal study requirements, policies and evaluation criteria which, in turn, often affect the individual teacher's behaviour both cognitively and normatively.

When governing bodies begin to discuss student culture on the basis of such proposed metaphors, it is likely that divergent views and inconsistent policies come to light. It is therefore relevant to ask whether the courses and study programs are evaluated according to content and/or stream-oriented parameters. And, if such parameters are mutually exclusive, it is important to discuss which goals are preferred.

Key point:
- Address student culture in diverse policy forums such as governing bodies, study boards, faculty groups and alumni groups.

University branding and student recruitment

Stevens and O'Connor (2005) describe how engineering students identify the university's role differently. Some students have an expectation that, corresponding to Vermunt's (2005) vocational learning orientation, the institution should clearly position and certify students' competencies for a future job. Other students perceive the institution as a place that develops the student as a whole person, corresponding to Vermunt's (2005) personal development and fulfilment orientation.

These two perspectives can provide ideas for university branding. Universities can choose to brand themselves as knowledge providers or learning partners. When the university markets its faculty as top researchers who have the newest (and best) knowledge, it supports the perception of the university as an education institution and knowledge provider. The same is the case with branding the university's alumni and business community relations to show that the university fulfils the need for knowledge.

Other students will be attracted to a more network-based "ambassador" model. They look for developmental relations between fellow students and faculty members. They need proof that personal investment is possible and that new knowledge can be developed and addressed by students in relation to their studies. When existing and former students, who have positively experienced the university's learning environment and acted like employees, become ambassadors of student and faculty integration, this will support the perception of the university as a workplace. At the same time, this kind of strategy is only possible if students actually experience workplace relations during their studies. This means that advanced branding through student communities only becomes possible if the university, through its curriculum development, has nurtured the creation of such communities.

This raises a couple of questions: Is it wise to brand a university as a learning partner and seek to recruit certain student profiles that match this ambition? Would existing and former students confirm that the learning processes, the challenges and the creativity in teaching and study methods support the university as a place for partnership?

Key points:
- Students' educational expectations and perceptions can provide ideas for university branding.

- Universities can brand themselves as knowledge providers or learning partners.

- Knowledge providers are likely to attract students that expect the university to provide an education that prepares and certifies them for a future job.

- Learning partners are likely to attract students that perceive the university as a place that develops the whole person.

- Existing and former students who have positively experienced the university's learning environment can act as ambassadors to support the branding.

- Questions remain about the wisdom of this type of branding and recruitment.

Conclusion

The aim of this chapter has been twofold: 1) to discuss matters of university student culture and its possible relationship with teaching and learning; and 2) to inspire a fruitful dialogue within the community of curriculum developers and teachers on how to develop "the learning university" where we see a move "from teaching to learning", where teaching goes "beyond transmission" and where students are "learning to learn".

In order to achieve this aim, we have drawn on both theory and practice. We have argued that perceptions by students and faculty of the university at large and of their own roles as students and teachers play an important part in creating the learning university. We have also argued that different types of curricula will lead to the creation of different perceptions of a university by students as well as faculty. If the curriculum is designed following the principles of the content stream, students are likely to be treated as pupils and thus act like pupils or customers. If the curriculum is designed following the principles of the process stream, students are likely to be seen as partners and thus act like partners or employees.

It is our hope that, by accepting our arguments of potential relationships between student culture and teaching and learning at universities, it may be possible to engage in a normative development of a teaching and learning environment in which the underlying culture is one of students as collaborative partners. It is our belief that this will benefit students and future employers as well as the university.

About the authors

Steffen Löfvall is Senior Consultant at the Dean's Office of Education at Copenhagen Business School, Copenhagen, Denmark. He can be contacted at this email: sl.edu@cbs.dk

Claus Nygaard is Professor in Management Education at Copenhagen Business School and Executive Director of LiHE. He can be contacted as this email: lihesupport@gmail.com

ePortfolios and the Twenty-first Century: Learning in Higher Education

Lori L. Hager

Introduction

As increasing numbers of faculty members across educational institutions utilise social-media tools for instructional purposes, it is imperative to identify indicators and evidence for resulting positive transformational shifts from faculty-centred instruction to student-driven learning. This chapter discusses what learning looks like in one such learning environment, based on learning outcomes from a three-year ePortfolio initiative at one American university.

The application of ePortfolio processes in higher education supports an iterative student-centred teaching and learning strategy responsive to changes in twenty-first-century learning. 'Learning ePortfolios' situate the student at the centre of the learning process, embedding critical skills such as collaboration, creativity and cross-disciplinary connections in an iterative cycle that is at the core of higher order thinking and learning. Daniel Pink (2006) asserts that the next generation of thinkers and leaders will be driven by creators, pattern recognisers, meaning makers, artists, designers, storytellers and big-picture thinkers. Learning ePortfolios provide a framework for faculty and students to embed twenty-first-century skills and make them visible.

This chapter illustrates how one ePortfolio project at an American research university seeks to make twenty-first-century learning visible in graduate education. The purpose of this chapter is to illustrate how ePortfolios have been used to support learning in one American graduate program in order to demonstrate that ePortfolios can be an effective strategy to address twenty-first-century learning and skills.

Evaluation of the ePortfolio project suggests that ePortfolios are clearly having an impact on pedagogy and the learning culture of the participating programs and departments (Bramhall *et al.*, 2011), fostering twenty-first-century workplace skills, including collaboration and creativity. Students report that participation in ePortfolios deepens connections between curricular and co-curricular learning, fostering the transfer of classroom learning to real-world challenges and promoting collaborative problem solving.

Henry Jenkins (2009:8) refers to an "ecological approach" toward learning with technology, which *"rather than dealing with each technology in isolation"* fosters *"thinking about the interrelationship among all of these different communication technologies, the cultural communities that grow up around them, and the activities they support."* The development of a cultural community or "digital commons", which functions as a point of daily departure and return, where community is formed, identities constructed and connections between the academy and the world are enriched and extended, is a central driver in the ecological approach of this unqiue ePortfolio project.

ePortfolios in higher education

The use of ePortfolios at institutions of higher education is proliferating. In the United States, 40 per cent of campuses are now utilising ePortfolios (Rhodes, 2011). From university system-wide implementation to individually owned sites built from publicly available web tools and platforms, ePortfolios are changing learning and assessment processes and structures in educational institutions.

Research (Cambridge, 2010; Cambridge *et al.*, 2009; Rhodes, 2011; Light *et al.*, 2011; Stefanakis, 2011) suggests that participation in ePortfolio learning in a web 2.0/3.0 environment enhances:

- Student engagement
- Critical reflection and analysis
- A collaborative teaching–learning environment.

Universities and colleges employ ePortfolios for a variety of purposes, including supporting students in professional and career advancements (professional portfolios), for student-centred assessment and reflection (academic portfolios that represent a student's "body of work") and for the purposes of institutional accreditation (to provide a means to archive and represent student achievement across schools):

"Portfolios for personal representation guide users in managing their virtual identities via online resumes, professional portfolios, and freeform portfolios. Portfolios for teaching and learning establish workflows that guide students in reflecting upon and sharing learning within and across disciplines. Portfolios for assessment and accreditation provide systematic reporting of results from courses and programs for institution-wide assessment."

(Cambridge *et al.*, 2008:492)

ePortfolios provide a way to track student progress through an academic degree program, serving as a compass through learning. The content of a student learning ePortfolio may include artefacts from courses, personal information, education and professional background, awards, instructor feedback, peer critique, reflective analysis, professional objectives, co-curricular activities, etc. However, ePortfolios are widely recognised not solely as a tool or a technology but as both a product and process (Light *et al.*, 2011; Barrett, 2009; Cambridge, 2008).

Universities that employ ePortfolios integrate them into instructional design, providing a means for student demonstrations of learning and evidence of skills development. Students document and legitimise their learning choices through a record in their ePortfolios. At the University of Minnesota, for instance, they are using ePortfolios for:

- Creating a system of tracking student work over time and in a single course

- Aggregating many students' work in a particular course to see how the students as a whole are progressing

- Assessing many courses in similar ways that are all part of one major and thus, by extension, assessing the entire program of study

- Encouraging continuity of student work from semester to semester in linked courses.

(Batson, 2002)

Integrating ePortfolios promotes cross-disciplinary connections, applications of theory to practice, greater student involvement in their own learning processes, and supports faculty to integrate social media and web 2.0/3.0 tools into the structures, resources and processes of instruction, fostering a collaborative teaching and learning environment. Participation in ePortfolios fosters communities of learning and of practice, extending classroom learning into the community and through both formal and informal pathways (Barrett, 2011; Batson, 2002; Cambridge, 2010; Cambridge *et al.*, 2009; Oliver *et al.*, 2009). ePortfolios that incorporate social media capitalise on the social networking behaviours of entering students, in support and enhancement of curricular and co-curricular meaning making, and multi-modal communication and interaction (Oliver *et al.*, 2009).

ePortfolios in action

An interdisciplinary learning ePortfolio initiative was begun in 2008 with three professional programs (Architecture, Business, and Arts and Administration) at the University of Oregon, building on a successful showcase ePortfolio project established in 2005 in the Arts and Administration Program (AAD). The project is part of a network of Higher Education institutions engaged in developing ePortfolio learning processes and a member of the fifth cohort of the Inter/National Coalition of Electronic Portfolio Research (I/NCEPR).

The mission of the Arts and Administration Program is to *"educate cultural sector leaders and participants to make a difference in communities"* (AAD, 2012). Composed of four full-time faculty and with an average of 55 regularly enrolled graduate student body, AAD is a small professional department in a large research university. ePortfolios began as a faculty initiative to connect coursework and learning objectives in two core components of the graduate curriculum: the professional development course sequence (internship) and information technology courses (graphic design and web development).

All entering Arts and Administration graduate students are required to create learning ePortfolios in a WordPress blogging platform. Students post their overall learning objectives and two-year academic plan, and for each participating class they post learning objectives that connect the course to their larger academic and career goals. Students are provided with ePortfolio templates, which they modify and update as they progress through the program and which become increasingly reflective of their personal learning journey. Periodically throughout and at the end of the term, students post artefacts and reflections that provide a narrative and evidence for their learning and how it connects with their overall learning objectives. During their summer professional internship placements, students create "field blogs", allowing them to demonstrate how they are connecting theory to practice, how their thinking is changing and how their research is connected to their developing professional practices.

As they are using an ePortfolio system in a blogging environment, students have the option to aggregate multiple web 2.0/3.0 tools that enhance their learning experience and, if they choose, maintain an active blog through posting assignments, reflections and professional development and research activities.

The vision of the AAD ePortfolio system is a comprehensive learning system that serves as a hub for the generation of dynamic learning communities between faculty, students and professionals, and centres the integration of demonstrations of excellence in academic objectives, participatory learning and professional development through digital communications.

The design of the system allows for a very robust aggregation of faculty and student uses, which includes course instructional blogs, project blogs that support student team assignments and an aggregated hub that provides a point of entry to course information, faculty and student information, tutorials and ePortfolio guidance. Through aggregating learning ePortfolios, program resource blogs, instructional blogs, faculty and student professional portfolios in a hub, or "digital commons", a community of practice is generated that supports multi-modal learning and application of communication technologies in a distributed cognition approach.

Twenty-first-century learning ePortfolios

The kinds of skills which are required for success in the twenty-first-century world require a radically different approach to learning and teaching and, consequently, suggest different roles for the student and teacher. As Nygaard *et al.* (2011, foreword) acknowledge, *"paradigms of learning are evolving, with concepts of 'knowledge transfer' becoming less important and co-production of knowledge becoming more widely accepted."* Learning ePortfolios place the student at the centre of the learning process, embedding critical skills such as collaboration, creativity, and cross-disciplinary connections in an iterative cycle that is at the core of higher-order thinking and learning. Learning ePortfolios also provide a mechanism for faculty and students to act as co-participants in twenty-first-century learning through fostering collaborative knowledge generation (Stefanakis, 2011).

With the emergence of new technologies that allow for the facile interplay of individuals in the collective global sphere, young people have moved from being "media consumers" to becoming "media producers" (Jenkins, 2009). The focus on the twenty-first-century citizen resituates learning and education well beyond traditional academic disciplinary distinctions, to cultivating lifelong learning skills in the abilities to:

- Synthesise (integrative and applied learning)

- Collaborate (work in teams/collective intelligence)

- Engage in ethical reasoning, lifelong learning

- Creative thinking and critical analysis

ePortfolios provide a mechanism for support and demonstration of learning and achievements in these critical areas.

The American Association for Colleges and Universities (AACU) advocates for ePortfolios as a strategy for twenty-first-century learning in higher education:

> *"The e-portfolio is an ideal format for collecting evidence of student learning, especially for those outcomes not amenable nor appropriate for standardized measurement. Additionally, e-portfolios can facilitate student reflection upon and engagement with their own learning across*

multi-year degree programs, across different institutions, and across diverse learning styles while helping students to set and achieve personal learning goals. E-portfolios provide both a transparent and portable medium for showcasing the broad range of complex ways students are asked to demonstrate their knowledge and abilities for purposes such as graduate school and job applications as well as to benchmark achievement among peer institutions."

(AACU, no date)

ePortfolios have, like any learning tool or process, a multitude of applications. From showcase/professional ePortfolios to personal learning environments (PLEs), flexible learning frameworks (Oliver *et al.*, 2009), evidence-based learning (Eynon, 2009) and differentiated assessment (Stefanakis, 2011), ePortfolios are adopted by a range of institutions for different purposes and have been appropriated by different sectors to reflect a range of applications:

"Primary and secondary teachers often use terms such as 'digital portfolios', 'digital storytelling' and 'digital learning portfolios'; higher-education practitioners prefer 'electronic portfolios', 'e-portfolios', 'web folio' and 'e-folio'; while in the corporate sector terms such as 'performance management tools', 'career management tools' and 'personal development planning records' refer to similar systems and activities."

(Editorial, 2009:1)

"Learning ePortfolio" is a term used to distinguish ePortfolios for learning from showcase or capstone ePortfolios, or ePortfolios used for assessment and accreditation purposes. "Learning ePortfolio" refers to both the process and product of engaging in ePortfolios as an embedded reflective and critical learning process which results in a demonstration of learning through tangible digital products. In the Arts and Administration Program, students create learning ePortfolios in the open-source blog-based platform and also create showcase ePortfolios using a standard web development program. The showcase ePortfolio is designed to be their capstone portfolio, where they designate the evidence for professional competencies matched with career objectives, which they may share with potential supervisors and employers. The learning ePortfolio is designed to be their "compass through learning", one that changes with the student as they progress through their degree program. Students have the option of "taking" it with them when they graduate, so that learning ePortfolios have the capacity to be lifelong (Barrett, 2011; Rhodes, 2011).

Student use their ePortfolios in vastly different ways depending on their career and degree emphasis, which the system and the project allows and encourages. Some students focus on the extension of their professional networks, utilising the blog feature to publish their work in the public domain. As a result, several students have been invited to be professional and guest bloggers with international associations and organisations. Students report on the use of ePortfolios in constructing their professional digital identities, the importance of its use as a marketing and branding tool, for personal expression, information collection, communication and distribution of work, and for job advancement. As one student said: *"I blog for other organizations already, and the entries can serve as writing samples for potential jobs. I use a variety of social media for research and making professional connections."*

The purposes, values and uses of ePortfolios are well-documented elsewhere (Jafari & Kaufman, 2006; Cambridge *et al.*, 2009; Barrett, 2011; Batson, 2002). However, Kathleen Yancey (2001:16) captures the essence of the ePortfolio learning process, stating: *"Created by the three principal activities of collection, selection, and reflection, student portfolios can be succinctly defined as collections of work selected from a larger archive of work, upon which the student has reflected. Portfolios can be created in many different contexts, serve various purposes, and speak to multiple audiences."*

In AAD, students use learning ePortfolios to aggregate and reflect on their academic work and course assignments, for information sharing and keeping track of resources, and as a simple and accessible hub for collecting work and sharing it with colleagues. In end-of-year surveys, which examined factors in student engagement and usage of the learning ePortfolios, students reported value for a multitude of uses:

- Aggregating all their academic work

- Posting course assignments

- Information sharing

- Keeping track of resources.

In an end-of-year anonymous survey, students reported that:

- *"It keeps all of my most important school work in one place and it is something to show to potential employers."*

- *"It is simple and provides an accessible hub for collecting work and sharing it with my colleagues in school."*

- *"Having a centralized place for all of my work and thoughts (learning goals/reflections) has helped me track my overall learning and draw conclusions/see themes over the quarters."*

Students value their ability to articulate and demonstrate growth over time. Students report that their learning has changed as a result of their use of learning ePortfolios:

- *"I am forced to look back on my work and reflect on how it informed my understanding of the course topics. I am also more organized in my documentation of work."*

- *"Classes that utilize the ePortfolio typically ask for pre and post reflections on the class, so it helps to identify how I learn and grow throughout the course."*

Light *et al.* (2011) report that these instrumental processes are reflected in ePortfolio learning in the concept of "folio thinking":

> *"Central to folio thinking and ePortfolios is the process of reflecting on the growth of one's knowledge and capabilities over time with an emphasis on metacognition by intentionally providing structured time and space for learners to consider and document the process of their learning and not just the product (assignments, tests, and so on). This process highlights the affordances of ePortfolios as not only potentially transformational with respect to individual learning and development."*
>
> (2011: Kindle locations 463–7).

ePortfolios are driven by the learning process, rather than the technological tool; however, the ability to "mash-up" a variety of learning tools and media supports and enhances the ways that learning is constructed in the ePortfolio process. One of the most immediate and unexpected results of the implementation is the widespread adoption of the blog-based ePortfolio platform across an array of applications. Students apply what they are learning from utilising their learning ePortfolios in the WordPress environment to:

- Create project blogs to demonstrate co-curricular work in their practice and internships

- Collaborate and represent projects in class and field-based assignments

- Keep field blogs when they are away on their internships to keep in touch with what each other is doing and experiencing and to develop a record of their accomplishments and experiences.

Students report that they value engagement in learning ePortfolios also for its importance as a marketing tool and for personal branding, personal expression, information collection, communication and distribution of work, and for job advancement. Many students create blog-based websites for internship and practicum sites, and research blogs where they aggregate resources, reflect and synthesise courses and research, and make multi-disciplinary connections between courses explicit, while connecting their co-curricular project-based learning.

ePortfolios cannot be defined as either product or process, but rather are an integrative approach that harnesses the learner as co-creator in knowledge generation, or in what Jenkins (2009:4) refers to as "distributed cognition" or *"the ability to interact meaningfully with tools that expand mental capacities."* This new media literacy, or "collective intelligence" (Jenkins 2009) fosters the ability to pool knowledge and compare notes with others toward a common goal or, in other words, to make twenty-first-century learning visible.

AAD Students are contributors on the graduate course instructional blogs, where they post analyses of readings and projects, respond to peer reflections and contribute course resources such as journals and websites, acting as co-contributors to the development of course content and resources. The discussion and blog features of the ePortfolio platform support students to engage in robust online discussion forums, which extend class discussions and enhance their team-based projects.

During the first year of utilising a blogging platform, AAD graduate students spontaneously re-appropriated blogs as a way to stay connected during their summer internships. In effect, they made use of the tools and technology that they had learned from the ePortfolios to create their own virtual dynamic learning community. Their informal reflective posts became one of the key features of the ways in which students constructed meaning from their professional experiences and connected their co-curricular and curricular learning.

Because of the visible nature of the platform, students designate what work they will make fully public, which has increased the peer-to-peer engagement, helping to promote collaboration and teamwork. Students post comments, reflections and other materials into a common instructional hub, which allows students to peer review each other's work and to post critiques and observations. Feeling part of a learning community, students are helping to guide their educative growth and development. Students are able to view each other's work, both in the same class and across classes. Faculty can designate that the instructional blog be viewable by just the students in the course, by all users in the system or completely publicly available. A rigorous privacy policy has been developed, in adherence to university requirements. Students and faculty maintain the greatest degree of control over visibility. So, the choice of what to make visible, or private, becomes an intentional choice with implications that become opportunities for discussion and analysis.

Students using learning ePortfolios in the blogging environment indicated a broad range of discomfort to comfort with negotiating their public digital identifies, and the educational use of what they associate with informal, and social networking tools. Students demonstrated discomfort when asked to transfer skills and tools employed in informal learning to formal learning contexts – these are domains that they have traditionally kept separate and this affects how they assert their digital selves and identities in different contexts. Yet these challenges have provided a critical opportunity to engage students in discussions around managing their digital identities, which has implications for a broad array of professional practices.

Twenty-first-century skills	Student ePortfolio usage
Communication and collaboration	Students voluntarily create collaborative spaces using the tools modelled in ePortfolios. For example, students will create project weblogs where they work together on products and processes. The visibility of the blogging environment allows students to see and build on each other's work. The ePortfolio "commons" fosters communication between students and faculty.
Creativity (synthesis, new knowledge, pattern making) and innovation	The versatility of the learning platform allows a wide range of re-mixing and "mashing up" skills and knowledge in new ways. Students re-appropriate the tools and remix them in new and innovative ways, which they bring back to the classroom and share with each other – both formally and informally.
Critical thinking (curricular and co-curricular connections/theory to practice)	Students capture "aha" moments in their reflections and as they synthesise learning throughout their degree program and courses. They are able to look back at where they started and track their progress through learning. Students match learning objectives with course and program objectives, and are involved in a process of reflective iteration about their learning journey, how they are making meaning, forming knowledge and skills, and extending and applying these skills and knowledge in new contexts and environments, both in the classroom and in the professional community. Through connecting curricular and co-curricular learning, students make the application of theory to practice visible and tangible. Students will question and analyse experiences in practice and internships and how they diverge or converge with what they learn in class. This fosters a dynamic approach to learning and discussion which informs class-based processes as well as professional development opportunities.

Table 1: Demonstrations of twenty-first-century learning skills through ePortfolios

Discussion – emergent outcomes

Emergent findings from student surveys and focus groups during the three-year initiative suggest that participation in ePortfolios leads to student-centred learning and pedagogical change, while applying real-world technology to the ways that student and faculty engage in learning (Bramhall *et al.*, 2011). For students:

- Peer-to-peer engagement increases as students share and view each other's work

- Self-assessment of change and development over time increases

- Ability to demonstrate and articulate growth over time improves

- Curricular and co-curricular learning connections are made that have implications for the applications of theory to professional practice and professional development

- Skills learned in the ePortfolio environment are transferable, and

- The level of critical reflection increases as a result of the unique digital environment.

The ways that participating faculty embed ePortfolios in their courses are widely varied. Faculty may aggregate all their courses and instructional materials onto a single instructional blog or create a different one for each class. Some faculty have created templates for specific courses, which they can customise for each unique course. Faculty may include in their instructional blogs any external resources, such as links to websites and web resources, diigo collaborative web bookmarking tools and other kinds of web 3.0 and social-media strategies – in effect, modelling the application of learning tools and strategies.

Discussion – unexpected outcomes

The ePortfolio project began with the vision of creating and fostering a digital neighbourhood, or what is now named the "commons", as a point of daily departure and return, where social capital is fostered through sharing thoughts, ideas, events and professional development. The participants sought a way to share what was happening in classes and for students and faculty to share how they were extending their thinking outside the classroom. Faculty wanted to see how students applied theory to practice, how they could make the learning visible. It was important to create and foster a space where students articulated value, a place where faculty, students and community partners could work together to foster connections between curricular and co-curricular work, and to help faculty see how students were transferring skills and knowledge across a range of experiences. The initiative outcomes were both more than anticipated, as well as disappointing.

Three years into the department-level integration, students are voluntarily generating new knowledge through a mediated convergence and participatory culture. They are showing the faculty new ways of working in the environment, making the connections across classes, so that transformative learning moments become more visible inside and outside the classroom. Students use it as a mechanism for peer-to-peer mentoring and as a way to learn from each other. Students are able to harness their co-curricular learning, connecting what is happening outside the classroom to ideas and reflections they are exploring in the classroom. This has the effect of improving the in-class as well as the professional experiences. Through setting intentional learning objectives, making these visible and reflecting on how they are meeting their learning objectives, students take greater responsibility for how they are charting their own learning path.

The ways in which both students and faculty engage in learning and in technology are widely varied. While higher-education institutions are put on notice to prepare for students fully conversant in web 2.0/3.0 and social media, the levels at which students are entering the university prepared are hugely varied, and comfort in engaging with new technologies and subsequent changes in pedagogical structures affects the time and effort that faculty give.

Integrating learning ePortfolios into the curriculum creates a need for visible curriculum mapping, making graduate learning outcomes visible, and an articulation of pedagogical practices. As Cambridge *et al.* (2008:500) assert: "*Integrative learning is supported by offering students broad latitude in composing their portfolios, while assessment requires gathering data that can be compared across programs and institutions. It is difficult to serve both these purposes at once.*" Helen Barrett (2009) discusses this as an "opportunity cost" of ePortfolios, for faculty and students. Not all faculty members perceive the benefits of participation, viewing the risks as greater than the benefits. The learning curve for faculty participation in ePortfolios can be steep and, unless the institution supports participation through incentives or rewards, faculty engagement can be a challenge.

As Coogan (2009) points out, blended learning at the graduate level comes with its own set of issues and challenges. The convergence of formal and informal learning processes through social-networking tools and blended learning environments raises unique challenges. Students demonstrate a degree of discomfort when asked to transfer skills and tools employed in informal learning to formal learning contexts; these are domains that they have traditionally kept separate and this affects how they assert their digital selves and identities in different contexts. Yet "digital citizenship" is becoming an increasingly important part of education and workplace preparation.

Research has suggested that participation in learning ePortfolios can lead to changes in learning and pedagogy (Cambridge *et al.*, 2009; Jafari & Kaufman, 2006). One of the factors is how faculty engage with it in their courses; another factor is the general climate for managing risk and innovation in the institution. Both faculty and students acknowledged that utilising it for innovation and change was high risk, from the publicly visible profile of the project and the implications for their academic, professional identity, and for faculty who experiment with varying degrees of success.

Conclusion

Technology already pervades every classroom in the United States, whether it is the use of content management systems such as Blackboard, clickers, mobile apps or YouTube. Advances in technology are allowing ePortfolio applications to demonstrate that ePortfolio learning is not about the technology but about learning and knowledge generation. Students are now entering the university fully equipped to utilise tool sets to generate knowledge collectively. ePortfolios help to harness these skill sets, to make learning (and knowledge generation) visible to students, to peers, to faculty and professionals. Technology fundamentally changes the way that young people go to school and learn, and the ways that higher-education institutions harness technologies for learning represent a sea change in how students will be preparing for college in the future. Empowering students to take charge of their own learning can have unintended and far-reaching consequences. ePortfolios can serve as an effective instructional and learning strategy to capture the kinds of learning that inevitably will envision this future.

Acknowledgements

The ePortfolio project was supported by a grant from the UO Educational Technology Committee, the UO Vice Provost for Academic Affairs, and with support from the Arts and Administration Program and the UO Center for Community Arts and Cultural Policy.

About the author

Lori L. Hager is Assistant Professor in Community Arts in the Arts and Administration Program at the University of Oregon where she founded and directs the ePortfolio project. She can be contacted at this email: lhager@uoregon.edu

The Development of "Learning to Be" in Higher Education

Yahui Su

Learning in higher education today

A wealth of literature concerning learning and education (e.g. Usher, 2001; Kivinen, 2002) suggests that we are currently facing uncertainty, diversity and changes that are unprecedented in their rapidity. These phenomena are characteristic of postmodern conditions. To meet these challenges, scholars have suggested that "challengeability", "contestability", "uncertainty" and "unpredictability" are the main concepts that we must consider in order to understand the environments within which higher education operates (Barnett, 1997). With the collapse of universal "metanarratives" (Lyotard, 1984), higher education institutions, instead of justifying themselves as places where knowledge is pursued for its own sake, must reconsider their students' learning practices by conceiving of students as the centre of epistemological authority – meaning that the decisions on what is learnt and which knowledge is relevant are left to students, according to how they reflect upon current and future lives of change.

Although the classic image of higher education involves *the gathering of teachers and learners in pursuit of the higher learning*" (Bauman, 1997:17), the meaning of higher learning today requires the constructive-developmental view of learning (Kegan, 1982; Baxter Magolda, 1999), which proposes that learners construct their view of reality by organising, accommodating and reflecting upon their individual experiences to meet the challenges of changing times. The dynamic, developmental character of learning requires the learner's mentality and behaviour to be taken into account, and the learning process cannot be reduced to a process of acquisition. Instead, the learner's subjectivity, which includes his or her perceptions, thoughts, feelings and actions (see Fast, 1998; Thompson, 2007:16), becomes central to the process. If the learner's subjectivity is not actively engaged in the learning process, the shaping of his or her authentic existences is not considered and the true medium of communication within the postmodern "supercomplex" world (Barnett, 1997) cannot be wholly and persistently addressed.

This chapter argues that the learning practices associated with modern higher education cannot be sustained only by the acquisition of skills and knowledge. Attention must be paid to the development of students' "learning to be", because higher education requires cultivating students to find their values and develop identities to confront the loss of certainty in a world of change in the long term.

This chapter begins by pointing out higher learning within the context of postmodern change as a basis for understanding why the ability of "learning to be" is required. Then, the significance and meaning of the pursuit of "learning to be" are addressed. Furthermore, learning for oneself by moving beyond disciplinary boundaries, rather than the pursuit of discipline-based knowledge in itself, is essential as students work to respond reflectively to the changing times and futures. Next, higher-education curricula, pedagogy and teacher roles that inspire and encourage students' "learning to be" are considered. The concept of being has implications for developing curricular and pedagogical strategies for developing student being and identity and generating more student-centred and engagingly reflective learning practices in higher education.

Higher education: the pursuit of learning to be

As meta-narratives (Lyotard, 1984), which used to be where the legitimacy of world certainty lay, can be themselves problematised today, higher education demands a different theory of learning that can help students to hold the meaning of their own existence in this context. The uncertainty and contestability of knowledge integration and renewal needed for everyday work and life reflect the accentuation of the "liquidity" and dynamism of the world (Bauman, 1997). To *have* knowledge seems to have become more irrelevant and less useful for living in an uncertain, changing world. Instead of having knowledge, "being-in-the-world" needs to become the focus of higher education (Barnett, 2005; Dall'Alba & Barnacle, 2007) in lifelong terms (Su, 2011). "Learning to be" differs from the traditional concept of "learning to have", which has tended to emphasise the universal and cognitive aspects of *the past*; indeed, "learning to be" helps students to progress towards *an unknown future* in which they will confront and influence changing real-life and career situations.

"Learning to be" is also different from "learning to do", which focuses on immediate thought and action intended to solve the problems of *the present* (see Table 1). The "learning to do" perspective assumes that learning by doing or through action is normally superior to other learning methods. This method focuses on the student's acquisition of competences and problem-solving skills that allow the student to cope effectively with temporality and indeterminacy. In contrast, "learning to be" is intrinsically rooted in the idea of the student's "being-in-the-world", as Heidegger phrases it (1996). "Being-in-the-world" refers to the development of relationships without some prior or eternal essence. This conceptualisation opposes the Cartesian understanding of subject and object as separate. In "being-in-the-world", according to Heidegger, one is "thrown" into one's own situation and, from there, projects oneself forward into the future, where one's identity is inevitably influenced by this process. Heidegger emphasised the confrontation of one's situation, as the particular, with the understanding of how one's being relates to the whole (Being) in an *authentic* sense. It is through the experience of being in his or her own situation that a student comes to understand the connections between himself or herself and the world; and herein lies the meaning of a student's existence in a state of change. The "learning to be" approach, accordingly, shifts the focus from the acquisition of knowledge and competences to their integration into the authentically specific, changing situations confronting students.

Learning type	Learning to have	Learning to do	Learning to be
Learning vision	The past	The present	The future
Learning outcome	Knowledge acquisition	Competence acquisition	Meaning and identity development
Learning focus	Knowledge	Practice	Person (student)
Learning philosophy	Epistemic learning	Pragmatic learning	Existential learning
Agency operation	Cognitive	Cognitive and physical	Cognitive, physical and affective
Agency medium	Mind	Mind and body	Mind, body and heart (the whole person)

Table 1: "Learning to have", "learning to do" and "learning to be"

Thus, learning in higher education, for "learning to be", is no longer fundamentally understood either as traditional (epistemic) learning (i.e. as primarily based on the operation of the mind and on cognitive aspects of student agency) or simply as pragmatic learning (i.e. as emphasising students' capacity for reflective thought and action) (see Table 1), although these abilities are understood as important. Higher education that cultivates a student's "learning to be" would instead encourage the participative exploration of meaning and the active creation of the student's own options, thus meeting students' particular, authentic needs as determined by their own personal situations. Students must provoke fundamental, existential questions that demand meaningful answers that indicate how they can co-participate in and commit to a changing life. As Boyer (1987) suggests, the focus of higher education must transition "from competence to commitment" such that students can become "*well-informed, caring individuals*" who "*learn from one another, to participate as citizens*" (Boyer, 1987:280) and who collectively commit to helping to transform a changing world. The students' "learning to be" is intrinsically connected to their experiences and connections with people and to the collective meanings that these experiences and connections generate under constant change.

The development of "learning to be": learning for oneself

The process of being-in-the-world facilitates the pursuit of learning *for oneself* by moving beyond disciplinary boundaries, unlike the pursuit of discipline-based knowledge, which is focused on rationality and knowledge *in itself*. This focus on knowledge in itself presupposes learning as a process of delivery and the learner as the "receptor". Rather than the knowledge content taken as central, with the learner and his or her situated context serving instrumental roles, the entire gestalt (learner, what is learned and the learner's situation) is integral to learning for oneself in the constitutive sense. Learning for oneself evolves from the self; it not only requires self-direction in a psychological sense but also invites self-authorship on the part of students (i.e. their capacity to coordinate, integrate, act upon or invent their own beliefs, values or generalisations based on who they are) (Kegan, 1994:185). Self-authoring students bring their subjectivities to bear on the learning process. They may wander aimlessly, indulge in speculation, review and consider the values and perspectives that they have learned, reserving for themselves the right to sense and judge possible thought for appropriate action. Students who learn for themselves are not hindered by traditional structures of authority and are expected to become more self-reliant because they must answer for their own knowledge, beliefs and value systems based on their respective contexts and experiences.

In learning for themselves, students do not simply think and act in order to solve the problems created by change, as pragmatists suggest. Rather, by involving the whole person, the *"willing–feeling–perceiving being"* (Dilthey, 1988:73), students apply all of their reflection on change and their resulting actions to their own existence. A mode of learning that engages the whole person in his or her quest to achieve meaningful relationships with confronting situations requires an existential sense of agency and thus becomes *"more than merely a cognitive activity"* (Gibson, 1986:57); this type of learning is deeply connected to all aspects of an individual's mind (cognition), body (action) and heart (affect) (Brillinger, 1997; Rogers, 1997). It requires deeper levels of feelings and commitment, generating a type of authenticity, in which the mind, body and soul of the student work symbiotically to facilitate relatedness and connection that is not "pieced" together but is instead "absorbed" into an intentional relationship to the whole. Intentional relatedness is described "*in terms of the sentient qualities of emotion, feeling, purpose, and desire*" (Schrag, 1959:45). Students, cognitively as well as affectively, intends to recognise the ultimate meaning of learning and their identities in change. All three domains – the cognitive, the physical and the affective (see Table 1) – are important for higher-education students' to meet the requirements of a changing life and their careers.

Curricula for "learning to be": developing student identity and meaning

Curricula that focus on knowledge for its own sake and emphasise discipline-based knowledge have become insufficient as they are only partially, temporally relevant to the challenges of our era. The curriculum in the "learning to have" mode has only one aim: students retain existing knowledge that can be delivered and taught by teachers. The curriculum in the "learning to do" mode, in contrast, is intended to develop students' reflection, action and problem-solving skills in practice. The aim of the practice-based curriculum is not to acquire or to "have" particular knowledge or content but to create a context within which to employ such knowledge to ensure that students develop competences and their ability to manage a given context. Curricular practice in the "learning to have" mode, for instance, is processed mainly by lectures and context-free knowledge delivered by teachers in the classroom; whereas the "learning to do" curricular practice may include students' experiences of going to a restaurant (in my hospitality education class, for instance) or practising in an internship programme to observe and learn how the manager thinks and takes action in specific situations. The "learning-to-do" curriculum focuses on required actions that one must perform in practice.

Alternatively, curricula that are designed to develop students' continuous "being-in-the-world" contribute to making students autonomous, active participants who develop their own "learning projects" (Tough, 1979). The curricular practice is designed for students to construct and find their own identities, values and meanings to confront future change. In the learning project, knowledge is thought of in terms of *concepts* rather than *content*. As Usher *et al.* (1997:90–1) stated: "[b]y adopting a critical posture, we can provide ourselves with the conceptual resources to develop our own discourse, a discourse which would ensure that disciplines have a place but one which is not that of mastery". To determine whether any concept or discourse is relevant requires the student's self-authorship rather than simply requiring the acquisition of knowledge and skills.

The focus on "being" does not diminish the significance of knowledge, skills or competence learning. The goal of developing students' ability to "learn to be" is not to replace the acquisition of important skills – of "learning to have" and "learning to do" – but rather to extend these skills by developing learning projects actively to optimise students' engagement (Hong & Weitman, this volume), in which students anticipate the consequences of integrating their knowledge of the past with their present actions and decisions and their possible future existence. The student-centred approach to student learning, in contrast to the knowledge- and practice-centred approaches (Table 1), focuses on developing students' identities and meanings by engaging situations based on their agentic reflections, attitudes, feelings and actions towards their possible futures. The curriculum in the being mode does not simply involve a set of cognitive and practical exercises; it is concerned with liberating students *"beyond the present and the particular"* (Bailey, 1984) by permitting a discussion, for instance, that engages the liberal arts in tandem with other disciplines. Such engagement can be an aesthetic, transformative experience that enhances the potential for personal growth and identity (Laff, 2005). Usher and Edwards (1994:107) posit that it is through liberal ideas that discourses of competence become more powerful than one's knowledge and skill development in securing employment (Harvey, 2000).

Thus, curricular practice must transition from its emphasis on discipline-centred content to learning what is valuable and meaningful. Teachers who design curricula within the framework of learning for oneself must focus on a "theme", "issue" or "project" that means something "real" in relation to the student's real life-situation and that is therefore relevant to the student (Beane, 1995). Because of the focus on themes or projects, the multi-narratives of knowledge coexist and interact with each other in complex ways and it is impossible to develop a common curriculum (Delanty, 1998:105). This becomes even more true under what Gibbons *et al.* (1994) call the Mode 2 form of knowledge production, which is cross-disciplinary, heterarchical and transient. From an empirical standpoint, the traditional boundaries between disciplines are not rejected (Nicoll & Edwards, 1997; Edwards & Usher, 2000). What is being rejected is not the disciplines themselves but rather "a foundationalist epistemological grounding in disciplines" (Usher at al., 1997:90). Accordingly, new boundaries will flourish, but none will be superior to the others. Although there is room for Mode 1 knowledge production, which may be appropriate as long as it is not conceived of as 'canonical', Mode 2 knowledge production as action-oriented, self-oriented and encouraging of cross-disciplinary work is essential to the curricular goals of learning for oneself, which them-selves are necessarily subject to change because the meaningfulness of Mode 2 knowledge production is ever-expanding and changing as students self-determine their ways of learning.

To nurture this new mindset, the inclusion of inviting learning projects in higher-education curricula encourages the long-term develop-ment of students' feelings, thinking and actions to generate and enhance the potential for being in change. While the associations of reflection and action (Schön, 1983, 1987) can explain *how* students can produce learning outcomes, students' affective engagement can explain *why* they engage in the process of associations and the acknowledgement of their responsibility for their learning. To help students develop authentic learning projects, the teacher should not only provide students with *what* they need to know and require them to reflect and act upon *how* the knowledge may be employed but should also ask students to propose and interpret *why* the learned knowledge has meaning for their present and future existence (see Table 2).

In "learning to be", students do not enter the class as *tabulae rasae*; they have different backgrounds and experiences, and they come with themes and issues that are important and interesting to them. Rather than being passive recipients of knowledge, as students develop their learning projects they are encouraged to self-direct and reflect upon certain existential questions, including "What have I learned?", "How is this learning linked to my current life situations or work practice?", "What does my learning today mean to me in terms of my future life and career development?", "How can my learning today help to develop my future potential?" and "What would I like to learn more about?" (see Table 2).

Curriculum type	Learning to have	Learning to do	Learning to be
Curriculum learning	Learning-what	Learning-what Learning-how	Learning-what Learning-how Learning-why
Curricular Questions	What have I learned?	1. What have I learned? 2. How is this learning linked to my current life situations or work practice?	1. What have I learned? 2. How is this learning linked to my current life situations or work practice? 3. What does my learning today mean to me in terms of my possible future life and career development? 4. How can my learning today help develop my future potential? 5. What would I like to learn more about?

Table 2: Curricula for "learning to be"

The pedagogical focus: students who become fully engaged

The transformation of the concept of learning into a mode of being makes it possible for pedagogy to *"take into care beings as a whole"* (Heidegger, 1998:39). The pedagogy for "learning to be" is on the right track when students become fully engaged and are regarded as the centre of the action, effectively acting upon their situation by being integrative and productive rather than compartmental and reproductive: by finding the meaningfulness of their own potential. Unlike with traditional pedagogy, which gives little credence to student learning as experiential engagement or that reinforces the dichotomy between the learner and the situation rather than challenging it, the type of pedagogy that focuses on engagement locates the learner with his or her situation as a whole. *"Situation is more than context*" (Feldman, 2002:1039): a situation includes what one experiences, whereas a context refers to the environment in which these experiences occur – the backdrop against which an ordered sequence of events or ideas is experienced or understood. The student's direct engagement as a felt, concrete experiential encounter situates the student as *"part of the environment rather than a detached spectator"* (Hager, 2003:5). Within this process of engagement, the student feels mentally focused in experiencing the 'flow', (Csikszentmihalyi, 1997), in which feeling, thinking and acting are very much related (Su, 2011). The process of flow through engagement is circular and, in this sense, the student's thoughts, feelings and willingness to act become the world *of* the student that forms a united whole.

When engaging in an experience of being, students penetrate the complex structures of the situation-based, authentic-oriented learning tasks or projects that closely relate to their inner enquiries, take a deep rather than a superficial approach to tasks (Entwistle, 2001) and look for meaningful patterns by probing beneath the surface. The holistic patterns of connection between the student and his or her situation vary based on the learning project or task at hand, as it is integrated with the student's personal interests and intentions. As a consequence of engagement, students' interpretations of situations "will always be something more or less than, but at least different from, the teacher's interpretations" (Gallagher, 1992:134). Students see themselves as creative (rather than receptive) subjects who engage in circular reflections and connections in their learning processes, and they ontologically feel these processes and connections (Sinnott, 2009) rather than only epistemologically receiving and constructing them. The processing of the connective experience is the self-authoring moment in which the student begins to use his or her reasoning and imagination to assess the situation, thus enabling the adjustment of his or her feelings, thoughts and actions towards a new "fusion of horizons" (Gadamer, 1989). This fusion, in turn, makes it possible to produce a more inclusive (vertical) view by transcending what has been previously learned or to produce an alternative (horizontal) view that may displace what the student has previously learned. As a consequence of engagement, both the student and the student's situation may change. Each successful engagement empowers the student's self-authoring capacity to feel, think and act, thereby increasing the student's capacity to "be".

What teachers do: letting students learn

The process of entering into the state of engagement and being cannot be taught explicitly and straightforwardly, nor can it be forced on the student. Learning to be involves the tacit dimension of knowing (Polanyi, 1966). What teachers say about "being" is always the articulated part of it. The articulated part of engagement and being is what students see when students are not a part of it, whereas the inarticulate part requires students to learn as "dwelling" (Plumb, 2008) within what they experience. If the teacher chooses to teach the internal "how" by "telling", the teacher is "attending *from* these internal processes *to* the qualities of things outside" (Polanyi, 1966:14; italics in original). These "outside" articulated qualities are what the processes of engagement and being can mean to students but are not what students can become. To simply "tell" a student how to "be" is to divert attention from the tacit, silent dimension of this concept to appearances, to the identifiable and to what can be expressed.

The liquid processes of experiencing, thinking, acting and feeling that constitute tacit and dynamic being cannot be fully controlled by rational individuals (e.g. teachers). What the teacher must consider when teaching "learning to be" is how to develop a process of "letting students learn", an idea borrowed from Heidegger (1968). To let learn is to provide students with opportunities to become fully engaged in learning as they complete a task or a project, as they solve problems, as they present or perform ideas or actions, as they turn the implicit into the explicit and as they eventually construct their own knowledge and being, thereby producing insight. Students' full engagement in their potential life and career situations come *"only when teachers let go"*, liberating students *"to experience the possibilities in terms of what their engagement might turn out to be"* (Su, 2009:713).

To let students learn does not mean to let them alone. The teacher serves as a facilitator and a designer of *"a set of course activities and assignments that responsibly give learners more control over decisions that affect learning"* (Weimer, 2002:41). A variety of pedagogical activities, including lectures, discussions, conversations, questions, problem solving and co-operative work, may be helpful in this context. For example, the teacher may redesign a lecture by adding small pauses that enable students to detect cognitive conflict and engage in questioning (Albergaria Almeida & Teix-eira-Dias, this volume). Teachers may invite students to design their own concepts of restaurants based on the situation of aesthetic economy; to apply management theories into a basketball team that project students in reality choose to join; or to develop a report on exploring the possibility of improving the library system they use every day. Students are empowered and significantly influenced not by the activities that teachers arrange but by their own ability to engage in and grow from these learning activities.

The positioning of the teacher as facilitator is anchored in the understanding that students are active subjects, the acknowledgment of their current identities and the design of pedagogical activities that provide room for students to use their own subjectivity. A student's "learning to be" does not simply arise from the transmission of knowledge from teachers; rather, it stems from *"the process of thought, discussion, writing, debate, [and] exchange"* (Lusted, 1986:4) that encourages students to engage in the authentic and the unfamiliar. The students enact their own learning activities using their values (feelings), beliefs (thinking) and everyday practices (actions), rather than acting as an audience in the classroom. Students learn not only to be in the sense of their physical presence but also to act as mental operators. They do not merely display and perform what they know; rather, they feel, think and act in ways they can integrate into their lives and careers through engagement and being, working to sustain their existence authentically and meaningfully, as they live with change.

Implications and conclusions

This chapter suggests that higher-education practices cannot be fully sustained through the simple acquisition of skills and knowledge, and that the "being" approach should be incorporated into higher-education learning to adjust to a changing future. Students are expected to learn to deal with authentic-oriented tasks or projects, as well as to construct and develop their personal meanings and existences in a more engaging and reflective mode, to meet the possible challenges of future life and career situations. Learning for oneself by moving beyond disciplinary boundaries ought to be the focus of higher education; this practice will enable students to live authentically and continuously in a reflexive world in an ontologically self-directing manner.

The concept of being has implications for curricula and pedagogy. In developing curricula and pedagogy, what is important and sustainable is not simply the learning of knowledge and skills but also the engagement of students in significant and integrative learning experiences that they will be able to employ when their course of study is over – and that, indeed, will become a part of the students' identities as time goes by. The student and the self, rather than the knowledge of disciplines, should be the focus of the curriculum. The former emphasises the development of students' "learning to be" by searching for relevancy and meaningfulness of learning tasks or projects that either the teacher or the student assigns and that closely relate to real-life complexities and occurrences. The latter, based on the scientific approach to learning by seeking disengaged universal truths, rules, laws, patterns and principles, instead becomes a conceptual resource rather than a set of authoritative narratives. Although contemporary higher education may continue to focus on delivering content, it is necessary to move beyond the current focus on how best to provide curricular content and instead to develop higher-education curricula that facilitate student success in times of change by providing meaningfulness and empowering students. Furthermore, the successful development of "learning to be" practices requires teachers to think differently about teaching and learning because there will be growing pressure from students who want their learning to be more aligned with their personal meanings and values.

Curricular and pedagogical strategies for developing students' being and identity might include the following:

- Explicitly stating the development of student being and identity as a curricular goal and as a process that will allow students to cope with change; this goal may be articulated through a series of teacher training and professional workshops or programmes to help curricular designers and teachers understand the goal of curriculum.

- Moving the goal of developing student being and identity from the periphery to the centre of the curriculum by not only delivering learning-what and learning-how to students but also by asking students to learn why. Teachers encourage students to question possible links between past knowledge and their present and future careers and lives. The design of teaching must move beyond the quantifiable transmission of knowledge and skills to focus upon the invisible development of dynamic action, affect and reflection. Prioritising the invisible student agency makes it possible for various considerations and learning activities to be incorporated into all areas of the curriculum and of teaching.

- Encouraging students, where appropriate, to be aware of their ability to "learn to be" as the key focus of the curriculum; increasing students' self-awareness and responsibility for their own personal development. Teachers help students understand and appreciate the concept of learning for themselves. This concept may be processed by encouraging students to question and reflect on the development of their learning and identity, which must be sustained to meet the challenges of the changing future.

- Developing flexible and liberating learning programmes that emphasise interdisciplinary, multidisciplinary or extra-disciplinary work and moving beyond traditional disciplinary boundaries will allow students to experience both structure and freedom as they learn to pursue and develop personal meanings and identities, empowering them to exercise their autonomy in coping with change. Teachers may consider, for instance, designing and implementing transdisciplinary pedagogical templates (Dobozy *et al.*, this volume).

- Providing a student-centred curriculum in which various pedagogical approaches are used to optimise student engagement, thus inspiring students to feel, reflect and act and thereby activating their abilities of being. Teachers' strategies to engage students' minds, bodies and souls (Brillinger, 1997) must be made meaningful by subjecting them to authentic tasks or projects based on students' life situations. Students integrate their knowledge, competences, values and intentions, and convert them into action within their personal situations.

- Ensuring that assessments are congruent with and reflect the goals of the curriculum. Assessing students' abilities formatively and dynamically by focusing on the dynamic, developmental, and complex character of learning may help to determine whether students are authentically developing effective modes of thought and action and appropriate affective attitudes that facilitate self-direction in the construction of existence.

Consideration ought to be given to the degree to which students and teachers alike perceive their roles in the teaching and learning process as active rather than passive. If students and teachers fail to recognise the importance of "learning to be", this lack of recognition could prevent essential foundational changes in the development of "learning to be" in higher education. The use of the framework of being within higher-education learning can benefit teaching and "learning to be", an ontological state whose dynamism and flexibility can help students to meet sustainably the challenges of changing times.

Acknowledgment

The author acknowledges the support of the National Science Council, R.O.C.

About the author

Yahui Su is Associate Professor at the Teacher Education Center of National Kaohsiung University of Hospitality and Tourism. She can be contacted at this email: yahuisu@hotmail.com

Chapter 12

Building Student Capacity for Reflective Learning

Kayoko Enomoto and Richard Warner

Introduction

In contemporary higher education (HE) contexts, a common aspiration in learning is to equip students with *the ability to self-produce and self-develop knowledge* (Nygaard *et al.*, 2008:34). We argue that this aspiration must be underpinned by a pedagogically viable strategy to shift students' focus away from marks and reduction in workload, towards their learning processes. We propose that building student capacity for reflective learning can lead to this shift in focus. In this chapter, we introduce a curriculum in which a reflective learning model is scaffolded in order to help precipitate this shift.

The aim of this chapter is to explore the pragmatic value of the proposed reflective learning model, as a mechanism for facilitating reflective capacity building on the part of students. Subsequently, it addresses the model's transferability beyond the course in question, given the potential usefulness and relevance of the findings to other discipline areas.

The chapter demonstrates a course curriculum, first-year Japanese, in which generic learning processes are systematically and effectively embedded and scaffolded to bring about reflective learning with a large, diverse student cohort (n=232), comprising traditional, non-traditional and international students. The chapter is principally concerned with students' perceptions of how they were learning, rather than the discipline-based content knowledge which they gained in the course. Therefore, it necessarily focuses on students' learning processes rather than learning product (final marks and achievement test scores). As such, the chapter utilises students' reflective writing as representing process data to understand what actually happened in the process of learning. The chapter begins, however, with a discussion of what the concept of reflective learning involves.

Transforming experience into learning through reflection

Reflective learning is defined here as learning processes facilitated through the practice of contemplation which transform individual experiences into learning. This definition draws upon Kolb's work (1984:41) on experiential learning in which: *"Learning is the process whereby knowledge is created through the transformation of experience. Knowledge results from the combination of grasping and transforming experience"*. Thus, we also consider such transformations in learning processes as valid manifestations of learning itself. In other words, learning is not just manifested through understandings but also in the processes which lead to such understandings. The practice of reflection necessarily involves the close examination of one's own experiences, whilst bringing together one's thoughts and actions in such processes (Bourner, 2003; Ertmer & Newby, 1996). This practice, in turn, can transform every experience into new potential learning. In this sense, reflective learning differs from learning of more discrete discipline-specific knowledge because what is learned in learning processes can be transferable to both planned and unplanned learning scenarios. This view of learning implies that 'what is learned' is potentially broader than 'what is taught' and, with this view, we can empower students to reach their own true learning potential in life.

However, there is a need for a pedagogy which can systematically target the development of reflective learning, because students' views of learning in HE can vary, as is outlined below.

Views of learning in the context of increasing student diversity

The variety of students' differing perceptions of what constitutes learning has become particularly evident in the current context of widening participation in Australian HE. Since the 2009 government implementation of the widening participation strategy, local students from a wide variety of non-traditional backgrounds are taking undergraduate courses, adding to the already existing international student diversity in the classroom. In 2010, after a first course orientation lecture, one non-traditional first-year student stated:

> *"I need to pass this course to get my degree. 50% is a pass. A pass is a degree. So, how much work do you think I need to do to pass this course?"*

In the context of increasing student diversity, such questions are not uncommon today and indicate that some students see the accumulation of prescribed credit units as their sole university learning goal. This evidences a lack of understanding that what they learn from their learning processes can ultimately help reduce their academic burden and improve their marks, whilst also being beneficial to both short- and long-term futures.

Therefore, it is crucial to unpack the value of learning processes as being directly relevant to both their present and future. To do so, we need to move students' focus away from their marks and workload reduction, towards their learning processes. We propose that building students' capacity for reflective learning can help bring about their focus shift. Facilitation of such a shift through reflective learning can be embedded in a scaffolded curriculum, with staged learning processes involving a gradual transfer of control from teacher to student as a course progresses (Enomoto, 2011; Pickard *et al.*, 2011; Warner, 2011). This transfer of control also paves the way for both planned and unplanned learning. As Bourner (2003:267), drawing upon earlier work on reflection by Boud *et al.* (1985), argues: *"Much learning across lifespan is unplanned, experiential and emergent. The key to this sort of learning is reflection, which turns experience into learning"*.

Thus, to prepare students for both planned and unplanned learning, a reflective learning model was designed to engage students in their practice of reflection, without compromising the development of discipline-specific knowledge and skills. Central to this model is the systematic integration into the curriculum of embedded components to facilitate and practise reflection and opportunities to experience interim successes as rewards for such practice. Furthermore, this reflective learning model seeks to decrease students' perceptions of academic burden, rather than adding to them, by scaffolding reflective practice to help students move away from a short-term focus on marks into a longer-term view of learning. However, before introducing our model, we consider three key attributes of the reflective learner that we aim to foster in our pedagogy.

Key attributes of the reflective learner

According to Ertmer and Newby (1996), reflection provides the crucial link between students' thoughts and actions, enabling them to learn from and to take control of their own learning processes. This means that, to begin the process of reflection, students must be able to link their thoughts and actions by reflection (Figure 1). Then, to learn through reflection, students must also be able to engage in reflective learning processes (Figure 1). These processes necessitate students developing autonomous self-regulation, to set goals for themselves, as well as self-efficacy to sustain their motivations and belief that reaching such self-goals is possible. In so doing, they use metacognitive skills to monitor, regulate and control their own thinking, motivations and behaviour, at various points in their learning processes (Pintrich, 2000).

Significantly, to develop such autonomous self-regulation, self-efficacy and metacognitive skills, students must also be able to exercise a deep approach to learning (Figure 1), which presupposes the intention to comprehend material to be learnt and incorporates strategies including breadth of reading and synthesis (Lizzio *et al.*, 2002). Students with such an intention and strategies come to class with some relevant background knowledge and questions to be answered, through conducting previewing and reviewing on a regular basis (Biggs, 1999). This deep approach also involves students developing generic learning skills, such as learning from their errors to create subsequent plans of action, including time management and organisational skills. If effective, these generic skills

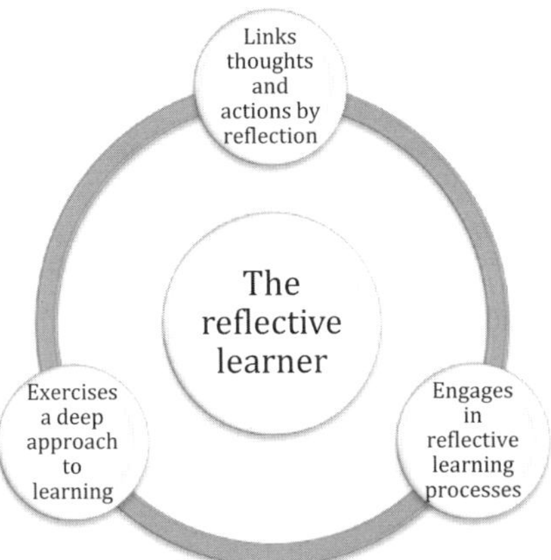

Figure 1: Key attributes of the reflective learner

can ultimately lead to reduction in workload and to increased marks. Furthermore, exercising a deep learning approach in one course can also bring about students' identification of generic/transferable learning skills, as applicable to other courses.

In contrast, a surface approach to learning is characterised more by the acceptance of ideas without critical engagement, utilising such techniques as rote learning, and through storage of ideas in unconnected silos (Lizzio *et al.*, 2002). For example, students with poor time management and organisational skills tend to adopt such rote-based-learning strategies to prepare for their immediate task and assessment (Biggs, 1999). Past research has identified learning environments that could or could not shift students into a deeper approach (Lizzio *et al.*, 2002; Kember & Leung, 1998) to ascertain how to encourage students with less-developed learning skills to adopt deeper processing strategies to achieve long-term quality learning outcomes (Lenstrup, this volume). In this respect, past studies (Bourner, 2003; Peltier *et al.*, 2005) argue that a deep approach to learning is associated with reflective thinking. *"Within the domain of reflective learning, the distinction between surface learning and deep learning is equally applicable… surface learning is associated with unreflective thinking and deep learners, like deep reflective thinkers, find more from their experience"* (Bourner, 2003:271).

Therefore, the ability to exercise a deep approach to learning is a key attribute of a reflective learner, in addition to the abilities of linking thoughts and actions by reflection and of engaging in reflective learning processes to learn through reflection (Figure 1). The nurturing of these three key attributes is crucial to the development of the reflective learner in a curriculum. Yet, in order for these attributes to be developed, we need to scaffold timely and appropriate teacher provisions within the curriculum.

Feeding forward towards reflection

It is not uncommon to see teachers include 'reflection' as an assignment in their courses. However, all too often, such reflection assignments seem to be given without requisite scaffolding, such as timely provision of feedback prior to reflection, objectives of such assignments, and clear instructions and expectations, in order to guide students appropriately to truly experience and benefit from reflective learning. For example, a vague instruction, such as *"Please reflect on what you learned in this project"*, is likely to draw an equally vague reflection, such as *"I learned a lot from this project"* – particularly in first-year courses. This is because many students do not yet know how exactly to reflect without any provision of concrete starter questions to prompt their reflection.

Specific starter questions, such as "Among the study methods you used in learning new vocabulary, which methods do you think worked best and least for you, and why?" or "Are there any study methods you would have liked to use but couldn't, and why?", are more likely to raise and direct students' awareness to reflect upon and cross-examine their own experiences. To ensure continual development of learning, we need to create an environment where students' awareness of reflection is prompted through scaffolded teacher provisions. This requires beginning our curricula with the explicit provision of reflective learning techniques.

Bourner (2003) proposes the use of "searching questions" as guiding questions that scaffold the students' reflective learning process in a curriculum. To build student capacity for reflective learning, we need to assist students to autonomously produce, develop and ask such searching questions of the content of their own experience, and then to translate their reflective thoughts into subsequent actions (Bourner, 2003; Ertmer & Newby, 1996). As such, it is imperative that we begin with explicit instructions, containing both usable teacher feedback and useful starter questions to prompt reflection. Then, to guide students to distinguish consciously between their reflective thoughts and the content of their experience (Bourner, 2003), students must be told they will not be assessed for the content of their experience but for their ability to reflect upon what they have done with such experiential content. At the same time, we must also make explicit to students the objectives and benefits of given reflective learning tasks, to ensure that they fully understand why they are asked to practise reflection in a discipline-based course. This is necessary because some students appear to believe that the sole learning goal of a discipline-based course is to develop those discipline-specific skills.

Thus, to help build students' reflective learning capacity, a reflective learning model should be designed to begin with the stage where these three teacher provisions (usable feedback, useful starter questions and explicit instructions) are scaffolded. The following section also describes these further; however, first, it presents the curriculum context where our reflective learning model was implemented with students, before discussing our model.

A reflective learning model

Japanese 1A, the largest foreign language course at the University of Adelaide (n=232 in 2011), is a first-year beginners' course for non-native speakers with no or little knowledge of Japanese. Around 50% of the cohort in 2011 were international students from various cultures and first-language backgrounds, whereas the remaining 50% consisted of local students from both traditional and non-traditional backgrounds. The non-traditional group included mature age, alternative pathway and first-generation university students, who also tended to be from low socio-economic and/or non-English-speaking backgrounds. At the same time, 80% of the same cohort were studying for various non-Arts degrees across the University (Engineering, Science, Health Science, Psychology, Finance, Commerce, Education, Law).

To build the capacity for reflective learning within the diverse cohort in this Japanese language course, three embedded components (Teacher Feedback, Study Action Plan (SAP) and Personal Reflections (PR)) were placed between assessment tests, in the order depicted in Figure 2. Completion of SAP (1 & 2) and PR (1 & 2) was counted as 3% of their final mark.

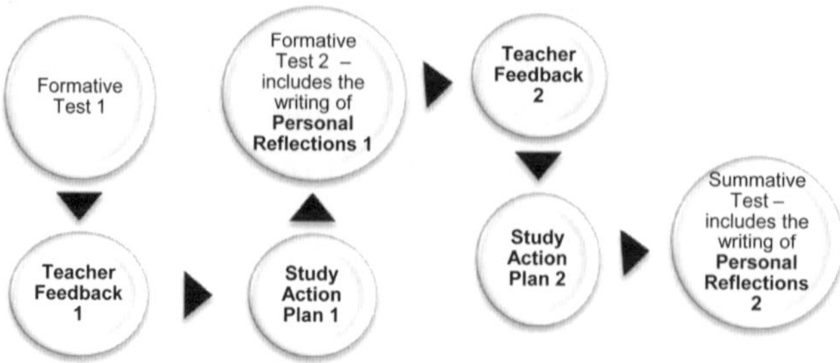

Figure 2: Order of embedded components in the Japanese course

Our reflective learning model draws on Kolb's (1984) model of experiential learning: 1. concrete experience, 2. reflective observation of that experience, 3. abstract conceptualisation based on that reflection, and 4. active experimentation of those new concepts (Figure 3). This reflective learning model mirrors the sequence of these four stages, through the two reflective learning cycles scaffolded in the Japanese curriculum (Figure 3). We now discuss details of the aforementioned three embedded components, referring first to Cycle 1, then to Cycle 2 (Figure 3).

Teacher Feedback: After students "experience" Formative Test 1, the test papers are returned in class to individual students together with the personalised Teacher Feedback 1 form completed by the teacher. Then, students are required to understand the teacher's feedback and this process facilitates their "reflection" of the "experience" (i.e. Formative Test 1) they had. The teacher feedback form is designed to make feedback timely, simple and clear. So, this form covers all specific skills areas tested in Formative Test 1 (kanji characters, vocabulary and grammar) and all areas of weakness to be worked upon for Formative Test 2 are marked by the teacher with a tick in the appropriate boxes.

Study Action Plan (SAP): An empty hard copy of the SAP 1 form is also distributed to students when the (above) Teacher Feedback 1 form is given to them. To help students establish clear linkages between their received feedback and SAP, both forms cover identical study areas (kanji characters, vocabulary and grammar). The SAP form shows a list of study methods and strategies in relation to each study area, as well as an empty space where students can create and write their original study methods and strategies. Using the given feedback, students are required to devise their own SAP, by deciding which study methods and strategies they

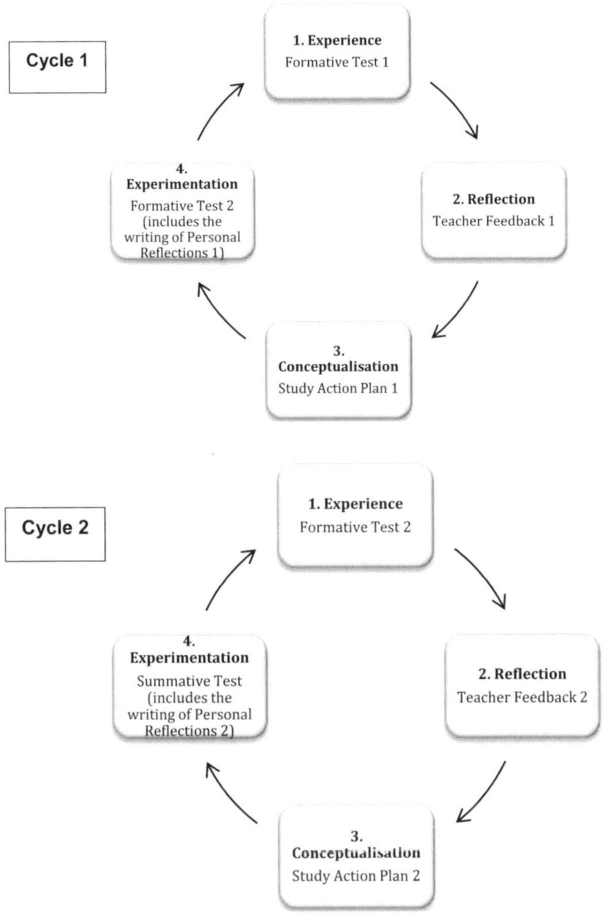

Figure 3: Reflective learning model scaffolded in the Japanese curriculum

choose to adopt to prepare for Formative Test 2. This is done by ticking boxes on the given list of study methods and strategies and/or by writing their original methods and strategies in the empty space. During this process, students are to "conceptualise" their subsequent study methods and learning strategies for themselves. Students complete the SAP form outside the class (they can consult the teacher if needed) and submit it to the teacher in class within one week of receiving the feedback and SAP forms. Students keep a copy of the submitted SAP to use to follow through and implement their own action plans.

Significantly, the study methods and strategies listed on the SAP form include both surface learning approach (e.g. rote writing of kanji characters and simple memorisation of textbook vocabulary lists) and deep learning approach (e.g. previewing, reviewing and relating new information to previous knowledge). This is done to allow students to "experiment" on their self-selected study methods and strategies (surface or deep approach) in Formative Test 2 at the end of Cycle 1. In doing so, they can discover for themselves the effects of the methods and strategies they adopted in relation to each study area (kanji characters, vocabulary and grammar). Then, in commencing Cycle 2, such "experience" (of discovery) in Formative Test 2 can be taken into consideration by students, when reflecting on Teacher Feedback 2 and when devising their SAP 2 to prepare for the final Summative Test.

Personal Reflections (PR): The submission of the SAPs is followed by the writing of Personal Reflections in English. Students write PR 1 during the Formative Test 2 in Cycle 1 and PR 2 during the Summative Test in Cycle 2. Each PR is designed to encourage students to follow through with their own SAP and to emphasise their accountability for their submitted SAP as a study contract. At the same time, the PRs provide students with opportunities to put into writing their reflections upon their behaviour, motivations and achievements, together with the relevance of different study methods and strategies to their own needs. Sufficient time (up to 30 minutes) is allocated specifically for the PR writing during the test. This is because students' perceptions of having a lack of time to write can result in blank or very brief reflective commentary (Enomoto, 2010).

Importantly, students are provided with explicit instructions and explanation of objectives in relation to the submission of SAP and the writing of PR in advance (when the Teacher Feedback and the blank SAP forms are given to them). Students are notified that they are assessed only on two criteria: the length of their commentary (200–250 words) and their ability to reflect upon how they are learning. They are also told that no marks will be deducted for linguistic errors or stylistic/structural shortcomings in their English writing. This is done to ensure that students do not see the PR writing as an 'English essay' assignment and to encourage students to practise reflection by focusing essentially on the content of their PRs. At the same time, they are also given a set of five starter questions for their PRs, to help both raise awareness of reflection and to prompt their reflection at the beginning of each reflective learning cycle (Figure 2), as follows:

You will be asked to write your own "personal reflections" on how you have been learning Japanese independently outside the class, involving reflective analyses of your own study methods you had chosen to adopt in your Study Action Plan 1. You may include:

1. *Any study methods that you devised which have worked or failed, and why?*
2. *Any difficulties that you may have had and/or overcome in your study, and how?*
3. *What you are happy to have done or what you regret not to have done in your study, and why?*
4. *Self-feedback on your progress and performance in relation to what you have done or not to have done in your study,*
5. *How and what areas in particular you are going to study for the next assessment.*

In this way, to build student capacity for reflective learning, this model was designed to enable students to follow Kolb's four stages of experiential learning (1984), using the three embedded components (Teacher Feedback, SAP and PR).

Findings and discussion

Of 232 students enrolled in Japanese 1A in 2011, 223 students wrote PR1 during the Formative Test 2 (Cycle 1 in Figure 3) and 216 students wrote PR 2 during the Summative Test (Cycle 2 in Figure 3). Overall, we found no discernible differences between the students' PR 1 and PR 2 writing in terms of their reflectivity, apart from one tendency – PR 1 tended to contain less specific details of a greater number of study methods, whereas PR 2 tended to contain more specific details of fewer study methods. This shows that many students had found, after trial and error, their own individual study methods suitable to their specific needs as the course developed.

A phenomenographic approach was used to analyse the students' reflective writing data. This qualitative approach enables a collective (as opposed to an individual) analysis of the range of experiences, perceptions and understandings held within any given group, by categorising perceptions of individuals which "emerge" from the data, into specific "categories of description" (Åkerlind, 2005). Thus, in this study, this phenomenographic approach involved the reading and re-reading of all PRs (n=439; [PR 1, n=223] + [PR 2, n=216]) to group the excerpts into the emerging categories of experiences, conceptualisations and understandings, searching for the key themes and issues widely recognised by the students. Five qualitatively distinct descriptive categories emerged from the analysis.

Category 1: Non-reflective learners

Firstly, although there were no blank or markedly brief PRs, we found a very small minority of students demonstrating little by way of reflection. These can be mainly characterised in two ways: those who merely listed what they did/did not do without reflection; and those who did not take ownership of their own learning strategies and failed to reflect upon this. It could be said that these students failed to link their thoughts and actions by reflection – the first key attribute of the reflective learner (Figure 1). Furthermore, such students typically followed rote-based surface approaches to learning, without engaging in reflective learning processes and exercising deeper learning approaches – the other two key attributes of the reflective learner. This correlates to not moving beyond the first "experience" stage of the reflective learning model (Figure 3).

> *"Although my score of Japanese is not high, I learnt a lot in Japanese class. Firstly, I read and write new vocabulary many times until I remember them. Secondly, I downloaded the voice tools…"*
> (PR 2, Student A, international student)

> *"To review grammar, I did all exercises in the book. The only problem I found is there are too few exercises for us to do… So, I didn't spend more time in reviewing Japanese… because I have an essay due and also a presentation to prepare."*
> (PR 2, Student B, international student)

All of these non-reflective commentaries were produced by students whose course attendance had been poor. Therefore, it is very unlikely that they had been fully utilising the three embedded components (Teacher Feedback, SAP and PR) to practise reflection in the course.

Category 2: Adopting a deep approach to learning

The second category that emerged from the vast majority of students' comments is that, in developing their reflectivity, they reported use of the provided starter questions to prompt their reflection, linking their thoughts and actions – the first key attribute of the reflective learner (Figure 1). Students also commented that they discovered, revised and even created their own study methods and learning strategies as a result of self-monitoring and assessing their own learning needs and actions. This is achieved through developing their autonomous self-regulation and metacognitive skills, while engaging in reflective learning processes to learn through reflection – the second key attribute of the reflective learner (Figure 1).

> *"I've taken advantage of some of the free downloadable applications on the iPhone. This technique I feel has yielded the best results for me… I feel I'm really strong with both in writing and recognising scripts."*
>
> (PR 1, Student C)

> *"I tried substituting some Japanese words into my daily vocabulary to have a stronger association between the words and their meanings."*
>
> (PR 1, Student D)

In addition, such students' comments characteristically showed the evidence of adopting and exercising a deep approach to their learning – the third key attribute of the reflective learner (Figure 1).

> *"In order to study the required vocabulary, I typed out all the words… and grouped them into groups that represent [groupings] such as jobs, places and objects… putting them into groups and studying them together makes better sense… In order to make sure I know my grammar well I came up with a few sentences of my own and translated them. I used Google Translate to check my answers."*
>
> (PR 1, Student E, international student)

> *"I had found many aspects of both grammar and vocabulary learning difficult... I overcome this by writing my own notes which grouped the grammar concepts as well as being written in a way that's easily understood by me."*
>
> (PR 2, Student F)

In adopting a deep approach to learning, it was clear from students' comments that they exercised 'critical' reflection. Students described that they effectively solved problems and issues by taking a critical attitude in monitoring and evaluating their own study methods, behaviour and motivations.

> *"My Japanese is comparable to a patchwork blanket eaten by the moths of ignorance. To solve this, I have tried using cue cards to help improve my vocabulary... study sentence structure by reading course materials and using the voice tools..."*
>
> (PR1, Student G)

> *"One main difficulty in learning Japanese was overcoming dependency on roma-ji [=romanised version of Japanese scripts], which was continually hinted as hindering to my progress. This was overcome by use of mnemonics in my study to create unique methods of remembering [Japanese] scripts."*
>
> (PR1, Student H, non-traditional student)

Thus, these comments provide strong evidence that the reflective learning model was effective in developing the students' reflective learning capabilities, which, in turn, encouraged them to engage in reflective learning processes and to exercise a deep approach to learning. Therefore, this category evidences that students were developing all of the three key attributes of the reflective learner (Figure 1), following the full cycles of the reflective learning model (Figure 3).

Category 3: Developing generic/transferable learning skills

This third category emerged from a majority of comments that the reflective learning model effectively developed students' generic learning skills. Even when students stated that they did not exactly achieve their self-set goals, they appeared to be learning from their errors to create future plans of action. They were transforming their experiences into learning, seeing their failure as a 'chance' to learn – an opportunity rather than an impediment to learning. Such an attitude towards one's own errors and failures is one essential facet of the resilient learner.

> *"I believe studying for Japanese has not only helped the subject itself, it has helped my study methods as a whole. Going from learning some in class to studying every day at home has improved my self-discipline and character as a whole."*
>
> (PR 2, Student I, non-traditional student)

> *"One method I've come up with is by putting cards with words from the vocabulary lists along with descriptive pictures, all around my room. This method has helped a lot… and now [I am] not being afraid to make mistakes."*
>
> (PR1, Student J)

Moreover, students' comments further demonstrated their identification of generic learning skills as transferable skills, by understanding through their own experience of success that such skills ultimately reduce workload and improve marks.

> *"I am content with the methods I had chosen, as they had given me a lot of free time to do other activities and continue with other studies."*
>
> (PR1, Student K, non-traditional student)

> *"I will also use the studying methods that I learned from Japanese on my other subjects."*
>
> (PR 1, Student L, international student)

> *"I learned a lot of study methods and experiences… I met many difficulties… but I finally overcome them. I am so happy to learn Japanese and from this learning process. I learned how to learn independently and how to study effectively, which are helpful to my further study."*
>
> (PR 2, Student M, international student)

Therefore, these comments indicate that the model was effective in unpacking the value of learning processes as directly relevant to both their present and future learning, suggesting that students were developing all of the three key attributes (Figure 1), completing the cycles of the reflective learning model (Figure 3).

Category 4: Strengthening self-efficacy in learning

One encouraging category also emerged from the majority of comments. That is, self-efficacy in learning was clearly strengthened through this reflective learning model, for many students. The majority of comments showed that both distinction-level and pass-level students alike were setting their learning goals at their own levels, taking ownership of their own learning. Students also described their experience of success in achieving their current goals and such descriptions of achieving interim successes were typically followed by their strong motivations and convictions to follow through with their SAP to achieve their next self-set goals. In so doing, they were developing all of the three key attributes of the reflective learner (Figure 1), following the cycles of the reflective learning model (Figure 3).

> *"I am more confident from my Japanese learning journey. I will continue my study methods as it helps me to build firm foundation."*
>
> (PR 1, Student N, international student)

> *"In order to get a better mark in the final exam, I'll take my strength to follow through with study plan, I will use my good approaches still after [the final exam]."*
>
> (PR1, Student O, international student)

These comments indicate that this model successfully allowed for the scaffolded development of self-efficacy on the part of the students. This is significant because students with higher self-efficacy are likely to believe in their ability to perform well and therefore be more willing to challenge themselves to accomplish more difficult tasks (Bandura, 1977).

Category 5: Identifying the need for time management and organisational skills

An interesting category also emerged from a minority of students' comments. They referred commonly to lack of time management and organisational skills preventing them from following their action plans.

> "I feel I am learning poorly due to my own terrible organisation skills; for example, I didn't even realise there was an exam on today… I regret not completing the homework as this has not given me a good base of knowledge to work from…"
>
> (PR 1, Student P)

> "The main problem I have is time management. I think if I arrange my time better I would be more than able to improve my test scores."
>
> (PR 1, Student Q)

In so doing, however, they were able to identify clearly through reflection why such skills are important for their success in learning, indicating that they were able to link their thoughts and actions by reflection – one key attribute of the reflective learner (Figure 1). Furthermore, because they did devise and submit their action plans through conceptualising (to varying degrees) their next study methods and strategies, it can be said that they had progressed to the third "conceptualisation" stage from the "reflection" stage, but failed to move beyond it (Figure 3). In other words, these students did not involve themselves in any action implementation to develop the other two key attributes of the reflective learner (Figure 1), to move forward towards the final "experimentation" stage (Figure 3).

Summary of findings

In summarising the findings, an important message can be gained from the students' reflective writing as a whole. With the systematic provision of the three embedded components, as set out in this reflective learning model (Figure 3), students can shift from a marks focus to a learning-process focus. This is encouraging, because the students seemed to be looking beyond the immediate tasks and seeing the relevance of reflective learning in something they could utilise over and above this particular learning context.

> *"I think this kind of learning will stay with me forever."*
>
> (PR1, Student R, non-traditional student)

> *"Independent learning and overcoming the difficulties are learned from last few months and my learning ability has improved and I hope that I will learn more from the future study, not only the knowledge, but also the ability of studying."*
>
> (PR 1, Student S, international student)

These comments clearly illustrate that the reflective learning model developed students' understanding and valuation of their own learning processes, so that they see learning as not all about marks and passing courses – 50 per cent is a degree! Thus, the findings from the students' reflective writing suggest that our reflective learning model, mirroring the four-stage sequence of Kolb's (1984) experiential learning theory (Figure 3), effectively developed students' ability for reflective learning to transform their individual experiences into new learning. Whilst successfully engaging the diverse student cohort with new ways of thinking and doing, the two reflective learning cycles enabled students both to feedback and to feed-forward. Students were integrating this new learning with the already known to prepare for their ongoing learning.

Conclusions and implications

This chapter has examined the pragmatic value of a reflective learning model in a first-year language course. Qualitative analyses of students' reflective writing demonstrate that the reflective learning model, integrating scaffolds to practise reflection with opportunities to experience interim successes as rewards, effectively developed students' reflective learning skills to learn how to learn. The students' reflective comments strongly indicate that the course curriculum design, integrating reflective learning, helped students transform individual experiences into learning. At the same time, the model encouraged students to understand and value their learning processes, not just marks, as valid manifestations of 'learning' directly relevant to their futures.

The specific implications of these findings indicate that, in order to build student capacity for reflective learning, it is necessary to:

- Provide opportunities for students to practise reflection and to be rewarded for it through experiencing a series of small successes in a scaffolded curriculum.

- Bring out and raise students' awareness consciously to ask reflective searching questions of their learning experiences to enable them to conceptualise 'how' they are learning.

- Unpack the value of learning processes, not just marks, as directly relevant to both students' present and future learning through scaffolded reflective learning practice.

This chapter has demonstrated that enabling students to build their capacity for reflective learning, transferable beyond the Japanese course to other subject/discipline areas, can be a realistic goal, even with a large first-year student cohort. This is with the proviso that such capacity building is systematically scaffolded within curricula, rather than an adjunct to each course. This chapter has also shown that such a reflective learning model (see Hager, this volume, and Holtham, this volume, for further reflective learning scenarios) can succeed in developing the reflective learning capabilities of different types of student groups (traditional, non-traditional and international). Whilst the findings presented here are limited to the context of a language course, we believe the scaffolding principle inherent in our reflective learning model is not language-course specific but has the potential for application and implementation in other disciplines.

About the authors

Kayoko Enomoto is a Lecturer at the Centre for Asian Studies at the University of Adelaide, Australia. She can be contacted at this email address: kayoko.enomoto@adelaide.edu.au

Richard Warner is a Lecturer in the School of Education at the University of Adelaide, Australia. He can be contacted at this email address: richard.warner@adelaide.edu.au

Preparing for Learning: Incorporating Academic Literacies in a Pathway Programme

Helen Benzie

Introduction: preparation for learning in higher education

This chapter focuses on the transitional space between a Pathway programme, providing academic preparation for international students, and the disciplinary programme they enter in an Australian university. The Pathway institution delivers a direct-entry programme referred to here as the "Pathway programme". The disciplinary programme, a coursework master's degree in Commerce, is referred to as the "Degree programme". The purpose of this chapter is to explore the relationship between the curricula in both programmes, highlighting some of their connections and approaches to learning. Specifically, it asks: to what extent, and in which ways, is the Pathway programme providing language and academic preparation suitable for learning in the Degree programme?

It is a common view that learners should possess academic skills, including the ability to think critically and analytically, and communicate ideas clearly, before they begin higher education. These skills form a significant part of the academic preparation provided in secondary school or in preparation programmes.

However, a social practices approach to academic preparation proposes that multiple and plural literacies are required in higher education, that they can only be acquired over time and that they are largely acquired within the academic discipline (Russell *et al.*, 2009). This approach, usually identified by the pluralised term "academic literacies", emphasises an awareness of the institutional context and of ideological and discursive features of the writing required of learners (Street, 2005).

Preparation for university study has come into focus with the shift from an élite to a mass higher-education system and the resulting increasing numbers of non-traditional entrants (Doherty & Singh, 2007). The presence on campus of students from a wide range of learning and social backgrounds has given rise to the notion that students need to learn how to learn in preparation for university, coming under the broader agenda of *"widening participation"* (Russell *et al.*, 2009:396). The expectation that students should be better prepared for academic learning is aligned with the idea that the responsibility is not theirs alone and that institutions should adapt to meet the needs of an increasingly diverse student body (Zepke & Leach, 2005). In Australia, one institutional response has been the provision of Pathway programmes.

Pathway programmes are situated within or outside higher-education institutions and often delivered by separate technical or English-language colleges. Some provide a foundation year of study and bridge students into a degree by including some content instruction. Others, like the one discussed here, are specifically for international students, providing linguistic, cultural and academic preparation for university study. These programmes are usually situated in the English Language Intensive Courses for Overseas Students (ELICOS) sector. This implies a specific curriculum focus on English for Academic Purposes as distinct from disciplinary content. Teachers are English Language specialists, often with limited control over curriculum, delivering *"pre-packaged curricular materials"* (Doherty & Singh, 2005:69). Universities and Pathway programmes have formalised relationships but this tends to refer to student movement from one to another and does not always extend to interaction or collaboration at curriculum level (Benzie, 2011). It has been noted that Australian education sectors tend to operate as silos, each delivering its own distinct product with little interaction between institutions (McLaughlin & Mills, 2011). This segregation provides a significant challenge for curriculum designers who might not have access to detailed information about learners' future studies.

Research on the first-year experience (Krause *et al.*, 2005) has not specifically focused on Pathway programmes, assuming rather that most students have completed high-school studies and then entered first-year undergraduate higher education. While specific cohorts, such as post-graduate coursework students, can make up significant numbers of the student body, it is often assumed that they are already familiar with the discipline they are entering and require only a brief introduction to the new learning culture.

Curricula in Pathway programmes are often based on imagined essentialised differences in learning cultures (Doherty & Singh, 2005). For example, the Western learning style is often viewed as being more critical, implying that non-Western learners are deficient (Doherty & Singh, 2005). This "othering" of international students works to position them, like other marginalised groups (see Branch & Martina, this volume) and like the Pathway college itself, as outside the mainstream, on the margins of the academic community. It denies learners cultural capital and might affect their ability to adapt to the processes and practices in the university.

At the same time, by teaching generic skills assumed to be transferrable, Pathway curricula aim to inculcate learners into a version of academic practice characterised by uniformity across contexts (Yazbeck, 2008). While transfer of skills might be an aspect of preparing for university learning, it has been shown to be inadequate as a model for the process of transitioning to higher education (Haggis, 2003; Wingate, 2006). Such approaches fail to factor in difference or allow for multiple points of view. They can, for instance, lead to learners gaining the impression that there is little variation across disciplines, ignoring the many different interpretations of practices and genres in the university such as tutorial participation and the academic essay.

From the perspective of the higher-education disciplines where the emphasis is on preparation for professional employment, learners' prior knowledge and experience are not always taken into consideration (Tran, 2010). As in Pathway contexts, assumptions are made about student learning styles based on perceptions of their cultural or learning backgrounds. The challenge for disciplinary curricula is to develop content which is accessible from a wide variety of prior learning experiences, while at the same time delivering content and skills required by the professions. This suggests that knowledge of learning in Pathway programmes could inform the development of disciplinary curricula which are more inclusive of the needs of international students and which prepare them more fully for their future professional lives.

Much current learning in Pathway contexts sees learners as requiring a set of skills that will be generally applicable and teachers as experts in English language and academic skills. In the Degree context, where there is a focus on disciplinary theory and practices, learners are assumed to be already prepared. The role of lecturers as disciplinary experts is to deliver content rather than to explain how that knowledge can be integrated into learners' individual experiences. Under these conditions, the existence of Pathway programmes relies on a perception that language and academic skills can be learned and ought to be taught outside the discipline.

However, other versions of preparatory learning are possible. One of these introduces learners to a meta-language which makes academic practices more explicit. According to Thesen (2001:143), acquiring meta-knowledge is a way of bridging into the abstract language of the academy. It involves teaching in such a way that learners verbalise what they already know in relation to the new ways of knowing that are being introduced. By being able to relate the discourses learners preparing for university already possess to those they are learning, and knowing how those relate to themselves and society, learners develop a meta-language. A meta-language offers an index of discourses, of cultural capital and identity, thus making more explicit the practices and approaches to be found in the context of the university. Such an approach would require explicit critique of tasks or at least an introduction to boundary practices (Wenger, 1998) which link learners' knowledge of genres and practices to those they will be expected to produce in future study. This linking could explore a meta-language, developing ways of making explicit and questioning the practices and genres of the academy. Also required would be bridging (James, 2010) or pushing learning to abstract levels through reflection on genres and how they require adaptation in different contexts.

Through an examination of curricula at both a Pathway programme and a Degree programme, this chapter offers some alternative approaches to the preparation for learning that takes place in a Pathway programme. I begin by introducing academic literacies in a framework which is applicable to analysis of approaches to learning. I then apply this framework to learning in the two programmes, suggesting changes to curricula. These suggestions could enable learners to adapt to the particular disciplinary practices and handle the social meanings and identity changes that may arise as they study in the new learning context. These changes could also better prepare learners for the complexity and fluidity of practices in their future employment.

Learning and academic literacies in higher education

Learning involves a complex mix of individual and interpersonal processes influenced by both intentional and incidental factors (Nygaard *et al.*, 2008). This chapter is influenced by contextual theories of learning (Bruner, 1996; Kolb, 1984; Lave & Wenger, 1991) which consider that the environment in which learning takes place and the learners' interaction with that environment are key factors in positive outcomes.

At postgraduate level, learning requires more than the development of advanced disciplinary knowledge and the skills to apply that knowledge (Bitzer, 2011). It involves the development of the learner over time, including the development of critical analytical thinking, reflective thinking, an expectation of independence and the ability to take responsibility for learning. The development of the capacity for reflective learning is a key consideration as it allows learners to integrate new knowledge and skills into those generated in prior learning and experiences (Kolb, 1984). Learners who can more easily incorporate new knowledge into existing frameworks in these ways are able to continue to apply that learning in their future experiences.

Language and learning

Preparation for learning involves many different processes but the development of academic language and learning is paramount as learning involves more than the development of disciplinary knowledge. A broad focus that goes beyond skills and socialisation and incorporates an awareness of institutional power structures can better prepare learners not only for learning in higher education but for future lives. The field of academic language and learning has arisen out of an assumption that learners, unfamiliar with academic contexts, can benefit from specific instruction in the practices of the academy. Underpinning much of the work in academic language and learning is the academic literacies approach (Lea & Street, 1998). Growing out of a series of studies of student writing practices, this approach has been widely used in subsequent investigations of student writing. However, it is also more generally applicable to understandings of learning, particularly when learners are transitioning to higher education – both because of the predominance of writing as a practice for assessment in higher education and because it is inextricably tied up with learning, meaning making and learner identity.

The academic literacies framework

The academic literacies approach is relevant to an investigation of curricula in Pathway programs as it draws on a continuum of different theories which have developed over time as new insights into preparing for learning in higher education have become available. This investigation into where and to what extent these theories are evident in the Pathway curriculum and in its future learning context: the Degree programme explores the potential for a shift to increased emphasis on academic literacies.

Table 1 shows Lea & Street's (1998) three-level framework for theorising student writing in higher education as (a) study skills, (b) socialisation into the academic culture and (c) academic literacies. Their original ideas have been further developed, particularly by Lillis (2003), who contributes the theories of language included in the table.

The first model in the framework, study skills, assumes learners need to acquire a set of skills which they can then apply in new learning contexts. This model, based in behavioural psychology, sees literacy learning as mainly technical and instrumental, and as positioned external to the learner (Lea & Street, 1998).

With insights available through constructivist education and anthropology, the academic socialisation model emerged as a counter to the insensitivity to learners' diverse backgrounds contained in the study skills model (Duff, 2007). Moving away from an emphasis on language form, this model takes account of the context of learning and learners' need to re-orient themselves to a new culture of learning as they begin to study in higher education.

Model	Issues with the model	Theory of language	Curriculum focus
(a) Study skills	Insensitive, treating learners as deficient	Language as a transparent and autonomous system, the elements of which are acquired by individuals	Explicit teaching of surface features of language
(b) Socialisation into academic culture	Assumes homogeneous academic culture	Language as discourse practices which individual learners must gradually come to learn implicitly	Teaching as implicit induction into established disciplinary discourse practices
(c) Academic literacies	No clearly defined pedagogy	Language as socially situated discourse practices which are ideologically inscribed	Literacy demands of the curriculum on learners are complex; it is necessary to switch practices among different settings, to use language appropriate to each setting, and to handle the social meanings and identities that arise

Table 1: The academic literacies framework
Adapted from Lea & Street (1998) and Lillis (2003)

Subsequent research into the genres of the academy exposed the myth of stable, predictable disciplinary cultures (Hyland, 2009; Swales, 2004) and gave rise to the third model: academic literacies. This view of learning appreciates the contested nature of disciplinary practices and the need for learners to negotiate a variety of genres, fields, practices and identities (Lea & Street, 1998). It underlines the importance of an awareness of learners' backgrounds and the unpredictability and internal variation of the learning context being entered. An issue with the academic literacies model is that it has focused more on critique of earlier models and less on outlining pedagogical approaches. This chapter attempts to fill that gap by providing some suggested changes in a Pathway programme incorporating features of an academic literacies model.

Influenced by research on situated learning (Lave & Wenger, 1991), the academic literacies model suggests that learning involves engaging in the social practices and contexts of a particular *"community of practice"* (Lave & Wenger, 1991:69). Jacobs (2005:476) defines communities of practice as *"groups of practitioners who work as a community in a certain domain"*, which in the university describes an academic discipline. Learning within a discipline requires access to specific discourses. Gee (2005:21) defines discourses as *"ways of combining and integrating language, actions, interactions, ways of thinking, believing, valuing"* and then using a range of tools to identify oneself and act as a member of a social group. The concept of discourse is important as it suggests communication is about more than language, is always situated in a context and involves identity.

Importantly, the academic literacies model is able to encapsulate the two earlier parts of the approach. With its focus on the surface features of language, the study skills model can only go so far to explain transition to learning in higher education. Researchers have alerted practitioners to the problems with teaching genres outside their disciplinary contexts (Wardle, 2009). Wingate (2006), for instance, claims that learning through separate study skills courses is ineffective because students have difficulty applying generic skills to the actual learning processes in the disciplines. However, the application of skills is included in the context of the academic socialisation model which is likewise included in the academic literacies model (Lea & Street, 1998). While the different models originate in different paradigms, keeping them all in play at the same time allows for an understanding of the complexity of academic practices. For example, this juxtaposition allows micro-aspects, such as a focus on surface features of language, to be retained in the macro-context inherent in the notion of academic literacies (Turner, 2003). Central to academic literacy is language and its use in a social context. These understandings of the contexts of learning and the concept of discourse thus help to overcome the difficulty of separating language from its contexts. They allow for multiple concurrent practices.

With this awareness of the situated nature of genres, work in academic language and learning has begun to focus on embedding academic literacies in the disciplines (Jacobs, 2005; Wingate *et al.*, 2011). A major issue in this work is how to make visible for learners the tacit knowledge which disciplinary practitioners have acquired in a gradual apprenticeship into the discipline. Strategies for unlocking that tacit knowledge include "*developing institutional discursive spaces*" (Jacobs, 2005:485) for collaboration between academic literacy and disciplinary specialists. Kokkinn and Mahar (2011), for instance, describe one such institutional space as a three-way collaboration between disciplinary, academic literacy and information literacy specialists.

The potential for collaboration is limited, however, when Pathway programmes are delivered in separate locations. This institutional structure is unlikely to change, given the convenience to internationalised higher education of an arrangement where learners from overseas, perceived to be underprepared, are provided with additional English and academic skills tuition. It is curriculum change, therefore, that can most easily provide more appropriate preparation for learners entering higher education via a Pathway programme.

The study

In this section, data selected from a larger study is analysed. The original study investigated the transition experiences of a group of learners who, in 2007, progressed from a Pathway programme into a postgraduate coursework Commerce degree in an Australian university. The aim was to understand how learning processes were presented and understood by learners in each context. Data were generated firstly from course information documents because they outlined requirements, indicating course content and processes. At the Pathway programme the document was called the *Pathway Coursebook*. In the Degree programme, *Course Information Booklets* from Accounting and Finance courses were selected as curriculum documents.

Perspectives on curricula were then obtained through semi-structured interviews with 11 student participants who discussed their experiences at two points in time, the first as they completed a Pathway programme (interview 1) and the second about ten-weeks later, after they had begun to study in the Degree programme (interview 2). For reasons of space, extracts are included here from only six of the participants. Pseudonyms were assigned as Kazuo, a Japanese male, Skye, Judy and Donna, three Chinese females, Clark, a Chinese male and Vijay, an Indian male.

Applying the academic literacies framework

The experience of studying in the Pathway programme provides a space where learners are able to prepare for further study. During the duration of a ten-week course they are able to make connections with other students from overseas. These friendships are important because they are likely to remain as they enter the university, providing social continuity at a time when academic learning aspects of their transition might be changing. Purely by spending some time living and studying in the Australian cultural environment, learners can adjust themselves to the context. These benefits of the Pathway learning experience can be further extended by incorporating academic literacies into the programmes.

In the discussion below, I explore aspects of the two programmes as they apply to the academic literacies framework described in Table 1. Drawing on curriculum documents and learners' interview responses, I address in turn the three models: study skills, socialisation into the academic culture and academic literacies.

Study skills

There are several indications in both Pathway and Degree programme curriculum documents that a study skills model is assumed. A comparison of reading sources, further discontinuity between the programmes and the way academic writing is described indicate the expectation that learners will apply a set of generic skills across programmes.

Reading sources

A comparison of the reading sources required of learners reveals very different choices. At the Pathway setting, required reading includes articles from popular magazines such as *New Scientist* and *The Economist*. Aside from the research report task, which expects learners to research sources in their own disciplines, discussion and writing tasks are based on these popular science sources. This choice of popular science reading sources has the potential to broaden learners' vocabulary and familiarise them with concepts of current interest in the community. While the popular science genre, according to Hyland (2009:173) *"must be seen as [a] key element of academic discourse"*, it is nevertheless absent from the reading lists of the Degree programme. Instead, the required readings listed for the Degree courses are commercially published textbooks on aspects of Accounting or Finance. This reliance on textbooks rather than magazines or journal articles as core reading is not indicated in the Pathway programme, where students are required to read between one and nine magazine articles on a range of different topics each week.

Participants commented on this difference between reading sources. Donna pointed out that, for her, the range of topics increased the level of difficulty:

> *"Ah no, I think   I, I found some [Pathway course] reading. It's more difficult than my textbook… My textbook is easy, is easy to understand."*
> (Donna interview 2)

Kazuo, who had mentioned in the first interview that he enjoyed the range of reading topics, explained why the textbook was more easily understandable:

> *"and also reading list I think easier than [Pathway course] because ah every time has same vocabulary again and again… so if I remember the word I can read easily more than [Pathway course] reading."*
> (Kazuo interview 2)

Hyland (2009) describes the popular science genre as journalism rather than science, written for entertainment rather than informational purposes. As Kazuo noticed, the range of vocabulary in these magazines is likely to be much wider than that found in a disciplinary textbook, with its predictable format and focus on specific topics. For English language learners, the textbook could be more easily understood than magazines which aim to reach a broad audience. Recent corpus linguistics research supports this suggestion, finding that language in extracts from popular science magazines used in textbooks for English language learners is not representative of language in university textbooks (Miller, 2011).

This illustration highlights the different discourses evident in the Pathway and the Degree contexts and the need for participants to gain the flexibility required to switch between different genres. A detailed critical analysis of the features of this genre compared with the reading genres commonly found in the university, such as textbooks and journal articles, could have better prepared learners for the immediate context of learning.

Discontinuity between programmes

There were significant differences between the content and tasks in the Pathway and the Degree programmes, without explicit explanation of the reasons for these differences. The Pathway programme, over a ten-week period, required learners to complete a seminar presentation, an essay, a research report, a critical review and a final examination, and also awarded grades for tutorial participation. The Degree programme courses ran for 11 weeks. During that time, the Accounting course required a workbook of calculations, a case study analysis and an exami-nation, while the Finance course asked learners to complete two multiple choice tests, a group case study report and a final examination. This lack of continuity of tasks across the courses might have suggested to learners that there was little relationship between the two programmes. Clark was most definite about this. At the time of the second interview, five weeks into the Degree programme, he said:

> *"maybe in the future we have some essay whatever we call it maybe useful but so far it's nothing, we don't use… you know for example eh like ah critical review we don't use that."*

(Clark interview 2)

This expectation of similar tasks across the two programmes suggests that there could have been more discussion of how learning in the Pathway programme connected with learning in the Degree programme. For instance, by being more explicit about how a critical review task is useful preparation for further study, the Pathway programme would have begun to provide a meta-language for learners to transfer learning from one context to another.

Responses from other participants also mentioned this discontinuity, indicating that they saw differences between the two settings principally in terms of disciplinary content. Kazuo points to this difference, saying:

> *"ah no because [Pathway programme] teacher is for teach – to teach English but lecturer is to teach specific subject."*
>
> (Kazuo interview 1)

He differentiates the disciplinary areas – English for Academic Purposes vs. Accounting and Finance – implying that the two have different levels of importance. This indicates a belief that English lies outside the realm of the disciplinary courses and is a separate skill that can be learned first and applied in a new context.

While the different disciplinary emphasis in the programmes noticed by Kazuo is an expected outcome in these segregated learning contexts, the place of English as inextricable from learning in the discipline could be made more explicit for learners. Without that distinction there is the potential that learners could consider that their English language learning is complete and thus loses importance as they enter the university. This separation between language and the (more highly valued) disciplinary content ties in with language being considered a technical skill, something prior to other aspects of life rather than the notion of language as always developing in the social world (Pennycook, 2010).

The participants demonstrated acceptance of an approach which saw academic genres as distinct and stable across contexts. Skye, for instance, related how she had learned to write an essay in a level one course at the Pathway programme but then been told that this way was *"incorrect"* in a level three course (Skye interview 2). This perceived inconsistency within the Pathway programme courses could have been used to alert her to the different and often conflicting writing practices in the university.

Instead of being reassured that now she knew how to write an essay, Skye could have learned to understand the university in less monolithic terms: *"like all institutions, as human, and constructed, rigid, fluid, hegemonous and negotiable – all at the same time"* (Johns & Swales, 2002:26). Research indicating not only variation within and between disciplines (Hyland, 2009) but also the ever-changing nature of disciplinary curricula (Quinn, 2010:124) suggests that any attempt to present academic tasks as monolithic or stable across contexts underestimates the complex nature of learning in higher education. Such approaches which leave commencing learners to find their own way (Haggis, 2003) tend to limit the effect of preparation for academic learning.

Academic writing tasks

The Pathway programme focused on developing learners' academic writing skills, emphasising academic discourse conventions such as evidence, intertextual references, tentativeness and nominalisation. However, links were not made to the particular writing requirements of the Master's in Commerce degree. This extract from the *Pathway Coursebook* (2007:11) introduction lists some features of academic writing in specific but incomplete terms:

> *"Academic language includes following gender inclusive language conventions, avoiding slang and colloquial language, minimal use of personal pronouns, hedging/vague language, and use of an appropriate academic tone."*

This list of some aspects of academic language does little to enlighten the learner or assist their writing in academic genres. Later in the document, further academic language development activities were included but without any explicit reference to expectations of academic writing in the discipline of Commerce. In the context of the Degree programme, documents indicate an assumption that learners will already know and be able to handle the academic literacy requirements of their studies. This can be seen in the assessment criteria for academic writing in the Accounting course:

Assessment criteria

Assessment of your assignments will take into account:

- *Relevance of your answer to the question or task set*

- *Clarity of expression*

- *Supporting documentation for arguments*

- *Proper acknowledgement of documentation and use of a bibliographic convention*

- *Logical planning and sequence*

- *Use of inclusive language*

- *Overall presentation, including correct grammar, spelling and punctuation*

- *Comprehensive coverage reflecting engagement with set readings, text(s) and other relevant materials.*

(Accounting Course Information Booklet, 2007:9–10)

While this list provides learners with some guidelines about how assignments will be graded, the fact that a general list of categories is to be applied to the different assessment tasks (a workbook of calculations; a case study report; and an examination) makes the criteria so general as to limit meaning. Notions such as *"clarity of expression"*, *"proper acknowledgement"* and *"correct grammar"* also suggest that there exists a well-known and understood standard for academic writing. There is no acknowledgement that these categories might have different meanings for the different people applying them in the assessment items for the course.

The criterion *"clarity of expression"*, for example, depends on how the reader understands the writing; and readers might have different standards. It implies that an agreed standard exists but is unstated because it is assumed to be common knowledge. Learners, as they address these criteria, must decide what constitutes clarity for their particular reader. Participants in this study could perhaps be expected to have some idea of how to achieve *"clarity of expression"* as they have completed the Pathway programme. However, the incomplete list of features of academic writing shown above does not make the requirements very explicit.

Turner (2003) calls for a return to teaching form in academic writing, saying that this requirement for clarity assumes an insider common-sense understanding of the criterion but fails to provide explicit instruction. She advocates teaching in such a way as to make visible the hegemony of notions such as clarity, and locating the norms of academic writing in their *"culturally constructed context"* (Turner, 2003:193). Others have questioned such transparency when it is interpreted in a narrow way that focuses on *"criteria compliance"* (Torrance, 2007:282), taking no account of the embodied nature of education (Mitchell, 2010) and the broader purposes of writing. The Degree programme could have made fewer assumptions about learners' prior knowledge by avoiding taking the norms of academic writing as given.

In both the Pathway and the Degree programmes, learners could be assisted to develop a meta-language if the different writing genres were deconstructed and their applications made explicit. This approach would allow learners more access to the tacit understandings implied in statements about what and how learning takes place.

Socialisation into the academic culture

When transition to learning in higher education is considered as socialisation into the academic culture of the discipline, it implies that there will be a gradual apprenticeship into the genres and practices of the discipline (Duff, 2007). This process of *"legitimate peripheral participation"* (Lave & Wenger, 1991:69) is difficult to reconcile with the pressured environment of the Pathway programme where learners were expected to complete six assessment tasks in ten weeks. The development of academic writing and English language are examples of cultural adjustments which provide most difficulty for learners. Each is discussed here as they are addressed in the programmes.

Developing academic writing skills

In the Pathway programme, while teachers commented on drafts of the written tasks such as the research report and the research essay, the need to complete so many tasks in a short period of time meant that gradual socialisation into academic writing practices would have been difficult. In the Degree programme courses there was no provision for learners to submit drafts of written work for comment by lecturers so learners were left alone to improve their writing skills, having assistance only through lecturer feedback on written assignments. As Haggis (2003:100) suggests, *"new ways of thinking and expressing oneself take some time to develop and need clear modelling and exploration."* The short timeframes of Pathway programmes as ten-week blocks tend to work against gradual learning over time.

Counteracting the effect of the time factor is difficult, but if learners are encouraged to self-manage their learning and use reflection to develop awareness of their own writing practices, they can continue to develop their writing as they progress into university. Changes to the Pathway programme could emphasise the importance of writing in academic practice and how it varies according to disciplinary practices. This might mean including fewer writing tasks but with more detailed analysis and feedback for each individual learner. More opportunities for learners to engage in writing, reflect on the kinds of writing expected in their discipline and evaluate their progress could be included. The development of peer writing groups would also help develop learners' meta-knowledge of themselves as writers and provide the potential for them to continue to develop writing skills.

Developing English language

The development of language skills is an important aspect of learning in a new cultural environment. The Pathway programme documents emphasised English language development but mainly in terms of completing the required oral and written tasks. One participant reported that he was learning, *"not English but the education system"* (Vijay interview 1). Others described the Pathway programme as an interruption to their goals of studying in Australia, a necessary preparation where they studied *"just English"* and not *"real"* subjects (Donna interview 2). It was also referred to as being *"like in elementary school"* (Judy interview 2). These comments imply a classroom experience where learning is closely monitored by the teacher and the expectation of independence is under-emphasised. It suggests that there is little appreciation of the knowledge that learners bring with them or that much learning takes place outside formal classroom contexts.

A certain level of English language proficiency is a prerequisite for learning in the disciplines. Indeed, the Degree programme documents made no mention of English language proficiency suggesting that there was an expectation that all learners would be fully prepared in terms of language. By attending the Pathway programme participants were able to develop language abilities but the short duration of the programme may not have allowed all learners to progress to sufficient levels for success. Additionally, preparation cannot cover every language need and inevitably learners would need to continue their language development. Accordingly, language learning needs to be promoted as a continuing, lifelong project for all learners rather than one of a range of generic skills which once learned are presumed to be transferable to any disciplinary context (Russell *et al.*, 2009).

In the Pathway programme, a greater emphasis on the importance of developing spoken English language would assist learners to adjust more quickly to the new learning culture. By addressing the inevitable barriers to social integration with native-speakers (Benzie, 2010), the programme could more explicitly introduce the cultural context of learning. The understanding that language learning must also take place outside the classroom could involve learners in guided activities requiring interaction in the wider community. Out of class activities which bring learners together with those already studying in the discipline, with academic staff and other members of the local community, would provide more opportunities for interaction in diverse environments.

Academic literacies

There was little evidence of awareness of the academic literacies model in either the Pathway or the Degree programme. While the inclusion of a task that required learners to select texts from their future discipline when writing a report indicated some awareness of future learning contexts, much more emphasis could have been made on the disparate changing nature of disciplinary learning.

So far this analysis has provided examples of how incorporating a focus on meta-language into curricula could assist a shift from the bounded study skills model to an academic literacies model. Implicit in the learning of a meta-language is *"conscious learning"* (Nygaard *et al.*,

2008:39), the ability to be self-reflexive and engage in thinking about what, how and why one is learning. Such an approach requires learners to engage actively in the learning process, rather than applying passive and reactive responses. An example is Wardle's (2009) three-part model which involves teaching learners how to extract principles explicitly from a given situation, use self-reflection to develop an alertness to the context and, in a supported environment, experiment with new genres. Bridges (1993) cautions that such an approach involves sophisticated higher-order skills, but these could be introduced in the Pathway programme with scaffolding so that learners are given the opportunity to learn how to select, adapt, adjust and re-apply skills, and also to question practices and processes.

Activities which involve learners becoming ethnographers of their discipline can also incorporate their experiences and ideas. Several studies have reported on different versions of this technique. In one study learners are provided with cameras and, in groups, leave the classroom to research difference (Grey, 1999). In another example, learners in a preparatory course form groups to research their future disciplinary learning contexts. They are supported through this process as they analyse the range of genres found in the university. Additionally, they interact with staff and learners in their future study destinations and, through this scaffolding, develop familiarity with the context they are about to enter (Pickard et al., 2011). These techniques allow learners to interact with, and question the practices of, the academy as they incorporate their existing knowledge. They indicate ways in which an academic literacies approach might be introduced in the Pathway programme.

Conclusion

The metaphor of a pathway suggests a guided transition from a Pathway programme into the Degree programme. While the experience of the Pathway programme provides participants with some preparation, the transition was not necessarily seen as a smooth trajectory. The many discontinuities suggest that the Pathway experience could more specifically provide preparation for academic practices in the disciplines of Accounting and Finance. The silence about English language in the Degree programme documents and the use of vague terms suggesting assumed knowledge of academic literacies indicate limited acknowledgement of learners' backgrounds and prior experience. These assumptions suggest that, to be successful in the Degree programme, participants would need to make significant adjustments in terms of language and academic literacies.

A focus on participant accounts of learning and curriculum documents in this study has provided only two perspectives in a broad field. Nevertheless, the analysis suggests that learning in the Pathway programme could be enriched by more explicit promotion of a deeper understanding of what it means to study at university. An approach has been described which suggests de-emphasising the narrow version of academic learning found in the Pathway programme and promoting preparation for the complexity and ambiguities inherent in academic study in any field, through more explicit understandings of disciplinary genres.

About the author

Helen Benzie is a Language and Learning Coordinator in the Learning and Teaching Unit at the University of South Australia. She can be contacted at this email: helen.benzie@unisa.edu.au

Collected Bibliography

AHEAD. Available online: http://www.ahead.org [Accessed June 30, 2012].

Åkerlind, G. (2005) Variation and commonality in phenomenographic research methods. *Higher Education Research & Development*, Vol. 24, No. 4, pp. 321–34.

Albergaria Almeida, P. (2012) Learning styles and disciplinary fields: is there a relationship? In N. Popov, C. Wolhuter, B. Leutwyler, G. Hilton, J. Ogunleye & P. Albergaria Almeida (eds) *International Perspectives in Education*, 391–6. Sofia, Bulgaria: Bulgarian Comparative Education Society.

Albergaria Almeida, P. & R. Mendes (2010) Learning style preferences across disciplines. *The International Journal of Diversity in Organizations, Communities & Nations*, Vol. 10, No. 2, pp. 285–302.

Albergaria Almeida, P., H. Pedrosa de Jesus & M. Watts (2008) Developing a mini-project: students' questions and learning styles. *The Psychology of Education Review*, Vol. 32, No. 1, pp. 6–17.

Albergaria Almeida, P., H. Pedrosa de Jesus & M. Watts (2011) Kolb's Learning Styles and Approaches to Learning through the Use of Students' Critical Questions. In S. Rayner & E. Cools (eds) *International Perspectives On Style Differences In Human Performance: Leading Edge Research, Theory And Practice*, 115–28. New York: Routledge.

Albergaria Almeida, P. & J. Teixeira-Dias (2011a) Implementing a constructivist learning environment: students' perceptions and approaches to learning. In C. Nygaard, N. Courtney & C. Holtham (eds) *Beyond Transmission – Innovations in University Teaching*, pp. 135–50. Oxfordshire: Libri Publishing Ltd.

Albergaria Almeida, P. & J. Teixeira-Dias (2011b) Education for sustainability: implementing research mini-projects in first year chemistry. *The International Journal of Science in Society*, Vol. 2, No. 1, pp. 117–31.

Albergaria Almeida, P., Teixeira-Dias, J. & J. Medina (2010) Building a culture of creativity while engaging students in questioning. In C. Nygaard, N. Courtney & C. Holtham (eds) *Teaching Creativity – Creativity in Teaching*. Oxfordshire: Libri Publishing.

Albon, R. & T. Jewels (2009) *Towards the development of a team learning theory for information systems: Implications for universities, academics, and academic developers*. 15th Americas conference on information systems (AMCIS), San Francisco, United States.

American Association of Colleges and Universities (AACU) (no date) *VALUE: Valid Assessment of Learning in Undergraduate Education, Project Description*. Available online: http://www.aacu.org/value/project_description.cfm [Accessed June 26, 2012].

Andersen, H. L. (2004) Eksamensformer: valg med konsekvenser. *Working Paper no. 128-04*, Centre for Cultural Research, University of Aarhus. Available online: http://www.hum.au.dk/ckulturf/pages/publications/hla/eksamensformeroglaering.pdf [Accessed January 11, 2011].

Anderson, L. W., C. R. Krathwohl, P. W. Airasian, K. A. Cruikshank, R. E. Mayer, P. R. Pintrich, J. Raths & M. C. Wittrock (eds) (2001) *A Taxonomy for Learning, Teaching, and Assessing – A Revision of Bloom's Taxonomy of Educational Objectives*. New York: Addison Wesley Longman.

Andrade, H. & A. Valtcheva (2008) Promoting Learning and Achievement through Self-Assessment. *Theory into Practice*, Vol. 48, No. 1, pp. 12–19.

Aoki, K. (2011) Reflection on the prospect of Learning Design adoption in Japan. *Learning Design Summit*. December 12–13, Sydney, NSW: Macquarie University.

Apple (2009) Challenge Based Learning. Cupertino. Available online: http://ali.apple.com/cbl/global/files/CBL_Paper.pdf [Accessed June 10, 2012].

Apte, U. M., U. S. Karmarkar & H. Nath (2008) Information Services in the U.S. Economy: Value, Jobs, and Management Implications. *California Management Review*, Vol. 50, No. 3, pp. 12–30.

Arts and Administration Program (AAD) (2012) *Mission and Objectives*. Available online: http://aad.uoregon.edu/about/history [Accessed June 20, 2012].

Awbrey, S. M. (2005) General education reform as organizational change: Integrating cultural and structural change. *The Journal of General Education*, Vol. 54, No. 1, pp. 1–21.

Bailey, C. (1984) *Beyond the Present and the Particular: A theory of liberal education*. London: Routledge & Kegan Paul.

Bailey, J. (2000) Students as clients in a professional/client relationship. *Journal of Management Education*, Vol. 24, No. 3, pp. 353–65.

Baker, T. & J. Clark (2010) Cooperative learning: a double-edged sword: A cooperative learning model for use with diverse student groups. *Intercultural Education*, Vol. 21, No. 2, pp. 257–68.

Balch, D., M. Manton & L. Masterman (2012) Phoebe: pedagogic planner. LDSE Project. Available online: http://www.phoebe.ox.ac.uk/ [Accessed June 10, 2012].

Ballantine, J. & P. McCourt Larres (2007) Cooperative learning: a pedagogy to improve students' generic skills? *Education + Training*, Vol. 49, No. 2, pp. 126–37.

Bandura, A. (1975) *Social Learning & Personality Development*. New Jersey: Holt, Rinehart & Winston, Inc.

Bandura, A. (1977) Toward a unifying theory of behavioral change. *Psychological Review*, Vol. 84, No. 2, pp. 191–215.

Bandura, A. (1986) *Social foundations of thought and action: a social cognitive theory*. Englewood Cliffs, NJ: Prentice Hall.

Bandura, A. (1994) Self-efficacy. In V. S. Ramachaudran (ed.) *Encyclopedia of human behavior*, Vol. 4, pp. 71–81. New York: Academic Press.

Barbosa, R., Z. Jofili & M. Watts (2004) Cooperating and constructing knowledge: case studies from chemistry and citizenship. *International Journal of Science Education*, Vol. 26, No. 8, pp. 935–50.

Barkley, E. F. (2010) *Student engagement techniques: A handbook for college faculty*. San Francisco: John Wiley & Sons.

Barnes, C. (2007) Disability, Higher Education and the Inclusive Society. *British Journal of Sociology of Education*, Vol. 28, No. 1, January, pp. 135–45.

Barnett, R. (1997) *Realizing the University*. London: University of London, Institute of Education.

Barnett, R. (2000) Supercomplexity and the Curriculum. *Studies in Higher Education*, Vol. 25, No. 3, pp. 255–65.

Barnett, R. (2005) Recapturing the universal in the university. *Educational Philosophy and Theory*, Vol. 37, No. 6, pp. 785–97.

Barrett, H. (2009) Limitations of eportfolios. *ePortfolios for Learning*. Available online: http://electronicportfolios.org/blog/2009/10/limitations-of-portfolios.html [Accessed June 26, 2012].

Barrett, H. (2011) *Balancing the Two Faces of E-portfolio*. Available online: http://electronicportfolios.com/balance/Balancing2.htm [Accessed June 26, 2012].

Barrie, S. (2006) Understanding What We Mean by the Generic Attributes of Graduates. *Higher Education*, Vol. 51, No. 2, pp. 215–41.

Barrouillet, P. & V. Gaillard (2011) *Cognitive development and working memory: A dialogue between neo-Piagetian theory and cognitive approach.* New York: Psychology Press.

Batson, T. (2002) *The Electronic Portfolio Boom: What's It All About?* Available online: http://www.msnc.la.edu/include/learning_resources/emerging_technologies/eportfolio/ePortfolio_boom.pdf [Accessed June 19, 2012].

Bauman, Z. (1997) Universities: old, new and different. In A. Smith & F. Webster (eds) *The postmodern university?: contested visions of higher education in Society.* Buckingham: SRHE & Open University Press.

Baxter Magolda, M. B. (1999) *Creating Contexts for Learning and Self-Authorship: Constructive-developmental pedagogy.* Nashville: Vanderbilt University Press.

Beane, J. (1995) Curriculum integration and the disciplines of knowledge. *Phi Delta Kappan*, Vol. 76, No. 8, pp. 616–22.

Bennet, A. & D. Bennet (2008) Engaging tacit knowledge in support of organizational learning. *VINE: The Journal of Information and Knowledge Management Systems*, Vol. 40, No. 1, pp. 1–25.

Benson, V. (2008) *Is the Digital Generation Ready for Web 2.0-Based Learning?* Paper presented at The Open Knowledge Society: A Computer Science and Information Systems Manifesto: First World Summit on the Knowledge Society, Wsks 2008, Athens, Greece, Sept. 24–26, 2008.

Benzie, H. J. (2010) Graduating as a "native speaker": International students and English language proficiency in higher education. *Higher Education Research & Development*, Vol. 29, No. 4, pp. 447–59.

Benzie, H. J. (2011) A pathway into a degree programme: Forging better links. *Journal of Academic Language & Learning*, Vol. 5, No. 2, pp. A107–A117.

Bergmann, J. & A. Sams (2012) *How the Flipped Classroom Is Radically Transforming Learning.* Available online: http://www.thedailyriff.com [Accessed June 4, 2012].

Bernacchio, C. & M. Mullen (2007) Universal Design for Learning. *Psychiatric Rehabilitation Journal*, Vol. 35, No. 2, pp. 167–9.

Biddulph, F. & R. Osborne (1982) Some issues relating to children's questions and explanations. LISP(P) working paper No. 106. Hamilton: University of Waikato.

Biggs, J. (1999) What the student does: teaching for enhanced learning. *Higher Education Research and Development*, Vol. 18, No. 1, pp. 57–75.

Biggs, J. (2003) *Teaching for Quality Learning at University.* Maidenhead: Open University Press, McGraw-Hill Education.

Bingham, C. & A. M. Sidorkin (2004) The pedagogy of relation: an introduction. In C. Bingham & A. M. Sidorkin (eds) *No education without relation*. Oxford: Peter Lang.

Birrell, B. (2006) Implications of low English standards among overseas students at Australian universities. *People and Place*, Vol. 14, No. 4, pp. 53–64.

Bitzer, E. (2011) Foreword. In C. Nygaard, N. Courtney & L. Frick (eds) *Postgraduate Education – Form and Function*. Oxfordshire: Libri Publishing.

Blumer, H. (1969) *Symbolic Interactionism: Perspective and Method*. Englewood Cliffs, N.J.: Prentice-Hall.

Bolden, R. (2004) *What is Leadership?* Available online: http://hdl.handle.net/10036/17493 [Accessed June 6, 2012].

Bolden, R. (2011) Distributed Leadership in Organizations: A Review of Theory and Research. *International Journal of Management Reviews*, Vol. 13, No. 3, pp. 251–69.

Bolhuis, S. (2003) Towards process-oriented teaching for self-directed lifelong learning: a multidimensional perspective. *Learning and Instruction*, Vol. 13, No. 3, pp. 327–47.

Bolton, C. & K. Kammeyer (1967) *The University Student: A Study of Student Behavior and Values*. New Haven, Connecticut: College and University Press.

Borg, S. (2003) Teacher cognition in language teaching: a review of research on what language teachers think, know, believe, and do. *Language Teaching*, Vol. 36, No. 2, pp. 81–109.

Borg, S. (2009) Language teacher cognition. In Burns, A. & J. C. Richards (eds) *The Cambridge Guide to Second Language Teacher Education*. Cambridge: Cambridge University Press.

Borg, S. (2010) Language teacher research engagement. *Language Teaching*, Vol. 43, No 4, pp. 391–429.

Bosch, T. E. (2009) Using online social networking for teaching and learning: Facebook use at the University of Cape Town. *Communication: South African Journal for Communication Theory and Research*, Vol. 35, No. 2, pp. 185–200.

Boud, D. & G. Felleti (1998) *The Challenge of Problem-based Learning*. London: Kogan Page.

Boud, D., R. Keogh & D. Walker (eds) (1985) *Reflection: Turning Experience into Learning*. London: Kogan-Page.

Bourner, T. (2003) Assessing reflective learning. *Education & Training*, Vol. 45, No. 5, pp. 267–72.

Boyer, E. (1987) *College: The Undergraduate Experience in America*. New York: Harper and Row.

Bramhall, R., N. Cheng & L. Hager (2011) *Inter/National Coalition of Electronic Portfolio Research Cohort V Final Report – University of Oregon*. Available online: http://ncepr.org/finalreports/cohort5/UO%20Final%20 Report.pdf [Accessed June 10, 2012].

Branch, J., L. Hershey & D. Vannette (2011) The use of RISK for Introducing Marketing Strategy. In C. Nygaard, N. Courtney & C. Holtham (eds) *Beyond Transmission – Innovations in University Teaching*. Oxfordshire: Libri Publishing Ltd.

Brew, A. (2010) *Enhancing undergraduate engagement through research and inquiry*. National Teaching Fellowship Report. Strawberry Hills, NSW: Australian Learning & Teaching Council.

Bridges, D. (1993) Transferable skills: A philosophical perspective. *Studies in Higher Education*, Vol. 18, No. 1, pp. 43–51.

Brillinger, M. F. (1997) Paths of learning, grieving and transforming. *Futures*, Vol. 29, No. 8, pp. 749–54.

Bruner, J. (1996) *The Culture of Education*. Cambridge, Massachusetts: Harvard University Press.

Burgstahler, S. (2007) *Equal Access: Universal Design of Instruction*. Seattle, USA: DO-IT, University of Washington.

Burgstahler, S. (2008) Universal Design of Instruction: From Principles to Practice. In S. Burgstahler & R. Cory. *Universal Design in Higher Education: From Principles to Practice*. Boston, USA: Harvard University Press, pp. 23–44.

Burgstahler, S. (2011) *Universal Design in Education: Principles and Applications*. Seattle, USA: DO-IT, University of Washington.

Calefati, J. (2009) College is Possible for Students with Intellectual Disabilities: New Support Programs and Federal Funds Can Help Students with Intellectual Disabilities. *U.S. News and World Report*, 13 February. Available online: www.usnews.com [Accessed June 15, 2012].

Cambridge, D. (2008) Audience, integrity, and the living document: eFolio Minnesota and lifelong and lifewide learning with ePortfolios. *Computers & Education*, Vol. 51, No. 3, pp. 1,227–46.

Cambridge, D. (2010) *Eportfolios for Lifelong Learning and Assessment*. John Wiley and Sons. Kindle Edition.

Cambridge, D., B. Cambridge & K. Yancey (eds) (2009) *Electronic Portfolios 2.0: Emergent Research on Implementation and Impact*. Sterling VA: Stylus.

Cambridge, D., L. Fernandez, S. Kahn, J. Kirkpatrick & J. Smith (2008) The Impact of the Open Source Portfolio on Learning and Assessment. *Journal of Online Learning and Teaching*, Vol. 4, No. 4, pp. 490–502.

CAST (2011) *Universal Design for Learning Guidelines Version 2.0*. Wakefield, USA: CAST.

CAST (2012a) UDL Guidelines 2.0 – Educator's Checklist. Available online: http://www.udlcenter.org/implementation [Accessed June 12, 2012].

CAST (2012b) Available online: http://www.udlcenter.org/aboutudl/whatisudl [Accessed June 12, 2012].

Chehore, T. & Z. Scholtz (2008) Exploring a Pedagogy that Supports Problem-Based Learning in Higher Education. In C. Nygaard & C. Holtham (eds) *Understanding Learning-Centred Higher Education*. Copenhagen: Copenhagen Business School Press.

Chen, H. & T. Light (2010) *Electronic Portfolios and Student Success: Effectiveness, Efficiency and Learning*. Association of American Colleges and Universities.

Chin, C. & L. Chia (2004) Problem-based learning: Using students' questions to drive knowledge construction. *Science Education*, Vol. 88, No. 5, pp. 1–21.

Chin, C. & J. Osborne (2008) Students' questions: a potential resource for teaching and learning science. *Studies in Science Education*, Vol. 44, No. 1, pp. 1–39.

Choo, S. S. Y., J. I. Rotgans, E. H. J. Yew & H. G. Schmidt (2011) Effect of worksheet scaffolds on student learning in problem-based learning. *Advances in Health Sciences Education*, Vol. 16, No. 4, pp. 517–28.

Choudhury, B. & I. Gouldsborough (2012) The use of electronic media to develop transferable skills in science students studying anatomy. *Anatomical Sciences Education*, Vol. 5, No. 3, pp. 125–31.

Christobal, F., C. E. Engel & J. Talati (2009) TUFH Position Paper: The Ultimate Challenge? Higher Education for Adapting to Change and Participating in Managing Change. *Education for Health*, Vol. 22, No. 3, pp. 1–7.

Chu, S. & D. Kennedy (2011) Using online tools for groups to co-construct knowledge. *Online Information Review*, Vol. 35, No. 4, pp. 581–97.

CIDEA. Available online: http://www.ap.buffalo.edu/idea [Accessed 12 May 2012].

Clark, B. & M. Trow (1966) The Organizational Context. In T. Newcomb and E. Wilson (eds) *College Peer Groups: Problems and Prospects for Research*. Chicago: Aldine.

Connell, B., M. Jones, R. Mace, J. Mueller, A. Mullick, E. Ostroff, J. Sanford, E. Steinfeld, M. Story & G. Vanderheiden (1997) *The Principles of Universal Design. Version 2.0.* Raleigh, USA: Center for Universal Design, North Carolina State University.

Conole, C., A. Brasher, S. Cross, M. Weller, P. Clark & J. Culver (2008) Visualising learning design to foster and support good practice and creativity. *Educational Media International,* 1,469–5,790, Vol. 45, No. 3, pp. 177–94.

Conole, G. (2011) *Learning Design workshop in Sydney.* Available online: http://e4innovation.com/?p=472 [Accessed June 24, 2012].

Conole, G. (2012) *Designing for learning in an Open World.* New York, NY: Springer.

Coogan, T. (2009) Exploring the Hybrid Course Design for Adult Learners at the Graduate Level. *Journal of Online Learning and Teaching,* Vol. 5, No. 2, pp. 316–24.

Costa, G. & N. Silva (2010) Knowledge versus content in e-learning: A philosophical discussion. *Information Systems Front,* Vol. 12, No. 4, pp. 399–413.

Cotten, S. R. & B. Wilson (2006) Student–Faculty Interactions: Dynamics and Determinants. *Higher Education,* Vol. 51, No. 4, pp. 487–519.

Cox, R., J. McKendree, R. Tobin, J. Lee & T. Mayes (1999) Vicarious learning from dialogue and discourse. *Instructional Science,* Vol. 27, No. 6, pp. 431–58.

Crandell, C., J. Smaldino & C. Flexor (1999) Sound Field Systems Improve Learning. *The Hearing Review,* Vol. 6, No. 6, pp. 40–2.

Crawford, T., G. J. Kelly & C. Brown (2000) Ways of knowing beyond facts and laws of science: an ethnographic investigation of student engagement in scientific practices. *Journal of Research in Science Teaching,* Vol. 37, No. 3, pp. 237–58.

Csikszentmihalyi, M. (1997) *Finding Flow: The psychology of engagement in everyday life.* New York: Basic Books.

Cuccio-Schirripa, S. & H. E. Steiner (2000) Enhancement and analysis of science question level for middle school students. *Journal of Research in Science Teaching,* Vol. 37, No. 2, pp. 210–24.

Currie, G. & A. Lockett (2011) Distributing Leadership in Health and Social Care: Concertive, Conjoint or Collective? *International Journal of Management Reviews,* Vol. 13, No. 3, pp. 286–300.

Dall'Alba, G. & R. Barnacle (2007) An ontological turn for higher education. *Studies in Higher Education,* Vol. 32, No. 6, pp. 679–91.

Dalziel, J. (2003) Implementing Learning Design: The Learning Activity Management System (LAMS). In G. Crisp, D. Thiele, I. Scholten, S. Barker & J. Baron (eds) *Interact, Integrate, Impact: Proceedings of the 20th Annual Conference of the Australasian Society for Computers in Learning in Tertiary Education*. Adelaide, December 7–10, 2003.

Dalziel, J. (2005) *From reusable e-learning content to reusable learning designs: Lessons from LAMS*. Available online: http://www.lamsfoundation.org/ CD/html/resources/whitepapers/Dalziel.LAMS.doc [Accessed June 18, 2012].

Dalziel, J. (2007) The Design and Development of the LAMS Community. In H. Beetham & R. Sharpe (eds) *Rethinking Pedagogy for a Digital Age: Designing and Delivering E-Learning*. London: Routledge.

Dalziel, J. (2008) Learning Design: Sharing Pedagogical Know-How. In T. Iiyoshi & M. Kumar (eds) *Opening up education: the collective advancement of education through open technology, open content and open knowledge*, pp. 375–88. Cambridge, MA: Massachusetts Institute of Technology.

Dalziel, J. (2009) Prospects for Learning Design Research and LAMS. *Teaching English with Technology – Special Issue on LAMS and Learning Design*, Vol. 1, No. 2, pp. i–iv.

Dalziel, J. (2010) *Practical eTeaching Strategies for Predict-Observe-Explain, Problem-Based Learning and Role Plays*. Sydney, NSW: LAMS International.

Dalziel, J. & B. Dalziel (2011) Adoption of Learning Designs in Teacher Training and Medical Education: Templates versus Embedded Content. In L. Cameron & J. Dalziel (eds) *Learning design for a changing world*. Proceedings of the 6th International LAMS & Learning Design Conference 2011, December 8–9, Sydney, NSW: LAMS Foundation.

Dalziel, B., G. Mason & J. Dalziel (2009) Using a template for LAMS in a medical setting. In L. Cameron & J. Dalziel (eds) *Opening Up Learning Design*. Proceedings of the 4th International LAMS Conference 2009, December 3–4, Sydney: LAMS Foundation.

Danielsen, O. & J. L. Nielsen (2010) Problem-oriented project studies: the role of the teacher as supervising/facilitating the study group in its learning processes. In L. Dirckinck-Holmfeld, V. Hodgson, C. Jones, M. de Laat, D. McConnell & T. R. Dirckinck-Holmfeld (eds) *Proceedings of the Seventh International Conference on Networked Learning 2010*.

Danielson, C. (2002) *Enhancing student achievement: A framework for school improvement*. Alexandria, VA: Association for Supervision and Curriculum Development.

Day, D. V. (2000) Leadership development: A review in context. *The Leadership Quarterly*, Vol. 11, No. 4, pp. 581–613.

Deci, E., R. Koestner & R. Ryan (2001) Extrinsic rewards and intrinsic motivation in education: Reconsidered once again. *Review of Educational Research*, Vol. 71, No. 1, pp. 1–27.

DeFillippi, R. J. (2001) Introduction: Project-Based Learning, Reflective Practices and Learning. *Management Learning*, Vol. 32, No. 1, pp. 5–10.

Delanty, G. (1998) Rethinking the university: the autonomy, contestation and reflexive of knowledge. *Social Epistemology*, Vol. 12, No. 1, pp. 103–13.

Deslauriers, L., E. Schelew & C. Wieman (2010) Improved Learning in a Large-Enrollment Physics Class. *Science*, Vol. 332, No. 6,031, pp. 862–4.

Dillon, J. T. (1988) Theory and practice of student questioning. In S. Karabenick (ed.) *Strategic help seeking: Implications for learning and teaching*, pp. 195–218. Mahwah, NJ: Lawrence Earlbaum Associates.

Dilthey, W. (1988) *Introduction to the Human Sciences: An Attempt to Lay a Foundation for the Study of Society and History*. Wayne State University Press

Dirckinck-Holmfeld, L. (2010) *ICT and Innovative Learning Environments in a National and European Perspective*. Presentation held at the Danish conference on IT and innovative learning environments by the Danish Ministry of Science and Technology, August 19–20, 2010.

DiTeodoro, S., S. Donders, J. Kemp-Davidson, P. Robertson & L. Schuyler (2011) Asking good questions: promoting greater understanding of mathematics through purposeful teacher and student questioning. *Canadian Journal of Action Research*, Vol. 12, No. 2, pp. 18–29.

Dobozy, E. (2008) The use and usefulness of non-assessed online learning: Tracking students' behaviour on LAMS. In L. Cameron & J. Dalziel (eds) *Perspectives on Learning Design*. Proceedings of the 3rd International LAMS & Learning Design Conference 2008, 5 December 2008. Sydney, NSW: LAMS Foundation.

Dobozy, E. (2011) Resisting Student Consumers and Assisting Student Producers. In C. Nygaard, N. Courtney & C. Holtham (eds) *Beyond Transmission – Innovations in University Teaching*. Oxfordshire: Libri Publishing Ltd.

Dobozy, E. (2012) Typologies of Learning Design and the introduction of a 'LD-Type 2' case example. In P. Ullmo & T. Koskinen (eds) *eLearning Papers – Special Edition 2012: Opening Learning Horizons*. Barcelona, Spain: eLearning Europa.

Dobozy, E., R. Reynolds & D. Schönwetter (2011) Metaphoric reasoning and the tri-nation classification of eTeaching and eLearning platforms.

Refereed proceedings of *the 23rd World Conference on Educational Media, Hypermedia and Telecommunication.* Lisbon, Portugal: AACE.

Doherty, C. & P. Singh (2005) How the West is done: Simulating Western pedagogy in a curriculum for Asian international students. In P. Ninnes & M. Hellsten (eds) *Internationalising Higher Education*, pp. 53–73. Hong Kong: Comparative education research centre, Springer.

Doherty, C. & P. Singh (2007) Mobile students, flexible identities and liquid modernity: disrupting western teachers' assumptions of "the Asian learner". In D. Palfreyman & L. McBride (eds) *Learning and Teaching Across Culture in Higher Education*, pp. 114–32. New York: Palgrave Macmillan.

Donaldson, M. (1978) *Children's Minds.* London: Falmer.

Duff, P. (2007) Problematising academic discourse socialisation. In H. Marriot, T. Moore & R. Spence-Brown (eds) *Learning Discourses and the Discourses of Learning,* pp. 01.01–01.18. Melbourne: Monash University ePress.

Dyball, M. C., A. Reid, P. Ross & H. Schoch (2007) Evaluating Assessed Group-work in a Second-year Management Accounting Subject. *Accounting Education: An International Journal,* Vol. 16, No. 2, pp. 145–62.

Editorial (2009) *Learning Communities: International Journal of Learning in Social Contexts,* December 2009, Issue 2 – ePortfolio Edition, pp. 1–3. Available online: http://www.cdu.edu.au/centres/spill//journal/ IJLSC_Dec_2009_eportfolio.pdf?q=centres/spil/journal/IJLSC_ Dec_2009_eportfolio.pdf [Accessed June 25, 2012].

Edwards, R. & R. Usher (2000) *Globalisation and Pedagogy.* London: Routledge.

Elstgeest, J. (1985) The right question at the right time. In W. Harlen (ed.) *Primary Science: Taking the Plunge,* pp. 36–46. London: Heinemann.

Enomoto, K. (2010) Promoting self-regulated learning: a feedback-based study skills action plan for students from diverse cultural, linguistic and disciplinary backgrounds. In E. Morrel & M. Barr (eds) *Crises and Opportunities: Proceedings of the 18th Biennial Conference of the ASAA, 2010, Adelaide.* Canberra: Asian Studies Association of Australia. Available online: http://asaa.asn.au/ASAA2010/index.php [Accessed June 12, 2012].

Enomoto, K. (2011) Fostering high quality learning through a scaffolded curriculum. In C. Nygaard, N. Courtney & C. Holtham (eds) *Beyond*

Transmission – Innovations in University Teaching. Oxfordshire: Libri Publishing Ltd.

Entwistle, N. (2001) Promoting deep learning through teaching and assessment. In L. Suskie (ed.) *Assessment to promote deep learning.* Washington, D.C.: American Association for Higher Education.

Entwistle, N. J., V. McCune & P. Walker (2001) Conceptions, styles and approaches within higher education: analytic abstractions and everyday experience. In R. J. Sternberg & L. F. Zhang (eds) *Perspectives on Thinking, learning and cognitive styles.* Mahwah, NJ: Lawrence Erlbaum Associates.

Erickson, J. A. & J. B. Anderson (1997) *Learning with the Community: Concepts and Models for Service-learning in Teacher Education.* American Association of Colleges for Teacher Education.

Erlandson, R. (2002) Universal Design for Learning: Curriculum, Technology, and Accessibility. In proceedings of ED-MEDIA 2002 World Conference on Educational Multimedia, Hypermedia & Telecommunications. Denver, Colorado, June 24–29, 2002, pp. 2–8.

Ernest, P., S. Heiser & L. Murphy (2011) Developing teacher skills to support collaborative online language learning. *The Language Learning Journal.* Available online: http://dx.doi.org/10.1080/09571736.2011.625095 [Accessed June 12, 2012].

Erskine, J., M. Leenders & L. Mauffette-Leenders (1998) *Teaching with cases.* Ontario: Richard Ivey School of Business, University of Western Ontario.

Ertmer, P. A. & T. J. Newby (1996) The expert learner: strategic, self-regulated and reflective. *Instructional Science*, Vol. 24, pp. 1–24.

Eynon, B. (2009) *It Helped Me See a New Me: ePortfolio, Learning and Change at LaGuardia Community College.* Available online: http://www.academiccommons.org/commons/essay/eportfolio-learning-and-change [Accessed June 30, 2012].

Falconer, A. S. & M. Pettigrew (2003) Developing added value skills within an academic programme through work-based learning. *International Journal of Manpower*, Vol. 24, No. 1, pp. 48–59.

Fast, I. (1998) *Selving: A relational theory of self organization.* Hillsdale: Analytic Press.

Feldman, A. (2002) Multiple perspectives for the study of teaching: knowledge, reason, social context and being. *Journal of Research in Science Teaching*, Vol. 39, No. 10, pp. 1,032–55.

Ferrell, G. (2011) *Transforming curriculum design – transforming institutions.* Briefing paper. Joint Information Systems Committee (JISC). Available online: www.jisc.ac.uk/publications/briefingpapers/2011/bpcurriculumdesign.aspx [Accessed June 18, 2012].

Fink, L. D. (2003) *Creating significant learning experiences: An integrated approach to designing college classes.* San Francisco: Jossey-Bass.

Fisher, D. & N. Frey (2007) *Checking for understanding: Formative assessment techniques for your classroom.* Alexandria, VA: Association for Supervision and Curriculum Development.

Franciosi, B. (2005) *Designing Curricula and Assessments for Universal Learning.* Center for Teaching Excellence. Durham, USA: University of New Hampshire.

Franz, R. (1998) Whatever you do, don't treat your students like customers! *Journal of Management Education,* Vol. 22, No. 1, pp. 63–9.

Gadamer, H.-G. (1989) *Truth and Method.* New York: Crossroad.

Gajar, A. (1992) Adults with Learning Disabilities: Current and Future Research Priorities. *Journal of Learning Disabilities,* Vol. 25, No. 8, October, pp. 507–19.

Gallagher, S. (1992) *Hermeneutics and Education.* New York: State University of New York Press.

Gardner, H. (2007) *Five Minds of the Future.* Cambridge: Harvard Business Review Press.

Garrison, D. R. (1991) Critical thinking and adult education: a conceptual model for developing critical thinking in adult learners. *International Journal of Lifelong Education,* Vol. 10, No. 4, pp. 287–303.

Garrison, D. R. (1992) Critical thinking and self-directed learning in adult education: an analysis of responsibility and control issues. *Adult Education Quarterly,* Vol. 42, No. 3, pp. 136–48.

Garrison, D. R., T. Anderson, & W. Archer. (2004) Critical thinking, cognitive presence, and computer conferencing in distance education. *American Journal of Distance Education,* Vol. 15, No. 1, pp. 7–23.

Garrison, R. D. & N. D. Vaughan (2008) *Blended Learning in Higher Education: Framework, Principles, and Guidelines.* San Francisco: Jossey-Bass.

Ge, X. & S. Land (2004) A conceptual framework for scaffolding ill-structured problem-solving processes using question prompts and peer interactions. *Educational Technology Research and Development,* Vol. 52, No. 2, pp. 5–22.

Gee, J. P. (2005) *An Introduction to Discourse Analysis: Theory and Method* (second edition). New York: Routledge.

Giannikis, G. & A. Daskalopulu (2009) The role of assumption identification in autonomous agent reasoning. *Proceedings of the 8th International*

Conference on Autonomous Agents and Multiagent Systems. Available online: http://dl.acm.org/citation.cfm?id=1558177 [Accessed June 18, 2012].

Gibbons, M., C. Limoges, H. Nowotny, S. Schwartzman, P. Scott & M. Trow (1994) *The New Production of Knowledge: The dynamics of science and research in contemporary societies*. London: Sage.

Gibson, R. (1986) *Critical Theory and Education*. London: Hodder and Stoughton.

Giddens, A. (1984) *The Constitution of Society: Outline of the Theory of Structuration*. Berkeley: University of California Press.

Gilson, S. (1996) Students with Disabilities: An Increasing Voice and Presence on College Campuses. *Journal of Vocational Rehabilitation*, Vol. 6, pp. 263–72.

Goffman, E. (1959) *The Presentation of Self in Everyday Life*. New York: Doubleday Anchor.

Goffman, E. (1961) *Asylums: Essays on the Social Situation of Mental Patients and Other Inmates*. New York: Doubleday Anchor.

Good, T. T., R. L. Slavins, H. K. Hobson & H. Emerson (1987) Student passivity: A study of question asking in K-12 classrooms. *Sociology of Education*, Vol. 60, No. 3, pp. 181–99.

Goodyear, P. & R. Ellis (2010) Expanding conceptions of study, context and educational design. In R. Sharpe, H. Beetham & S. De Freitas (eds) *Rethinking learning for the digital age: how learners shape their own experiences*. New York: Routledge.

Gradel, K. & A. Edson (2010) Putting Universal Design for Learning on the Higher Ed Agenda. *Journal of Educational Technology Systems*, Vol. 38, No. 2, pp. 111–21.

Graesser, A. C. & C. L. McMahen (1993) Anomalous information triggers questions when adults solve problems and comprehend stories. *Journal of Educational Psychology*, Vol. 85, No. 1, pp. 136–51.

Graesser, A. C. & B. A. Olde (2003) How does one know whether a person understands a device? The quality of the questions the person asks when the device breaks down. *Journal of Educational Psychology*, Vol. 95, No. 3, pp. 524–36.

Graesser, A.C. & N. K. Person (1994) Question asking during tutoring. *American Educational Research Journal*, Vol. 31, No. 1, pp. 104–37.

Grey, M. (1999) Ethnographers of difference in a critical EAP community-becoming. *Journal of English for Academic Purposes*, Vol. 8, No. 2, pp. 121–33.

Grigal, M., D. Hart & M. Paiewonsky (2010) Postsecondary Education: The Next Frontier for Individuals with Intellectual Disabilities. In M. Grigal

& D. Hart (eds) *Think College: Postsecondary Education Options for Students with Intellectual Disabilities*. Baltimore, USA: Paul H. Brookes Publishing, pp. 1–28.

Gronn P. (2002) Distributed leadership as a unit of analysis. *The Leadership Quarterly*, Vol. 13, No. 4, pp. 423–51.

Hager P. (2003) Changing pedagogy: productive learning. *OVAL Research Working Paper 03-16*. Sydney: OVAL Research UTS.

Haggis, T. (2003) Constructing images of ourselves? A critical investigation into "approaches to learning" research in higher education. *British Education Research Journal*, Vol. 29, No. 1, pp. 89–104.

Hall, D. T. (1968) Identity Changes during the Transition from Student to Professor. *The School Review*, Vol. 74. No. 4, pp. 445–69.

Harper, S. R. & S. J. Quale (2009) *Student engagement in higher education: Theoretical perspectives and practical approaches for diverse populations*. New York: Routlege.

Harvey, L. & P. T. Knight (1996) *Transforming Higher Education*. Bristol: Taylor and Francis for Open University Press.

Harvey, L. (2000) New realities: the relationship between higher education and employment. *Tertiary Education and Management*, Vol. 6, No. 1, pp. 3–17.

Hassanien, A. (2007) A Qualitative Student Evaluation of Group Learning in Higher Education. *Higher Education in Europe*, Vol. 32, No. 2, pp. 135–50.

Healey, M. & A. Jenkins (2009) *Developing undergraduate research and inquiry*. York, UK: Higher Education Academy.

Heidegger, M. (1968) *What is Called Thinking?* New York: Harper & Row.

Heidegger, M. (1996) *Being and Time*. Albany: State University of New York Press.

Heidegger, M. (1998) *Basic Concepts*. Bloomington: Indiana University Press. (Original work published 1981.)

Henriksen, T. D. & S. Löfvall (2012) Current and past experiences with games at business schools. In C. Nygaard, N. Courtney & E. Leigh (eds) *Simulations, Games and Role Play in University Education*. Oxfordshire: Libri Publishing Ltd.

Hmelo-Silver, C. E., R. G. Duncan & C. A. Chinn (2007) Scaffolding and achievement in problem-based and inquiry learning: A response to Kirschner, Sweller, and Clark (2006) *Educational Psychologist*, Vol. 42, No. 2, pp. 99–107.

Ho, S. T. K. (2009) Addressing Culture in EFL Classrooms: The Challenge of Shifting from a Traditional to an Intercultural Stance. *Electronic Journal of Foreign Language Teaching*, Vol. 6, No. 1, pp. 63–76.

Hofstede, G. (1980) *Culture's Consequences: International differences in work-related values.* London: SAGE Publications.

Hofstede, G. (1986) Cultural differences in teaching and learning. *International Journal of Intercultural Relations*, Vol. 10, No. 3, pp. 301–20.

Huann-Shyang, L., H. Zuway & C. Ying-Yao (2009) The interplay of the classroom learning environment and inquiry-based activities. *International Journal of Science Education*, Vol. 31, No. 8, pp. 1,013–24.

Huba, M. E. & J. E. Freed (2000) *Learner-centered assessment on college campuses: Shifting the focus from teaching to learning.* Boston: Allyn & Bacon.

Hughes, J. (2008) *Letting in the Trojan mouse: Using an eportfolio system to re-think pedagogy.* Conference Proceedings. Ascilite, Melbourne, 2008.

Hughes, R. L. & S. K. Jones (2011) Developing and Assessing College Student Teamwork Skills. *New Directions for Institutional Research*, Spring, No. 149, pp. 53–64.

Hunt, J. & J. Andreasen (2011) Making the Most of Universal Design for Learning. *Mathematics Teaching in the Middle School*, Vol. 17, No. 3, October, pp. 166–72.

Hyland, K. (2009) *Academic Discourse: English in a Global Context.* London: Continuum.

IDEA. Available online: http://www.gpo.gov/fdsys/pkg/PLAW-108publ446/html/PLAW-108publ446.htm [Accessed June 12, 2012].

Ivanic, R. (2004) Discourses of writing and learning to write. *Languages and Education*, Vol. 18, No. 3, pp. 220–45.

Izzo, M., S. Rissing, C. Andersen, J. Nasar & L. Lissner (2011) Universal Design for Learning in the College Classroom. In W. Preiser & K. Smith (eds) *Universal Design Handbook.* New York, USA: McGraw Hill, pp. 39.1–39.6.

Jacobs, C. (2005) On being an insider on the outside: New spaces for integrating academic literacies. *Teaching in Higher Education*, Vol. 10, No. 4, pp. 475–87.

Jafari, A. & C. Kaufman (eds) (2006) *Handbook of Research on ePortfolios.* Hershey, PA: Idea Group.

James, M. A. (2010) An investigation of learning transfer in English-for-general-academic-purposes writing instruction. *Journal of Second Language Writing*, Vol. 19, No. 4, pp. 183–206.

Jarvis, P., J. Holford & C. Griffin (1998) *The Theory and Practice of Learning.* London: Kogan Page.

Jee, M.J. (2011) Web 2.0 Technology Meets Mobile Assisted Language Learning. *The IALLT Journal of Language Technologies*, Vol. 41, No. 1, pp. 161–75.

Jenkins, H. (2009) *Confronting the Challenges of Participatory Culture.* Available online: http://www.digitallearning.macfound.org [Accessed June 30, 2012].

Johns, A. M. & J. M. Swales (2002) Literacy and disciplinary practices: opening and closing perspectives. *Journal of English for Academic Purposes*, Vol. 1, No. 1, pp. 13–28.

Johnson, L. (1997) *Risking Learning.* Ph.D. thesis, Queen's University Belfast. Available online: http://www.qub.ac.uk/mgt/papers/risklearn/ [Accessed June 10, 2012].

Johnson, L. & S. Adams (2011) *Challenge Based Learning: The Report from the Implementation Project.* Austin, Texas: The New Media Consortium. Available online: http://www.challengebasedlearning.org/public/admin/docs/NMC_CBLi_Report_Oct_2011.pdf [Accessed June 10, 2012].

Juang, Y., T. Liu & T. Chan. (2008) Computer-supported teacher development of pedagogical content knowledge through developing school-based curriculum. *Educational Technology & Society*, Vol. 11, No. 2, pp. 149–70.

Kansanen, P. (1999) Teaching as Teaching-Studying-Interaction. *Scandinavian Journal of Educational Research*, Vol. 43, No. 1, pp. 81–9.

Karmarkar, U. S. & U. M. Apte (2007) Operations Management in the Information Economy: Information Products, Processes, and Chains. *Journal of Operations* Management, Vol. 25, No. 2, pp. 438–53.

Katchadourian, H. A & J. Boli (1985) *Careerism and intellectualism among college students.* Jossey-Bass Publishers.

Kegan, R. (1982) *The Evolving Self: Problem and process in human development.* Cambridge: Harvard University Press.

Kegan, R. (1994) *In Over Our Heads: The mental demands of everyday life.* Cambridge: Harvard University Press.

Kember, D. & D. Leung. (1998) Influences upon students' perceptions of workload. *Educational Psychology*, Vol. 22, pp. 293–307.

Kennedy, D., A. Hyland & N. Ryan (no date) Writing and Using Learning Outcomes: a Practical Guide. Available online: http://www.bologna-handbook.com/docs/downloads/C_3_4_1.pdf [Accessed June 16, 2011].

Kirkpatrick, D. L. (1994) *Evaluating Training Programs: The Four Levels*. San Francisco, CA: Berrett-Koehler.

Kirschner, P. A., J. Sweller & R. E. Clark (2006) Why minimal guidance during instruction does not work: An analysis of the failure of constructivist, discovery, problem-based, experiential, and inquiry-based teaching. *Educational Psychologist*, Vol. 41, No. 2, pp. 75–86.

Kivinen, O. (2002) Higher learning in an age of uncertainty: from postmodern critique to appropriate university practices. In J. Enders & O. Fulton (eds) *Higher education in a globalizing world: international trends and mutual observations*. Dordrecht: Klüwer.

Kokkinn, B. & C. Mahar (2011) Partnerships for student success: Integrated development of academic and information literacies across disciplines. *Journal of Academic Language & Learning*, Vol. 5, No. 2, pp. A118–A130.

Kolb, D. A. (1984) *Experiential Learning: experience as the source of learning and development*. Englewood Cliffs, New Jersey: Prentice Hall.

Komives, S. R., S. D. Longerbeam, F. Mainella, L. Osteen, J. E. Owen & W. Wagner (2009) Leadership Identity Development: Challenges in Applying a Developmental Model. *Journal of Leadership Education*, Vol. 8, No. 1, pp. 11–47.

Kotterman, J. (2006) Leadership versus management: what's the difference? *The Journal for Quality and Participation*, Vol. 29, No. 2, pp. 13–17.

Kouzes, J. & B. Posner (2002) *The leadership challenge*. San Francisco: Jossey-Bass.

Krathwohl, D. R., B. S. Bloom & B. B. Masia (1964) *Taxonomy of Educational Objectives, The Classification of Educational Goals Handbook II: Affective Domain*. New York, McKay Company, Inc.

Krause, K., R. Hartley, R. James & C. McInnis (2005) *The First Year Experience in Australian Universities: Findings From a Decade of National Studies*. Melbourne: University of Melbourne.

Kuh, G. D. (1993) In Their Own Words: What Students Learn outside the Classroom. *American Educational Research Journal*, Vol. 30, No. 2, pp. 277–304.

Kuh, G. D. (2008) *High-Impact educational practices: What they are, who has access to them, and why they matter*. Washington, DC: American Association of Colleges and Universities.

Laff, N. S. (2005) Setting the stage for identity, learning, and the liberal arts. *New Directions for Teaching and Learning*, Vol. 2005, No. 103, pp. 3–22.

Laurillard, D. (2008) The teacher as action researcher: Using technology to capture pedagogic form. *Studies in Higher Education*, Vol. 33, No. 2, pp. 139–54.

Laurillard, D. (2009) The pedagogical challenges to collaborative technologies. *International Journal of Computer-supported Collaborative Learning*, Vol. 4, No. 1, pp. 5–20.

Lave, J. & E. Wenger (1991) *Situated learning: legitimate peripheral participation*. Cambridge: Cambridge University Press.

Lea, M. R. & B. V. Street (1998) Student writing in higher education: An academic literacies approach. *Studies in Higher Education*, Vol. 23, No. 2, pp. 157–72.

Light, P., H. Chen & J. Ittelson (2011) *Documenting Learning with ePortfolios: A Guide for College Instructors*. John Wiley and Sons. Kindle Edition.

Lillis, T. (2003) Student writing as "Academic Literacies": Drawing on Bakhtin to move from critique to design. *Language and Education*, Vol. 17, No. 3, pp. 192–207.

Lizzio, A., K. L. Wilson & R. Simons (2002) University students' perceptions of the learning environment and academic outcomes: Implications for theory and practice. *Studies in Higher Education*, Vol. 27, No. 1, pp. 27–52.

Löfvall, S. (2008) *Students' Perception of University*. Unpublished manuscript. CBS Learning Lab, Copenhagen Business School.

Long, S. (1976) Academic Attachment: Predicting Students' Affective Reactions to the University, *Research in Higher Education*, Vol. 5, No. 3, pp. 233–41.

Long, S. (1977) Student Types and the Evaluation of the University. *Higher Education*, Vol. 6, No. 4, pp. 417–36.

Lusted, D. (1986) Why pedagogy? *Screen*, Vol. 27, No. 5, pp. 2–14.

Luth, A. (2010) Fremtiden mangler sprogstuderende. *Urban*, pp. 36–7, May 11, 2010. Available online: http://www.e-pages.dk/urban/84/42 [Accessed June 30, 2012].

Lyotard, J.-F. (1984) *The Postmodern Condition: A report on knowledge*. Manchester: Manchester University Press.

Management Review, Vol. 50, No. 3, pp. 12–30.

Mangrum, C. & S. Strichart (1988) *College and the Disabled Student: Program Development, Implementation and Selection*. Philadelphia, USA: Grune & Stratton.

Markauskaite, L. & P. Goodyear (2009) Designing for complex ICT-based learning: understanding teacher thinking to help improve educational design. *Same places, different spaces*. Available online: http://www.ascilite. org.au/conferences/auckland09/procs/markauskaite.pdf [Accessed June 26, 2012].

Marton, F. & R. Säljö (1976) On qualitative differences in Learning – Outcome and process. *British journal of Educational Psychology*, Vol. 46, No. 1, pp. 4–11.

Maskill, R. & M. H. Pedrosa de Jesus (1997) Pupils' questions, alternative frameworks and the design of science teaching. *International Journal of Science Education*, Vol. 19, No. 7, pp. 781–99.

Mauffette-Leenders, L., J. Erskine & M. Leenders (1999) *Learning with cases.* Ontario: Richard Ivey School of Business, University of Western Ontario.

McGuire, J, S. Scott & S. Shaw (2006) Universal Design and Its Application in Educational Environments. *Remedial and Special Education*, Vol. 27, No. 3, pp. 166–75.

McInnis, C., R. James & R. Hartley (2000) *Trends in the First Year Experience in Australian Universities.* Centre for the Study of Higher Education, University of Melbourne.

McLaughlin, P. & A. Mills (2011) Combining vocational and higher education studies to provide dual parallel qualifications – an Australian case study. *Journal of Vocational Education and Training*, Vol. 63, No. 1, pp. 77–86.

McTighe, J. & G. Wiggins (1999) *The understanding by design handbook.* Alexander, VA: Association for Supervision and Curriculum Development.

Medland, J. & B. Evans (2011) PGT Teaching Review Report. Oxford: Oxford University Student Union. Available online: http://www.ousu.org/about/Teaching Review Report.pdf [Accessed June 10, 2012].

Meier, F. & C. Nygaard (2008) Problem Oriented Project Work in Higher Education. In C. Nygaard & C. Holtham (eds) *Understanding Learning-Centred Higher Education.* Copenhagen: Copenhagen Business School Press.

Miers, M. E., B. A. Clarke, K. C. Pollard, C. E. Rickaby, J. Thomas & A. Turtle (2007) Online interprofessional learning: The student experience. *Journal of Interprofessional Care*, Vol. 21, No. 5, pp. 529–42.

Miller, D. (2011) ESL reading textbooks vs. university textbooks: Are we giving our students the input they may need? *Journal of English for Academic Purposes*, Vol. 10, No. 1, pp. 32–46.

Miller, K. J. (2005) Attention and learning problems: When you see one, look for the other. Available online: http://www.ncld.org/ld-basics/related-issues/adhd/attention-and-learning-problems-when-you-see-one-look-for-the-other [Accessed June 5, 2012].

Mitchell, S. (2010) Now you don't see it; now you do. *Arts and Humanities in Higher Education*, Vol. 9, No. 2, pp. 133–48.

Mitsis, A. & P. Foley (2010) Psychographic Antecedents to the Creative Learning Style Preference. In C. Nygaard, N. Courtney & C. Holtham (eds) *Teaching Creativity – Creativity in Teaching*, Oxfordshire, Libri Publishing Ltd.

Miyake, N. & D. A. Norman (1979) To ask a question, one must know enough to know what is not known. *Journal of Verbal Learning and Verbal Behaviour*, Vol. 18, No. 3, pp. 357–64.

Mondahl, M., L. Pals Svendsen, L. Ingstad & J. Rasmussen (2011) Sociale medier som læringsredskaber. *Dansk Universitetspædagogisk Tidsskrift*, No 10, 2011.

Moon, J. (2002)*The Module and Programme Development Handbook*. London: Kogan Page Ltd.

Morgeson, F. P., D. S. DeRue & E. P. Karam (2010) Leadership in Teams: A Functional Approach to Understanding Leadership Structures and Processes. *Journal of Management*, Vol. 36, No. 1, pp. 5–39.

Morison, J. & D. R. Newman (2001) On-line citizenship: consultation and participation in New Labour's Britain and beyond. *International Review of Law, Computers & Technology*, Vol. 15, No. 2, pp. 171–94.

Morris, R. & C. Hayes (1997) Small Group Work: Are group assignments a legitimate form of assessment? *Learning Through Teaching Proceedings of the 6th Annual Teaching Learning Forum*, Murdoch University.

Mull, C., P. Sitlington & S. Alper (2001) Postsecondary Education for Students with Learning Disabilities: A Synthesis of the Literature. *Exceptional Children*, Vol. 68, No. 1, pp. 97–118.

Murray, N. (2010) Considerations in the post-enrolment assessment of English language proficiency: Reflections from the Australian context. *Language Assessment Quarterly*, Vol. 7, No. 4, pp. 343–58.

Naft, J. (2010) *Cognitive presence*. Available online: http://www.innerfrontier. org/InnerWork/Archive/2010/20100208_Cognitive_Presence.htm [Accessed June 5, 2012].

Nater, S. & R. Gallimore (2006) You haven't taught until they have learned: John Wooden's teaching principles and practices. Morgantown, WV: Fitness Information Technology.

NCLD. Available online: http://www.ncld.org [Accessed June 12, 2012].

Newman, D. & C. Holtham (2008) Emergent knowledge – pedagogies and technologies to support group learning. In C. Nygaard & C. Holtham (eds) *Understanding Learning-Centred Higher Education*. Copenhagen: Copenhagen Business School Press.

Newman, D. R., C. Johnson, B. Webb & C. Cochrane (1997) Evaluating the quality of learning in computer supported co-operative learning. *Journal of the American Society for Information Science*, Vol. 48, No. 6, pp. 484–95.

Nicoll, K. & R. Edwards (1997) Open learning and the demise of discipline. *Open Learning*, Vol. 12, No. 3, pp. 14–24.

NJCLD (1999) Learning Disabilities: Issues in Higher Education. Available online: www.ldonline.org [Accessed June 12, 2012].

November, A. & B. Mull (2012) *Flipped learning: A response to five common criticisms.* eSchool News, Bethesda, MD. Available online: http://www.eschoolnews.com/2012/03/26/flipped-learning-a-response-to-five-common-criticisms/ [Accessed June 10, 2012].

NSLC (2012) *What is Service-Learning?* National Service-Learning Clearinghouse. Available online: www.servicelearning.org/what-service-learning [Accessed June 4, 2012].

Nygaard, C. & P. Bramming (2008) Learning-centred Public Management Education. *International Journal of Public Sector Management*, Vol. 21, No. 4, pp. 400–16.

Nygaard, C., N. Courtney & C. Holtham (eds) (2010) *Teaching Creativity – Creativity in Teaching.* Oxfordshire, Libri Publishing Ltd.

Nygaard, C., N. Courtney & C. Holtham (eds) (2011) *Beyond Transmission – Innovations in University Teaching.* Oxfordshire: Libri Publishing Ltd.

Nygaard, C., T. Højlt & M. Hermansen (2008) Learning-Based Curriculum Development. *Higher Education*, Vol. 55, No. 1, pp. 33–50.

Nygaard, C. & C. Holtham (eds) (2008) *Understanding Learning-Centred Higher Education.* Frederiksberg: Copenhagen Business School Press.

Nygaard, C., C. Holtham & N. Courtney (eds) (2009) *Improving Students' Learning Outcomes.* Copenhagen: Copenhagen Business School Press.

Nygaard, C. & M. Serrano (2010) Students' Identity Construction and Learning. Reasons for developing a learning-centred curriculum in higher education. In L. E. Kattington (ed.) *Handbook of Curriculum Development*, Nova Publishers.

Oakley, B., R. M. Felder, R. Brent & E. Imad (2004) Turning Student Groups into Effective Teams. *Journal of Student Centered Learning*, Vol. 2, No. 1, pp. 9–34.

OECD (1996) *The knowledge based economy.* Paris: OECD.

OECD (2009) Teaching Practices, Teachers' Beliefs and Attitudes. In *Creating Effective Teaching and Learning Environments: First Results from TALIS*, 16 June 2009, pp. 87–136.

Oliver, B., B. von Konsky, S. Jones, S. Ferns & B. Tucker (2009) Curtin's iPortfolio: Facilitating Student Achievement of Graduate Attributes

Within and Beyond the Curriculum. *Learning Communities: International Journal of Learning in Social Contexts*, December 2009, Issue 2, ePortfolio Edition, pp. 4–15.

Oliver, R. (2002) *The role of ICT in higher education for the 21st century: ICT as a change agent for education.* Perth: Edith Conan University. Available online: http://elrond.scam.ecu.edu.au/oliver/2002/he21.pdf [Accessed June 25, 2012].

Papadimitriou, A. (2009) Improving Students' Learning Outcomes via Teamwork & Portfolios. In C. Nygaard, C. Holtham & N. Courtney (eds) *Improving Students' Learning Outcomes.* Copenhagen: Copenhagen Business School Press.

Patton, J. (2005) Foreword. In E. Getzel & P. Wehman (eds) *Going to College: Expanding Opportunities for People with Disabilities.* Baltimore, USA: Paul R. Brookes Publishing, pp. xiii–xv.

Pedrosa de Jesus, H., J. J. C. Teixeira-Dias & M. Watts (2003) Questions of Chemistry. *International Journal of Science Education*, Vol. 25, No. 8, pp. 1,015–34.

Pedrosa de Jesus, H., P. Almeida, J. J. C. Teixeira-Dias & M. Watts (2006) Students' questions: building a bridge between Kolb's learning styles and approaches to learning. *Education + Training*, Vol. 48, No. 2/3, pp. 97–111.

Peltier, J., A. Hay & W. Drago (2005) The reflective learning continuum: reflecting on reflection. *Journal of Marketing Education*, Vol. 27, No. 3, pp. 250–63.

Pennycook, A. (2010) *Language as a Local Practice.* London: Routledge.

Pickard, M., R. Warner & L. Velautham (2011) Enabling postgraduate students to become autonomous enthnographers of their disciplines. In C. Nygaard, N. Courtney & L. Frick (eds) *Postgraduate Education – Form and Function.* Faringdon, Oxfordshire: Libri Publishing Ltd.

Pink, D. (2006) *A Whole New Mind: Why right-Brainers will Rule the World.* New York, NY: Riverhead Books.

Pinker, S. (2009) *How the mind works.* New York: W. W. Norton & Co.

Pintrich, P. R. (2000) The role of goal orientation in self-regulated learning. In M. Boekaerts, P. R. Pintrich & M. Zeidner (eds) *Handbook of Self-regulation.* San Diego: Academic Press, pp. 451–502.

Pliner, S. & J. Johnson (2004) Historical, Theoretical, and Foundational Principles of Universal Instructional Design in Higher Education. *Equity & Excellence in Education*, Vol. 37, pp. 105–13.

Plumb, D. (2008) Learning as dwelling. *Studies in the Education of Adults*, Vol. 40, No. 1, pp. 62–79.

Polanyi, M. (1966) *The Tacit Dimension*. London: Routledge and Kegan.

Poldrack, R. (2007) *How multitasking affects human learning*. Interview on National Public Radio with Lynn Neary. Available online: http://www.npr.org/templates/story/story.php?storyId=7700581 [Accessed June 16, 2012.]

Pollack, D. (ed.) (2009) *Neurodiversity in Higher Education: Positive Responses to Specific Learning Differences*. Chichester, England: John Wiley & Sons.

Prensky, M. (2001) Digital Natives, Digital Immigrants. *On the Horizon*, Vol. 9, No. 5, n.p.

Prensky, M. (2012) Teaching the Right Stuff. Not Yesterday's Stuff or Today's, but Tomorrow's. To be published in *Educational Technology Magazine*. Available online: http://marcprensky.com/writing/Prensky-TheRightStuff-EdTech-May-Jun2012.pdf [Accessed June 25, 2012].

Proshansky, H. M., A. K. Fabian & R. Kaminoff (1983) Place identity: physical world socialization of the self. *Journal of Environmental Psychology*, Vol. 3, pp. 57–83.

Quinn, J. (2010) Rethinking "failed transitions" to higher education. In K. Ecclestone, G. Biesta & M. Hughes (eds) *Transitions and Learning Through the Lifecourse*. London: Routledge, pp. 118–29.

Raiker, A. (2009) A Personalised Approach to Improving Students' Learning Outcomes. In C. Nygaard, C. Holtham & N. Courtney (eds) *Improving Students' Learning Outcomes*. Copenhagen: Copenhagen Business School Press.

Ramsden, P. (1988) *Improving Learning: new perspectives*. Kogan Page.

Ramsden P. & E. Martin (1996) Recognition of good university teaching: Policies from an Australian study. *Studies in Higher Education*, Vol. 21, No. 3, pp. 299–315.

Rassow, L. C. (1998) Assessing the Under Graduate International Business Major. *Journal of Studies in International Education*, Vol. 2, No. 1, pp. 59–80.

Reid & Petocz (2008) A Tertiary Curriculum for Future Professionals. In C. Nygaard & C. Holtham (eds) *Understanding Learning-Centred Higher Education*. Copenhagen Business School Press.

Reilly, V. & T. Davis (2005) Understanding the Regulatory Environment. In E. Getzel & P. Wehman (eds) *Going to College: Expanding Opportunities for People with Disabilities*. Baltimore, USA: Paul R. Brookes Publishing, pp. 25–46.

Rhodes, T. (2011) Making Learning Visible and Meaningful Through Electronic Portfolios. *Change*. January–February. Available online: http://www.changemag.org/Archives/Back%20Issues/2011/January-February%202011/making-learning-visible-full.html [Accessed June 17, 2012].

Roberts, D. (2010) Vicarious learning: a review of the literature. *Nurse Education in Practice*, Vol. 10, No. 1, pp. 13–16.

Rogers, M. (1997) Learning about the future: from the learner's perspective. *Futures*, Vol. 29, No. 8, pp. 763–8.

Rose, D. (2011) Universal Design for Learning. *Journal of Special Education Technology*, Vol. 15, No. 4, pp. 47–51.

Rose, D., W. Harbour, C. Johnson, S. Daley & L. Abarbanell (2006) Universal Design for Learning in Postsecondary Education: Reflections on Principles and Their Applications. *Journal of Postsecondary Education and Disability*, Vol. 19, No. 2, pp. 135–51.

Rose, D. & A. Meyer (2002) *Teaching Every Student in a Digital Age: Universal Design for Learning*. Alexandria, USA: Association of Supervision and Curriculum Development.

Roselli, R. J. & S. P. Brophy (2006) Effectiveness of challenge-based instruction in biomechanics. *Journal of Engineering Education*, Vol. 95, No. 4, pp. 311–24.

Russell, D. R., M. R. Lea, J. Parker, B. Street & T. Donahue (2009) Exploring notions of genre in "academic literacies" and "writing across the curriculum": approaches across countries and contexts. In C. Bazerman, A. Bonini & D. Figueiredo (eds) *Genre in a Changing World*. Colorado: Parlor Press, pp. 459–91.

Savin-Baden, M. & C. Major (2004) *Foundations of Problem-based Learning*. Maidenhead: SRHE and Open University Press.

Saxon, W. (1998) Ronald L. Mace, 58, Designer of Buildings Accessible to All. *The New York Times*, 13 July.

Scanlon, L., L. Rowling & Z. Weber (2007) 'You don't have like an identity… you are just lost in a crowd': Forming a Student Identity in the First-year Transition to University. *Journal of Youth Studies*, Vol. 10, No. 2, pp. 223–41.

Schacter, D. L. (2002) *The seven sins of memory: How the mind forgets and remembers*. New York: Houghton Mifflin.

Schein, E. H. (1992) *Organizational Culture and Leadership*. Jossey-Bass Publishers.

Schlechty, P.C. (2011) *Engaging students: The next level of working on the work.* San Francisco: Jossey-Bass.

Schmidt, H. G., S. M. Loyens, T. van Gog & F. Paas (2007) Problem-based learning is compatible with human cognitive architecture: Commentary on Kirschner, Sweller, and Clark (2006). *Educational Psychologist,* Vol. 42, No. 2, pp. 91–7.

Schmidt, S. (2010) Radical constructivism: A tool, not a super theory! *Constructivist Foundations,* Vol. 6, No. 1, pp. 6–11.

Schön, D. A. (1983) *The Reflective Practitioner.* New York: Basic Books.

Schön, D. A. (1987) *Educating the Reflective Practitioner.* San Francisco: Jossey-Bass.

Schrag, C. O. (1959) Whitehead and Heidegger: process philosophy and existential philosophy. *Dialectica,* Vol. 13, No. 1, pp. 42–56.

Schroeder, A., S. Minocha & C. Schneider (2010) The strengths, weaknesses, opportunities and threats of using social software in higher and further education teaching and learning. *Journal of Computer Assisted Learning,* Vol. 26, No. 3, pp. 159–74.

Scott, S. & J. McGuire (2005) Implementing Universal Design for Instruction to Promote Inclusive College Teaching. In E. Getzel & P. Wehman (eds) *Going to College: Expanding Opportunities for People with Disabilities.* Baltimore, USA: Paul R. Brookes Publishing, pp. 119–38.

Scott, S., J. McGuire & T. Foley (2003) Universal Design for Instruction: A Framework for Anticipating and Responding to Disability and Other Diverse Learning Needs in the College Classroom. *Equity & Excellence in Education,* Vol. 36, Iss. 1, pp. 40–9.

Scoufis, M. (2000) Graduate Attributes Projects: A focus for grass roots change in teaching and learning practices. *Teaching and Learning Forum,* Western Australia.

Silver, H. (2007) *Boredom and its opposite: The role of active engagement in improving student achievement.* Association for Supervision and Curriculum Development Conference on Teaching and Learning: Connecting Instruction and Assessment, Atlanta, Georgia.

Silver, P., A. Bourke & K. Strehorn (1998) Universal Instructional Design in Higher Education: An Approach for Inclusion. *Equity and Excellence in Education,* Vol. 31, No. 2, pp. 47–51.

Sims, R. (2006) Beyond instructional design: Making learning design a reality. *Journal of Learning Design,* Vol. 1, No. 2, pp. 1–7. Available online: http://www.jld.qut.edu.au/ [Accessed June 18, 2012].

Sinnott, J. D. (2009) Cognitive development as the dance of adaptive transformation: Neo-Piagetian perspectives on adult cognitive development. In M. Smith & N. DeFrates-Densch (eds) *Handbook of research on adult learning and development*. New York: Routledge.

Small, G. & G. Vorgan (2009) *IBrain: Surviving the technological alteration of the modern mind*. New York: HarperCollins Publishing, Inc.

Smith, F. (2008) *Perceptions of Universal Design for Learning (UDL) in College Classrooms*. Unpublished dissertation. Washington, USA: George Washington University.

Sousa, D. A. (2006) How the brain learns. In E. F. Barkley (2010) *Student engagement techniques: A handbook for college faculty*. San Francisco: Jossey-Bass.

Sprogkernen (2011) Available online: www.sprogkernen.dk [Accessed June 30, 2012].

Sprogkernen (2012) Available online: www.sprogkernen.dk [Accessed June 30, 2012].

Stahl, S. (2004) *The Promise of Accessible Textbooks: Increased Achievement for All Students*. Wakefield, USA: National Center on Accessing the General Curriculum (NCAC).

Stainback, W., S. Stainback & G. Bunch (1989) Introduction and Historical Background. In S. Stainback, W. Stainback & M. Forest (eds) *Educating All Students in the Mainstream of Regular Education*. Baltimore: Paul H. Brookes.

Stassen, M. L., A. Herrington & L. Henderson (2011) Defining thinking in higher education. In J. E. Miller & J. E. Groccia (eds) *To improve the academy*, 30. San Francisco: Jossey-Bass.

Stefanakis, E. (2011) *Differentiated Assessment*. Hoboken: Jossey-Bass.

Stevens, K. & L. G. O'Connor (2005) *Engineering student identities in the navigation of the undergraduate curriculum*. Reed University of Washington, Seattle, WA, USA, Proceedings of the 2005 American Society for Engineering Education Annual Conference & Exposition.

Stogdill, R. M. (1950) Leadership, membership and organization. *Psychological Bulletin*, Vol. 47, No. 1, pp. 1–14.

Stone, G. P. (1962) Appearance and the Self. In A. M. Rose (ed.) *Human Behavior & Social Process*. Boston: Houghton Mifflin, pp. 86–118.

Story, M. (2011) *The Principles of Universal Design*. In W. Preiser & K. Smith (eds) *Universal Design Handbook*. New York, USA: McGraw Hill, pp. 4.3–4.6.

Strayer, J. (2007) *The effects of the classroom flip on the learning environment: a comparison of learning activity in a traditional classroom and a flip classroom that used an intelligent tutoring*. Doctor of Philosophy, Ohio State

University, Educational Theory and Practice. Available online: http://rave.ohiolink.edu/etdc/view?acc_num=osu1189523914 [Accessed April 15, 2012].

Street, B. (2005) Introduction: New Literacy Studies and literacies across educational contexts. In B. Street (ed.) *Literacies Across Educational Contexts: Mediating learning and teaching*. Philadelphia: Caslon, pp. 1–21.

Strobel, J. & A. van Barneveld (2009) When is PBL more effective? A meta-synthesis of meta-analyses comparing PBL to conventional classrooms. *Interdisciplinary Journal of Problem-based Learning*, Vol. 3, No. 1, pp. 44–58.

Stupans, I. (2012) Promoting collaborative leadership development. *Academic Exchange Quarterly*, Vol. 16, No. 1, pp. 79–85.

Stupans, I., G. March & S. Owen (in press) Enhancing learning in clinical placements: Reflective practice, self-assessment, rubrics and scaffolding. *Assessment & Evaluation in Higher Education*.

Stupans, I., S. Owen, G. Ryan, J. Woulfe & L. McKauge (2010) Scaffolding patient counselling skills in Australian University Pharmacy programs. *Asia Pacific Journal of Cooperative Education*, Vol. 11, No. 2, pp. 29–37.

Su, Y. H. (2009) Idea creation: the need to develop creativity in lifelong learning practices. *International Journal of Lifelong Education*, Vol. 28, No. 6, pp. 705–17.

Su, Y. H. (2011) The constitution of agency in developing lifelong learning ability: the 'being' mode. *Higher Education*, Vol. 62, No. 4, pp. 399–412.

Svendsen, L. P. (2011) Didactic Experiments Suggest Enhanced Learning Outcomes. *International Journal of Business and Social Science*, Vol. 2, No. 22, pp. 35–44.

Svendsen, L. P. (2012) How Social Media Enhanced Learning Platforms Challenge and Motivate Students to Take Charge of Their Own Learning Processes – A Few Examples. In L. Wankel & P. Blessinger (eds) *Increasing Student Engagement and Retention Using Social Technologies: Facebook, E-portfolios and Other Social Networking Services* – in press.

Svendsen, L. P. & M. Mondahl (2011) Tools for Teaching the "Digital Natives". *Læring & Medier*, No 7/8, 2011.

Swales, J. M. (2004) *Research Genres: Explorations and applications*. New York: Cambridge University Press.

Tagg, J. (2003) *The Learning Paradigm College*. John Wiley & Sons.

Teixeira-Dias, J. J. C., H. Pedrosa de Jesus, F. Neri de Souza & M. Watts (2005) Teaching for quality learning in chemistry. *International Journal of Science Education*, Vol. 27, No. 9, pp. 1,123–37.

Thesen, L. (2001) Modes, literacies and power: A university case study. *Language and Education*, Vol. 15, No. 2 & 3, pp. 132–45.

Thompson, E. (2007) *Mind in Life: Biology, phenomenology, and the sciences of mind*. Cambridge: Belknap Press of Harvard University.

Thorne, G. & A. Thomas (no date) *What is attention?* Available online: http://www.cdl.org/resource-library/articles/attention2.php [Accessed June 6, 2012].

Tinkler, D., B. Lepani & J. Mitchell (1996) *Education and Technology Convergence. A Survey of Technological Infrastructure in Education and the Professional Development and Support of Educators and Trainers in Information and Communication Technologies*. Commissioned Report No. 43, National Board of Employment Education and Training. Canberra: Employment and Skills Council, Australian Government Publishing Service.

Torrance, H. (2007) Assessment in post-secondary education and training: editorial introduction. *Assessment in Education: Principles, Policy & Practice*, Vol. 14, No. 3, pp. 277–9.

Tough, A. M. (1979) *The Adults Learning Projects, a Fresh Approach to Theory and Practice in Adult Learning*. Toronto: Ontario Institute for Studies in Education.

Tran, L. T. (2010) Embracing prior professional experience in meaning making: Views from international students and academics. *Educational Review*, Vol. 62, No. 2, pp. 157–73.

Turner, J. (2003) Academic literacy in post-colonial times: Hegemonic norms and transcultural possibilities. *Language and Intercultural Communication*, Vol. 3, No. 3, pp. 187–97.

UFO Group (2010) Available online: www.ufogroup.dk [Accessed June 30, 2012].

UniversalDesign.com. Available online: http://www.universaldesign.com/about-universal-design.html [Accessed June 12, 2012].

Usher, R. (2001) Lifelong learning in the postmodern. In D. Aspin, J. Chapman, M. Hatton & Y. Sawano (eds) *International handbook of lifelong learning*. Dordrecht: Kluwer.

Usher, R., I. Bryant & R. Johnston (1997) *Adult Education and the Postmodern Challenge: Learning beyond the limits*. London, Routledge.

Usher, R. & R. Edwards (1994) *Postmodernism and Education*. London: Routledge.

Verenikina, I. (2008) *Scaffolding and learning: its role in nurturing new learners. Learning and the Learner: exploring learning for new times*. P. Kell, W.

Vialle, D. Konza and G. Vogl. University of Wollongong: 161–80. Wollongong.

Vermunt, J. D. (1995) Process-oriented instruction in learning and thinking strategies. *European Journal of Psychology of Education*, Vol. 10, No. 4, pp. 325–49.

Vogt, E. E., J. Brown & D. Isaacs (2003) *The Art of Powerful Questions: Catalyzing Insight, Innovation, and Action*. Mill Valley, CA: Whole Systems Associates.

Vygotsky, L. (1962) *Thought and Language*. Cambridge, U.S.A.: MIT Press.

Vygotsky, L. S. (1987) *The collected works of L. S. Vygotsky. Volume 1: Problems of general psychology*. London, Plenum Press.

Waite, S., R. Cutting, R. Cook, J. Burnett & M. Opie (2009) Learning Outside the Classroom: Environments for Experiential Enrichment. In C. Nygaard, C. Holtham & N. Courtney (eds) *Improving Students' Learning Outcomes*. Copenhagen: Copenhagen Business School Press.

Wardle, E. (2009) "Mutt genres" and the goal of FYC: Can we help students write the genres of the university? *College Composition and Communication*, Vol. 60, No. 4, pp. 765–89.

Warmelink, H., C. Harteveld, G. Bekebrede & S. Meijer (2012) Lessons learnt from a decade of game development for higher education in Delft. In C. Nygaard, N. Courtney & E. Leigh (eds) *Simulations, Games and Role Play in University Education*. Oxfordshire: Libri Publishing Ltd.

Warner, R. (2011) Giving feedback on assignment writing to international students: the integration of voice and writing tools. In W. M. Chan, K. N. Chin, M. Nagami & T. Suthiwan (eds) *Media in Foreign Language Teaching and Learning*. Boston: Mouton de Gruyter.

Watts, D. M., S. J. Alsop, G. F. Gould & A. Walsh (1997) Prompting teachers' constructive reflection: Pupils' questions as critical incidents. *International Journal of Science Education*, Vol. 79, No. 9, pp. 1,025–37.

Wegner, E. (1998) *Communities of Practice: Learning, Meaning, and Identity*. Cambridge: Cambridge University Press.

Wehlburg, C. M. (2006) *Meaningful course revision: Enhancing academic engagement using student data*. Bolton, MA: Anker.

Weimer, M. (2002) *Learner-Centered Teaching: Five key changes to practice*. San Francisco: Jossey-Bass.

Weimer, M. E. (2010) *Inspired college teaching: A long-career resource for professional growth*. San Francisco: Jossey-Bass.

Wenger, E. (1998) *Communities of Practice: Learning meaning and identity*. Cambridge: Cambridge University Press.

Weston, C. & P. A. Cranton (1986) Selecting Instructional Strategies. *The Journal of Higher Education*, Vol. 57, No. 3, pp. 259–88.

Wierstra, R. F. A., G. Kanselaar, J. L. van der Linden, H. G. L. C. Lodewijks & J. D. Vermunt (2003) The Impact of the University Context on European Students' Learning Approaches and Learning Environment Preferences. *Higher Education*, Vol. 45, No. 4, pp. 503–23.

Wiggins, G. & J. McTighe (1998) *Understanding by design*. Alexandria, VA: Association for Supervision and Curriculum Development.

Wilkerson, L. A. (1998) Strategies for Improving Teaching Practice – A Comprehensive Approach to Faculty Development. *Academic Medicine*, Vol. 73, No. 3, pp. 387–96.

Willingham, D. T. (2004) *Cognition: The thinking animal*. Upper Saddle River, NJ: Merrill/Prentice Hall.

Willingham, D. T. (2010) *Why don't students like school: A cognitive scientist answers questions about how the mind works and what it means for the classroom*. San Francisco: John Wiley & Sons.

Wingate, U. (2006) Doing away with "study skills". *Teaching in Higher Education*, Vol. 11, No. 4, pp. 457–69.

Wingate, U., N. Andon & A. Cogo (2011) Embedding academic writing instruction into subject teaching: A case study. *Active Learning in Higher Education*, Vol. 12, No. 1, pp. 69–81.

Woods, P. A., N. Bennett, J. A. Harvey & C. Wise (2004) Variabilities and Dualities in Distributed Leadership. *Educational Management Administration & Leadership*, Vol. 32, No. 4, pp. 439–57.

Xyrichis, A. & E. Ream (2008) Teamwork: a concept analysis. *Journal of Advanced Nursing*, Vol. 61, No. 2, pp. 232–41.

Yancey, K. B. (2001) Digitized Student Portfolios. In B. L. Cambridge (ed.) *Electronic Portfolios: Emerging Practices in Student, Faculty, and Institutional Learning*, pp. 15–30. Washington, D.C.: American Association for Higher education.

Yazbeck, B. (2008) Towards a new EAP: Managing diversity in university preparation courses. *EA Journal*, Vol. 24, No. 2, pp. 38–45.

Yorke, M. (2003) Formative assessment in higher education: Moves towards theory and the enhancement of pedagogic practice. *Higher Education*, Vol. 45, No. 4, pp. 477–501.

Zepke, N. & L. Leach (2005) Integration and adaptation: approaches to the student retention and achievement puzzle. *Active Learning in Higher Education*, Vol. 6, No. 1, pp. 46–59.